Changing Bodies

Theory, Culture & Society

Theory, Culture & Society caters for the resurgence of interest in culture within contemporary social science and the humanities. Building on the heritage of classical social theory, the book series examines ways in which this tradition has been reshaped by a new generation of theorists. It also publishes theoretically informed analyses of everyday life, popular culture and new intellectual movements.

EDITOR: Mike Featherstone, *Nottingham Trent University*

SERIES EDITORIAL BOARD
Roy Boyne, *University of Durham*
Scott Lash, *Goldsmiths College, University of London*
Roland Robertson, *University of Aberdeen*
Bryan S. Turner, *National University of Singapore*

THE TCS CENTRE
The Theory, Culture & Society book series, the journals *Theory, Culture & Society* and *Body & Society*, and related conference, seminar and postgraduate programmes operate from the TCS Centre at Nottingham Trent University. For further details of the TCS Centre's activities please contact:

The TCS Centre
School of Arts and Humanities
Nottingham Trent University
Clifton Lane, Nottingham NG11 8NS, UK
email: tcs@ntu.ac.uk
web: http://sagepub.net/tcs/

Recent volumes include:

The Body and Society: Explorations in Social Theory, Third Edition
Bryan Turner

The Media City: Media, Architecture and Urban Space
Scott McQuire

The Dressed Society: Clothing, the Body and Some Meanings of the World
Peter Corrigan

Informalization: Manners and Emotions Since 1890
Cas Wouters

The Culture of Speed: The Coming of Immediacy
John Tomlinson

Consumer Culture and Postmodernism, Second Edition
Mike Featherstone

Changing Bodies

Habit, Crisis and Creativity

Chris Shilling

Los Angeles • London • New Delhi • Singapore

First published 2008

SAGE Publications Ltd
1 Oliver's Yard
55 City Road
London EC1Y 1SP

SAGE Publications Inc.
2455 Teller Road
Thousand Oaks, California 91320

SAGE Publications India Pvt Ltd
B 1/I 1 Mohan Cooperative Industrial Area
Mathura Road
New Delhi 110 044

SAGE Publications Asia-Pacific Pte Ltd
33 Pekin Street #02-01
Far East Square
Singapore 048763

Library of Congress Control Number: 2007940150

British Library Cataloguing in Publication data

A catalogue record for this book is available from the British Library

ISBN 978-1-4129-0831-3
ISBN 978-1-4129-0832-0 (pbk)

Typeset by Newgen Imaging Systems (P) Ltd, Chennai, India
Printed in India at Replika Press Pvt. Ltd
Printed on paper from sustainable resources

To Debbie, Max and Kate
With Love

Contents

Acknowledgements

This study could not have been completed without the support and assistance of a number of people. Philip A. Mellor has, as always, been an invaluable source of advice and friendship throughout this entire project, while the comments of Michael Erben and Mike Hardey have done much to improve particular chapters. More generally, analysis has benefited from discussions with all those colleagues involved in the International Body Pedagogics Project, and those who participated in the stream of papers on Embodying Sociology at the ISS World Congress in Stockholm, 2005 (particular acknowledgement here must go to Kathy Davis and Anna Aalton for their support). The *Theory, Culture & Society* editorial group continue to provide essential encouragement for my project and so too, at Sage Publications, does Chris Rojek. I should also like to thank Stephen Mennell and John Solomos for their advice and good sense over the years. The largest debt of gratitude I have accrued while working on this project, however, is to my family. Thanks to Debbie for her love and friendship (and help with the bibliography!), and to Max and Kate for their energy, openness, love... and noise.

1

Introduction

Body modification and transformation have exerted a growing fascination in contemporary consumer culture. This is partly because science and technology continue to weaken the boundaries separating flesh and machines and, in so doing, prompt us to revisit and revise our ideas about what it is to be a human being. It is also because the agents of bodily change – from cosmetic surgeons and tattooists, to personal trainers and style consultants – populate the high street and television schedules in ever greater numbers. People have long decorated and moulded their bodies in various ways, but the growth and variety of businesses designed to exploit the malleability of the flesh and its contents have turned bodywork into a hugely profitable industry.

The popularity of this cultural phenomenon raises a number of questions about the impact that bodily change has on people's identities and capacities for action. It also raises wider issues concerning the morality of social orders in which so much money, time and energy are devoted to the aesthetics of embodiment. These are important matters, but it would, I think, be an error to restrict discussion of them to the most visible or novel ways in which bodily modification occurs. Our bodies change, develop and age from the womb through to our death and decomposition. The institutions that surround us, the relationships we enter into, and the habits we develop, all impact upon the appearances, capacities and meanings associated with our bodies. Bodily change sometimes occurs as a result of consciously formulated actions undertaken in situations of considerable autonomy, but it also happens frequently in circumstances over which individuals have little control. In these and in other situations, the ways in which bodily change occurs are related inextricably to people's social actions as well as to the wider social structures in which they live.

It is this broad and general relationship between bodily change and social action that concerns this book. In what follows, I seek to develop an analytical framework, informed by pragmatism's account of the external and internal environments of human action, that explores how people's embodied appearances, identities and capacities are shaped by various combinations of habit, crisis and creativity. As a way of introducing this study, however, I want to start with a paradox. In coming to terms with the corporeal dimensions of social action, any adequate sociological approach to the subject has to go *beyond* bodily behaviour if it is to demonstrate the social consequentiality of our physical being. As Karen Fields (1995: lvi) implies, simply recognising bodily impulses and movements has the socio-logical significance of 'so many potatoes in a sack'. This observation helps us understand why Weber (1968: 24–6, 65) defined meaningful social action as action oriented towards the behaviour of *others*, and distinguished action that was rational within a social context from mere affectual and habitual bodily reactions to events. It was the former rather than the latter that most identified us as humans, able to intervene creatively and inten-tionally in the flow of social life. Yet contemporary attempts to harness embodied action to society often travel so far from the biological organism – in their concern with such issues as discourse and image – that the material-ity of their acting subjects disappears altogether (e.g. Butler, 1993). There is a balancing act to perform here. Sociology needs to account for the impact of society and culture on embodied actions, while also acknowl-edging that the embodied constitution of human action (an embodiment forged over the *longue durée* of human evolution that cannot simply be derived from current social orders) is itself consequential for these wider relationships, norms and values.

In seeking to meet this challenge, the rapidly growing and otherwise diverse collection of sociologically informed 'body studies' that emerged since the early 1980s has drawn in the main on two broad theoretical approaches. On the one hand, there are those who identify the governmental management of the body as setting key parameters to the overarching *external environment* in which social action occurs. Bryan Turner (1984), for example, draws on the distinctive concerns of Thomas Hobbes, Talcott Parsons and Michel Foucault with 'the problem of order' and 'disciplinary regimes' as a way of identifying the reproduction and regulation of populations through space and time, the restraint of desire, and the representation of bodies, as key action issues that face all societies. On the other hand, analysts have identified the body as central to the *internal environment* of social action. Arthur Frank (1991a: 43, 1991b), for example, views the opportunities and constraints of action as given by 'the problems of bodies themselves'. Such action-oriented studies develop typically by being attentive to 'the body's own experience of its embodiment' in various social contexts, and by drawing on interactionist, phenomenological and existentialist resources provided by such figures as Georg Simmel and Maurice Merleau-Ponty (Leder, 1990; Frank, 1991a: 48; Csordas, 1994).

Given the use of these traditional resources it should come as no surprise that while sociology's focus on embodiment may be relatively new (at least in its present incarnation), contemporary approaches remain indisputably related to, and in certain respects recapitulate, those sociologies of order and of action that have long characterised the discipline (Dawe, 1970). Thus, the focus on bodies as providing the 'core problems' confronted by the external environment in which action occurs conceptualises human phys-icality as an object ordered by society. Bodies, irrespective of how they act, are essentially a structural problem. The interest in the body as central to the internal environment of social action, in contrast, highlights how human behaviour involves subjects who engage sensorially and emotionally (as well as cognitively) with their social world. The body is here viewed as integral to, and sometimes coterminous with, social action.

These approaches have done much to bring 'body matters' to the centre of academic debate about the nature and contexts of social action, but they face continuing challenges. Studies that begin their inquiries with the external environment confront the difficulty from this analytical ground of grasping embodied action as an active determinant of social systems, while those whose chosen starting point is the internal environment struggle to incorporate into their analyses a comprehensive sense of the wider social and cultural factors affecting embodied action and bodily changes. Theorists who have sought to draw a bridge between these approaches have fared little better. The writings of Pierre Bourdieu, for example, have proven highly influential, but his conception of *habitus* places the reproduction of the external environment at the very heart of his conception of action (Bourdieu, 1984). The problem with this is that embodied action appears predetermined – it both echoes and replicates existing structures – leaving those who operationalise Bourdieu's work in their research employing strategies to modify its reproductive logic (see Shilling, 2005a).

Against this background, it is somewhat puzzling that the embodied focus on writers such as Hobbes, Parsons, Weber, Durkheim and a host of more recent theoretical figures including Foucault, Butler and Haraway, has not been accompanied by an equivalent interest in pragmatism. Pragmatism drew on various philosophical antecedents (Malachowski, 2004), but it was first formulated as an identifiable approach by Charles Sanders Peirce in the early 1870s, and named as a distinctive position by William James in an address to the Philosophical Union at the University of California, Berkeley, in 1898. It was developed further and deployed within substantive studies at the Chicago School of Sociology in the early decades of the twentieth century. John Dewey and George Herbert Mead were especially prominent in this respect. Only a few body theorists have taken this work seriously (e.g. Shusterman, 1992), however, despite more general theoretical studies highlighting the potential utility of pragmatism for analysing the social significance of corporeality (Joas, 1996). This is a serious oversight, I would suggest, as pragmatism's recognition and explorations of the distinctive properties of, and the dynamic relationship that exists between, the external and internal environments of human action can help avoid the dangers of conflation. This tradition of inquiry can also usefully inform substantive studies of embodied subjects in their social and material contexts, as evident in the work of the Chicago School, thus helping to address what some critics have described as the relative lack of empirically informed work in the field of body studies.

In explicating how pragmatism explores the corporeal dimensions of social action, it is useful to first clarify how it differs from the dominant traditions in sociology. During the early years of the twentieth century, sociology was still coming to terms with how to translate the a priori assumptions central to its various philosophical foundations into methods and procedures that would facilitate empirical research. The French sociological tradition took as its starting point the primacy of the collectivity, for example, while the German tradition began with the self-directing individual (Levine, 1995). Yet both presented problems to sociologists interested in examining *interactions* between social actors and their environment without reducing one to the other. This was because the former tended to derive the capabilities of the subject from the properties of social structures, while the latter usually conceived the social environment in terms of the dispositions of (inter)acting individuals.

Pragmatism, in contrast, offered an alternative foundation for sociology. Instead of identifying either the collectivity or the individual as absolute starting points, it recognised that action was undertaken by individuals *always already within* a social and natural context, yet possessed of *emergent capacities and needs* that distinguished them from, and also enabled them to shape actively, their wider milieu. In this context, action, experience and identity arise from the ongoing interactions and transactions that occur between the internal environment of the embodied organism and its external social and physical environment.

It is this ability to maintain a view of the external and internal environments of action as distinctive, yet interacting, phenomena that is of particular utility for sociological studies of embodiment. Thus, pragmatism's insistence on the human potential to 'make a difference' turns what sociologists have sometimes treated as exclusively socially determined organisms into phenomenologically aware, active body-subjects whose corporeal properties enable them to intervene creatively in the world. At the same time, pragmatism's recognition that embodied actions are shaped in part by the distinctive properties of the social and natural world also avoids the dangers of viewing action as emanating from monadic subjects who are hermetically sealed from other people and from the material contexts in which they live (Burkitt, 1991). It is these characteristics that provide sociological studies into the corporeal dimensions of social action with a *potential* framework for investigation that differs in important respects from its classical antecedents.

I emphasise the word 'potential', because pragmatism provides us with no single theory ready to be applied in its totality to substantive studies of embodiment. Those most closely associated with pragmatism developed their work in distinctive directions, while the body-relevant studies conducted in the Chicago School were also characterised by much diversity. More radically, contemporary writers have harnessed the insights of pragmatism to theories which sometimes appear to have little in common with their antecedents (e.g. Rorty, 1982; Shusterman, 1992; see Halton, 1995). Rescher (1997) goes so far as to conclude that pragmatism has undergone a remarkable deformation from its original conception. Rather than condemning these developments, we might see them instead as tributes to the continuing creative potential of an approach possessed of greater flexibility than many other theories. In the spirit of this flexibility, my own concern is not to seek to identify or promote any single 'authentic' pragmatist theory, but to explore how some of the key insights developed by the likes of John Dewey, George Herbert Mead and William James can be drawn together within a broad and flexible framework that facilitates sociological investigations into the *interactions* that exist between the external and internal environments of embodied action. It is these investigations into the external social and physical milieu (that contextualise and shape action), on the one hand, and the internal needs and capacities (that inform action), on the other, that enable us to explicate and explore the relationship between social action and bodily change that lie at the heart of this book. My focus on action is intended to complement the current emphasis in body studies on utilising theory not as an end in itself, but as a means of expanding those empirically informed accounts that add to our knowledge of body-subjects in their social contexts.

Chapter 2, *Embodying Social Action*, begins this process in detail by focusing on how pragmatism can aid our understanding of the environments of social action, and of the common sociological concern with identity or character. Chapter 3, *Embodying Social Research*, explores how this paradigm of thought was developed and deployed in the empirically oriented writings of the Chicago School of Sociology. These chapters illustrate and explore the promise of pragmatism, but there is still much to be done if we are to maximise its capacity to assist sociological explorations into areas of human life in which embodiment is centrally visible. This issue is perhaps particularly pressing in cases where the external or internal environments seem to place overwhelming constraints on individual action and on people's capacity for developing an integrated character or engaging in collective forms of moral action. It is also significant in relation to those cases in which the boundaries between these environments of action become particularly blurred or even, apparently, effaced.

This is the background against which Chapters 4–9 undertake a series of case studies which focus on embodied actions and bodily changes within radically different environments. The subjects covered in these substantive chapters provide illustrations of actions emanating from different contexts, and undertaken in situations characterised by wildly different constraints and opportunities. In terms of the contexts, three of them (Competing, Presenting and Moving) focus on actions associated with the contemporary, technological world. These deal respectively with the international significance of sport, transformations of the body involved in transgenderism, and the migrations undertaken by 'dispossessed travellers' in the global economy. The chapters on Ailing, Surviving and Believing, in contrast, analyse what might be described as more anthropological features of what it is to be an embodied human (albeit within specific milieu). These concentrate respectively on illness, the confrontation with death and belief. In terms of the constraints and opportunities dealt with by these chapters, Surviving, Ailing and Moving focus on situations in which people's actions are *heavily circumscribed*, while Competing, Presenting and Believing switch attention to areas of life associated with the *cultivation* and *expansion* of at least a selection of human potentialities.

Chapter 4 focuses on a type of action which requires a *surplus* of energy over that required for mere survival, and is associated with the structured accumulation of skills in an area of life which receives considerable social recognition. *Competing* explores embodied action and change in sport. Sport has flourished in benign as well as in virulent social orders such as the Nazi state, tends to be associated in the public mind with health and fitness, and has been associated over the centuries with a broad range of social and political goals. In the contemporary era, sport also provides a particularly interesting example of how the competitive action that lies at its core mediates the relationship between individual character and national identity. Chapter 5, *Presenting*, explores the centrality of action to appearance by examining how transgendered individuals negotiate cultural norms surrounding the presentation of self. Sociologists have long suggested that presentational norms exert a major effect on a person's identity, but the stories of those possessed of a profound sense that they are inhabiting the 'wrong' body shows how people can negotiate these norms in a manner which provides them with new opportunities for development. Chapter 6, *Moving*, focuses on those dispossessed travellers who constitute the underbelly of human migration. It explores how the actions and identities of refugees, asylum seekers, low-paid migrant workers and others excluded from global wealth, are forged through the travels in which they engage.

Chapter 7, *Ailing*, is concerned with illness and impairment in the context of an external environment that is shaped on the basis of the performative priorities embedded in a 'health role' (Frank, 1991a). Visions of healthy and aesthetically perfect bodies pervade consumer culture, but the ideal they project is a myth. Sooner or later virtually all of us get sick (defined biomedically as involving a diseased organism) and experience illness (defined sociologically as the subjective encounter with the symptoms and suffering associated with sickness). Entry into the 'kingdom of sickness', as Susan Sontag (1991) puts it, or into the world of physical or mental impairment, can have a devastating impact on our capacities for action and on our identities. Chapter 8, *Surviving*, explores social action oriented towards maintaining existence in the face of overwhelming odds. There can be fewer cases where social action is so constrained, or where life is so precarious, than in the 'killing factories' of the Nazi concentration camps or in the Soviet Gulag. Despite the vital differences between these systems – the Soviet camps were not established with the aim of facilitating genocide – millions died in them and the accounts of survivors provide us with a harrowing insight into embodied action at the extremes of life.

Chapter 9, *Believing*, picks up on some of the religious undercurrents of Chapter 8 and addresses an important consequence of migration in the current era. Since the twentieth century, the West has been dominated by a technological culture predicated on the rational 'enframing' of society and nature (Heidegger, 1993 [1954]), yet this culture has confronted challenges to its hegemony. These have ranged in severity and scale from direct attacks on symbols of its authority (by terrorist groups who justify their actions on the basis of religious affiliation) to the growth of 'new age' spiritualities, which seek to ameliorate the effects of technological culture on people's lives and on the viability of the planet. In this context, Chapter 9 explores what belief means to different peoples, identifies contemporary attempts to utilise belief-systems as a means of mitigating technological culture in the West, and examines how the embodied bases of these forms of belief are central to the increasing religious conflicts that exist in the world today.

Chapter 10 concludes this book by drawing together the disparate threads of these substantive chapters as a way of assessing the general approach that has informed them. The framework employed here is not intended to provide a single, 'closed', theory of the body. Pragmatism's concern with the change occasioned by the dynamically interacting environments of action, and the phases of habit, crisis and creativity that cycle into and out of people's lives, runs against the spirit of such a totalising aim. Nevertheless, it does provide us with an approach which enables us to analyse the interaction that occurs between embodied subjects, and the environments in which they act, without conflating the properties of social or physical structures with those of human beings. Taken together, the substantive chapters in this book also raise issues which are key to the field of body studies and to sociology more generally. The conclusion focuses on these in more detail in its discussions of how our existence as embodied beings enables us to *transcend* the parameters of our basic bodily needs. This is a central theme which runs throughout this study. In contrast to those who accuse 'body studies' of engaging in an 'inverted Cartesianism', I draw on the analysis in this book to argue that while we are not simply our organic bodies, it is by *living in, attending to* and *working on* our bodies that we become fully embodied beings able to realise our human potentialities in a variety of ways. The first step in my analysis, however, is to show in more detail how I am intending to interpret and harness the insights of pragmatism to a framework which allows us to analyse the environments of embodied action.

2

Embodying Social Action

Introduction

The aim of this chapter is to outline a general framework for analysing the environments of embodied action which avoids the reductionism characteristics of many existing approaches in the field of body studies. Pragmatism is useful in this context, as its concern with the interactions and transactions that occur between people and their surroundings provides us with a more dynamic conception of the relationship between bodily change and social action than is evident in reproduction models, possibly static typologies, or rational choice visions of preference maximising subjects. In their place, pragmatism adopts a processual approach to the phases of habit, crisis and creativity that mark (in various combinations and at various times) people's lives. These orientations towards action are important not only for what they have to say about the ability of people to respond to and/or change their surroundings, but because they impact cumulatively on the formation and development of individual character, and also on the collective capacities of social groups.

The environments of embodied action

The social and physical milieu

There is no better place to begin exploring pragmatism's view of the *external environment* of embodied action than with Mead's conception of a group of interdependent human organisms cooperating together and building a *social milieu* as they seek to survive. According to Mead, this cooperation encourages the development of gestures, inter-gestural understanding and, eventually, language as means for the efficient coordination of action. In turn, human communication welds people together into a purposeful society, possessed of normative standards and identities that develop as individuals become able, with the assistance of interaction and symbols, to 'take the role of the other'. This capacity is fostered from birth by the elementary structures of role-taking engaged in by care givers and pre-linguistic infants (Mead, 1962 [1934]), explored further by children in games, and taken-for-granted amongst adults socialised into experiencing and managing their actions and identities 'from the particular standpoints of other individual members of the same group, or from the general standpoint of the social group as a whole' (Mead, 1962 [1934]: 138). Mead refers to this group standpoint as the *'generalised other'*; an 'other' which places a pressure on the individual to conform to the standards of the group in terms of how they act, and which filters the development of embodied identity. As Dewey (2002 [1922]: 316) argues, 'Gradually persons learn by dramatic imitation to hold themselves accountable' for their actions and identities according to the standards of their social group, and on the basis of the common social activity in which all are implicated. This 'organised set of attitudes of others', assumed by individuals towards themselves, is how society exerts normative control over its members (Mead, 1962 [1934]: 175).

The social milieu is vital to the external environment in which embodied action occurs, but pragmatism insists it be considered in conjunction with the constraints and opportunities afforded by the *physical milieu*. Social interactions themselves develop as people seek to survive in their material surroundings, and are often based around 'the manipulation of physical things' that occur within these settings. It is in this context that Mead talks about the human capacity to 'take the role' of *objects* as well as other people. This is essential if we are to adjust ourselves to, and survive within, our physical environment, and is integrally involved in the sense we acquire of our bodily capacities and competencies (Archer, 2000).

The external environment (in its social and physical dimensions) is for pragmatism essential for understanding embodied action. The generalised standards that develop with regards to communicative acts, for example, affect our appearance, diet and action, while the social shaping of people's identities does not occur 'in a void' but through 'prolonged and cumulative interaction' with the peculiarities of their physical environment (Dewey, 1980 [1934]: 28). Similarly, the body's schema, postures, muscle tensions, techniques and textures also develop as a result of us 'bumping into' and undertaking navigations through our physical milieu. Having recognised the significance of the external environment, however, pragmatism is also concerned with the *internal environment* of bodily being, and acknowledges the importance of the body's emergent needs and potentialities.

Body needs and capacities

In examining the internal environment of embodied action, pragmatism takes account of biological necessities (e.g. the need for food, water, and protection from the elements and other threats that may endanger survival) through its analysis of 'impulses' which proceeded 'from need' and evolved into a 'congenital tendency to react in a specific manner to a certain sort of stimulus' (Mead, 1904: 337; Dewey, 1980 [1934]: 13). The existence of these impulses entails that there exists a 'pre-reflective intentionality of the human body', directed initially towards survival, which means that people do not just react to stimuli but intentionally select which stimuli are relevant depending upon the specific circumstances they encounter (Dewey, 1896; Mead, 1903).

This pre-reflective intentionality raises the issue of the *potentialities* of the organism as it implies that humans not only have needs they must meet in order to survive, but also are able to search out people and objects enabling them to meet these needs. Key to these potentialities is the capacity we have to manipulate things *outside* the topographical boundaries of our bodies. This is facilitated by the most basic features of embodiment. In an analysis which has strong affinities with phenomenology, pragmatism explores how the human senses extend from the individual to the environment. As Dewey (1980 [1934]: 13) notes, no creature lives within the confines of its skin and our senses are a 'means of connection' with 'what lies beyond [our] bodily frame'. The eye, the ear, and the senses of touch, taste and smell, unfold themselves onto, connect in their particular ways with, and gain information from, the environment (Dewey, 1980 [1934]: 237). Embodied subjects combine, utilise and deploy these senses in ways that give rise to multi-layered perspectives on social and physical situations (James, 1950 [1890]). The senses thus involve and contribute to the development of the body and the mind. They also provide the embodied basis on which it is possible for emotions to be 'called out' by physical and social objects, and to 'mark out' our particular relationship to the environment (Dewey, 1980 [1934]: 207; Siegfried, 1996: 164).

The interacting environments of action

Pragmatism's recognition that the sensory subject actively engages with, as well as being 'called out' by, the external environment, demonstrates that its acknowledgement of biological impulses and pre-reflective intentionality does *not* entail the assumption that human behaviour is genetically determined. Impulses are neither as extensive nor as unmalleable for humans as they are for other animals, while their specific manifestations and the objects they encompass are affected by the social as well as the physical milieu. Certain kinaesthetic and other experiences may be perceived as peculiarly 'private' phenomena (Mead, 1962 [1934]: 225). Nevertheless, while modern individuals may feel a strong sense of separation from others, even the smallest expressions of selfhood constitute 'expansive acts' that result in a 'breaking down of the walled-in self' as it responds to and is affected by social relationships and the physical environment (Dewey, 1958: 244). As we develop from childhood, these sensory dealings we have with the world around us become part of us. They shape our biological being and have a profound impact on our actions and identities. This means that social relationships are crucial in shaping the goal-directedness of impulses and intentions, and for adding to the human repertoire a range of non-impulsive bases for desire and action (Mead, 1962 [1934]).

If pragmatism is careful not to reduce action to its biological foundations, it is also determined not to conflate action with the external environment. This is clearly illustrated by its recognition that we possess the capacity to reflect practically on our dealings with the world, and to exert a degree of control over how we view ourselves and choose to act on our environment. The source of this practical reflection is related to the intentional orientation that we adopt to our surroundings – an orientation which requires regular adjustment and change as a result of the dynamism of life itself – and is founded on the immediate response of embodied subjects to their dealings with their world (Mead, 1962 [1934]: 175; Dewey, 2002 [1922]: 249). This capacity to reflect imparts to people a sense of 'freedom', 'initiative' and 'conscious responsibility', and is best known through Mead's account of how individuals engage in an internal dialogue with the group standpoint or 'generalised other'.

For Mead (1962 [1934]: 215, 202), there is 'always a *mutual* relationship of the individual and the community', and the 'I' is the term he uses to describe the creative source of 'the constant reaction of the organism to its socialised selfhood'. It is this 'I' that provides subjects with the capacity to react to, and depart from, the socialisation processes and cultural norms which have helped shape their bodily selves and actions (Scheffler, 1974: 165). The embodied subject can draw on perspectives marginalised by society or on their own experiences with the physical environment in order, for example, to act in ways which challenge the status quo (Mead, 1962 [1934]: 168). Thus, it is quite possible for those stigmatised within a community because of a physical disability or their sexual orientation to reflect critically on their 'spoiled identity', discover they are more capable than society assumes, and seek to develop an alternative sense of self which can in turn have positive consequences for their health and physical capacities. For Mead (1962 [1934]: 217), it 'is in such reactions of the individual, the "I" over against the situation in which the "I" finds itself, that important social changes take place'. Indeed, the long-term viability of any 'generalised other' impinging on people's embodied identities is significantly dependent on its ability to facilitate successful interventions in the social *and* physical milieu (Mead (1962 [1934], 1938; Joas, 1997). Without proposing an intellectual Darwinianism, it should not be surprising if norms and ideals that prove singularly unsuccessful in allowing a collectivity to engage successfully with its surroundings have a limited life expectancy (Rochberg-Halton, 1987: 197). Once again, it is the *interaction* between, as well as the existence of, the external and internal environment that is vital to our understanding of embodied action. This emphasis on interaction is reinforced further when we explore pragmatism's analysis of the distinctive modalities, or phases, of social action.

The phases of embodied action

Concerned as it is with pre-reflectively active individuals who face the demands and contingencies of their social and physical surroundings, pragmatism views humans as *always already* active. It is not the initiation of action that has to be explained, but the characteristics of how people act in particular situations. In undertaking this explanation, pragmatism rejects the tendency in sociology to construct rigid typologies of action, and the propensity in rational choice theory to regard all action as maximising the realisation of pre-set preferences. Instead, pragmatism approaches action in terms of its orientation to phases of *habit, crisis* and *creativity*, modalities associated with degrees of conflict or equilibrium that exist within and between the environments of human being. Habits, crises and creative actions emerge as pre-reflectively intentional subjects engage with the complexities and contingencies of the world around them, and discover the possibilities of action made available to them by their bodily potentialities and situated lives.

Habitual continuity

Habitual action is associated with a relative equilibrium in the relationship between the social and physical environment, biological need and bodily potentialities. It involves embodied subjects discovering *routinised* modes of behaviour that are more or less effective in 'joining' them to, and enabling them to manage, their surroundings. This does not mean all habits are healthy, but routinisation is vital for humans to operate effectively. As Dewey (1980 [1934]: 15) notes, the embodied subject cannot be engaged constantly with what is novel and indeterminate. To do so would be biologically disastrous and socially unproductive as the very 'structure of the relation between organism and environment ... typical for human beings' entails that a certain 'stability' in action is 'essential to living'. People need to be able to bracket out stimuli as non-threatening and establish a minimally ordered relationship with their environment if they are to flourish, and habits enable us to 'economise and simplify our actions' by storing 'the fruits of past experience' so that we can act without having to devote heightened attention and consciousness to every move we make (James, 1950 [1890]: 114; Scheffler, 1974: 123). In planning a journey, for example, we may have a set of 'related habits' such as 'packing our bags, getting our railroad tickets, [and] drawing out money for use' which enable us to reduce the intellectual and emotional energy that would otherwise be expended and to focus instead on unexpected occurrences within the journey or on what we plan to do at the journey's end (Dewey, 1958: 285; Mead, 1962 [1934]: 126).

Sociology has tended to forget the enormous analytical significance that habit held for the subject, but such matters were key to the founding assumptions of the discipline and have been kept alive by pragmatism's enduring concern with the 'durable and generalised disposition that suffuses a person's action throughout an entire domain of life or, in the extreme instance, throughout all of life' (Camic, 1986: 1046; see also Joas, 1996: 175; Kilpinen, 2000: 37; Dewey, 2002 [1922]: 199). It would be a mistake to view habits as the bare reoccurrence of acts, however, as they involve much more of the embodied subject and have significant consequences for physical being and identity. Habits involve a 'special sensitiveness' to 'certain classes of stimuli', and are 'a potential energy needing only opportunity to become kinetic and overt' (James, 1900: 134; Dewey, 2002 [1922]: 44). They demand 'certain kinds of activity' and help 'constitute the self' by forming 'our effective desires' and 'working capacities' and determining which of our thoughts 'shall appear and be strong and which shall pass from light into obscurity' (Dewey, 2002 [1922]: 25). Habits seep into the furthest recesses of the body. They have a structural basis in the nervous system, shape the selections our senses make, condition our preferences, predate and provide a basis for our deliberative orientations to the environment, direct our muscular responses, and structure our identities (Mead, 1962 [1934]: 116; Dewey, 2002 [1922]: 30; see also James, 1900: 134). Once constituted, habits are *almost* self-perpetuating insofar as they 'stimulate, inhibit, intensify, weaken, select, concentrate and organise' our impulses and activities into 'their own likeness' (Dewey, 2002 [1922]: 125). Habits lie at the very base of our sense of self.

This conception of habit enables us to see how routines are both necessary but can also function to enlarge or restrict our relationship with the world. In terms of those that restrict our horizons, Dewey (2002 [1922]: 35) notes that 'bad habits' can exert a hold over us and override 'our formal resolutions, our conscious decisions'. He begins with the seemingly innocuous example of poor posture and notes that simply trying to *think* one's way to standing up straight is doomed to failure as the body is already committed to 'an established habit of standing incorrectly', and is bound to use existing muscle tensions as a (wholly inadequate) basis on which to avoid slouching (Dewey, 2002 [1922]: 35).

The reason a habit can exert this influence is not because it is some external imposition, but because 'it is so intimately *a part of ourselves*. It has a hold on us because *we are the habit*' (ibid.: 24; emphasis added). Furthermore, habits have consequences for the wider environment. The example of posture that Dewey discusses may seem inconsequential, but in the West back problems cost health services millions of dollars a year and mean that significant personal, occupational and public resources are devoted to issues that are nowhere near as widespread in countries such as China that promote different techniques of standing, sitting and walking (Mauss, 1973 [1934]).

In contrast to habits that damage and constrain are those that effect an increase in the capacities of the embodied actor. When a child learns to walk, for example, the assistance, examples and models set by others are encouragements, incitements and reinforcements for the child's own efforts at establishing an empowering habit. Habits can enlarge one's agential field of action (Dewey, 2002 [1922]: 70). Indeed, James (1950 [1890]) argued that habits are not opposed to rational action, but constitute its bedrock, while Peirce eventually came to understand habits as 'logical and rational operations' and opposed this mode of action to the 'mere slothful repetition of what has been done' (cited in Kilpinen, 2000).

If habits can variously enable and constrain action, Dewey (2002 [1922]: 67) proposes a further distinction between 'routine, unintelligent habit, and intelligent habit or art'. The advantage of this distinction is that it dispenses with the conventional opposition between habit and reason without removing the means of judging the effectiveness of particular habits. While intelligent habits are informed by thought, unintelligent habits are rigid and unresponsive to changing circumstances. Thus, Dewey holds that habits can constitute 'mere responsive adjustment[s] to physical stimulus', or 'intentional responsive activities' based on the underlying structure of a situation and directed towards the achievement of particular goals (Siegfried, 1996: 96). A labourer with acquired dispositions and the theoretically informed reflection required to criticise and adjust them, for example, is possessed of habits that are intelligent because they have the flexibility to be effective in new situations (Mead, 1968: 57). This distinction between intelligent and more routinised forms of habit is elaborated further in Dewey's comments on the 'unmistakable' difference between the artist and the mechanical performer.

> The artist is a masterful technician. The technique or mechanism is fused with thought and feeling. The 'mechanical' performer permits the mechanism to dictate the performance. It is absurd to say that the latter exhibits habit and the former not. We are confronted with two kinds of habit, intelligent and routine. (Dewey, 2002 [1922]: 71)

This is not to underestimate the difficulties of acquiring routinised technical skills, or to denigrate the capacities for action afforded by them. Any adult who has attempted to learn a new physical skill can probably appreciate Mead's (1962 [1934]: 355) description of the 'bungling, awkward, hesitating play of the beginner at tennis or on the violin' as the novice struggles to acquire the most rudimentary competence in his or her chosen activity. Nevertheless, most of us will have experienced the distinction between mechanical and artistic habit in either acquiring a skill ourselves or in watching or listening to the performance of another. Our appreciation of dance, music, football or any number of skills, is based on at least an implicit appreciation of what it is like to witness a true artist (who executes their skills with flair, ease, feeling and originality) as opposed to a mechanistic performance characterised by a 'lack of soul'. Sudnow's (1978) experience of learning to become a jazz pianist provides a good example of the crossover from routinised to intelligent habit. Comparing his early efforts with his eventual acquisition of a degree of ease in the execution of performance, Sudnow (1978: 85) likens the difference to that between a student's first attempt to put together a sentence in a foreign language and a native speaker's speech. More generally, in the case of the artist, a 'flexible, sensitive habit grows more varied, more adaptable by practice and use' *irrespective* of whether it is deployed by 'the cook, musician, carpenter, citizen or statesman' or even jazz pianist (Dewey, 2002 [1922]: 72).

The initial development of habits starts early in infancy, and childhood routines usually leave an indelible mark on adult actions. Crystallising our capacities in line with early experiences, habits can make it exceptionally difficult for adults to effect changes in themselves. We become 'caught, as it were, by the consequences of our early habit formation' (James, 1950 [1890]). This is why societies place such great store on schooling. As Dewey (1969 [1916]) argues, the control, guidance and direction provided by education forms intellectual and emotional dispositions in children, and imparts them with habits of reasoning and judging that exert a profound influence over how they adjust to the natural and social environment. The significance of this becomes clearer when we look at how habits *incorporate within themselves* social expectations, physical objects, tools and technologies in the natural and social environment. Habits are *modes of connection* to the world, shaping us and the environment according to their specific logic and affordances. As Dewey (2002 [1922]: 15, 26) argues, assimilating and directing the energies of the individual, habits unify the body with the natural and social world in particular ways, having specific objects and technologies as their target, and exerting a certain command over the environment. Furthermore, while individuals die, habits can live on in objects and technologies, and also in customs and traditions. Once forged in conjunction with habits, the shape and accessibility of technological objects is not infinitely flexible, but offers a limited range of 'affordances' to future generations which structure how they are likely to encompass and shape the social and natural world (Gibson, 1979; Pels et al., 2002: 9). This is why habits can function as massively important conserving agents which not only economise and simplify our actions, but which have the potential to reproduce social structures.

Habits reside in and shape the deepest recesses of the embodied subject. Despite their conserving power, however, habits are subject to change and so too are the objects, technologies and social and natural environments encompassed by them. Individuals can also seek intentionally to change habits and, while we have noted how difficult this can be, such efforts are usually most successful when there is a corresponding change in the contextual and environmental conditions that form part of their routinised behaviours. (This is a good example of the relationship and interaction that exists between the internal and external environments of action.) In the case of poor posture, for example, therapies such as Pilates and the Alexander Technique involve individuals in a set of exercises that seek to alter the tensions and alignment of their bodies. In the case of the addict, Alcoholics Anonymous helps to provide individuals with a change in routine and a support system which can act as a substitute for previously habitualised patterns of drinking. Drug rehabilitation clinics provide similar types of support, and may prescribe substitute drugs which act as material replacements for the object of addiction. More generally, it is possible to learn new habits. This may be a painstaking process, involving a reorientation of the embodied subject to new external environmental conditions, but it can and does happen.

Habits may restrict or expand one's relationship to the world but are fundamental to the embodied subject's ability to act on and make a difference to the environment. However, there are times when even the most successful of habits are blocked, when the flow and routinised actions of embodied subjects is interrupted by personal conflict, physical obstacles or social circumstances, and shown to be inadequate to the task at hand. Even the most 'intelligent' and creative habit is not infinitely flexible, or else it would not be a habit. It is on such occasions that a whole realm of action that the embodied subject has taken for granted is called into question, and that their habitually accumulated 'practical consciousness' faces failure (Giddens, 1984). Habit, from being successful, enters a state of crisis (Dewey, 2002 [1922]: 190–1).

Crisis

Crisis occurs when there develops a significant mismatch or conflict between the social and physical surroundings in which individuals live and their biological needs and bodily potentialities. In these circumstances, certain routine ways of acting become impossible or ineffective. As Joas (1996: 128) notes, the routines of action based on our belief in a world of self-evidently given facts can be shattered by experience. In terms of changes occasioned in the external environment, customary ways of inter-acting with others may suddenly become unacceptable (e.g. as children grow up and demand to be treated 'like adults'), or climatic changes may render infertile a piece of land a family depended on for crops. In terms of changes occasioned by the internal environment, aging can throw our actions out of equilibrium with our bodily needs. A health regime may no longer prevent ill-health, a diet may become ineffective, and new body frailties and disabilities may restrict stamina, movement and the capacity to act in routinised ways. Finally, crisis can also occur when previously successful habits clash. When there is an *impasse* between habits, regularised action is brought to a halt and the individual is placed in a situation of deliberation. Choices have to be made so that there can emerge 'a unified preference out of competing preferences' (Dewey, 2002 [1922]: 193). This more deliberative mode of orientation towards the environment does not constitute the cessation of activity, or the replacement of a practical engage-ment with the environment by a purely cognitive process of thinking, or a type of rationality which can be contrasted with traditional habitual behaviour as in Max Weber's typology of social action. Instead, it repre-sents a form of 'intra-organic' activity in which there occurs 'a dramatic rehearsal (in imagination) of various competing possible lines of action' and a 'laborious' process of practical reasoning in an attempt to achieve a 'working harmony among diverse desires' (ibid.: 191, 196, 198).

These distinctive types of crisis are each characterised by a conflict either within or between the external and internal environments. Experience confronts us with cruel practical jokes and surprises (Peirce, 1997 [1903]), our stream of thought is interrupted by 'obstruction' (James, 1950 [1890]) and habit 'swells with resentment' (Dewey, 2002 [1922]: 44). Habits may continue in these circumstances, but are condemned to ineffectiveness and may damage the individual who stubbornly rejects the need to change.

This damage is evident when we look at the various consequences that crises can have for embodied actors. First, and most inconsequentially, the blockage of minor habits may be a relatively insignificant source of individual irritation, resulting in a slight refocusing of behaviour. Having to reduce one's coffee intake as a result of medical advice, for example, can produce short-term headaches and the difficulty of forgoing a regular early morning caffeine fix, but is hardly a major life event. The crisis here is for a particular habit. Having to walk an extra five minutes to go to the shops, because the corner shop has shut down, may be more of an inconvenience. Nevertheless, new routines can soon become habituated into behaviour without usually causing major disruptions to a person's life or sense of identity.

Second, the blockage of habits can result more seriously in a personal, practical *doubt* about one's capacities, and this may even extend into a crisis of identity. Doubt is a response to the interruption of successful habits, and Peirce contrasts doubt with the 'calm and satisfactory' state of belief. Blocked habits may continue to operate, seeking to reattach themselves successfully to the environment and release the embodied subject from doubt, but their 'demand for a changed environment' is usually futile (Dewey, 2002 [1922]: 53). The impact that blocked habits can have on the embodied subject's identity is evident in Sparkes and Silvennoinen's (1999) collection of articles centred around auto/biographical experiences of sporting injury and disability. These accounts detail how injuries may result in practical doubts which invade every element of the individual's previously taken-for-granted routines and identities. Such blockages of habitual ways of being in the world led to 'shattered masculinities', the 'loss of athletic identity', 'disrupted selves', 'failed bodies', and the ending of sporting careers. The crisis here challenges an individual's identity by destroying their confidence in their bodies and their world.

Third, and relatedly, individuals characterised by mechanised, unresponsive habits may find themselves buffeted by circumstances, alienated by the sudden obsolescence of their actions, and forced to fall back on ad hoc actions. This is illustrated by the fate of the IBM programmers in Sennett's (1998) study of the corrosion of character. Sennett (1998) examines how changes in the computer industry encouraged many programmers and operatives to expand their taken-for-granted stocks of knowledge in order to be able to deal actively with the technological changes sweeping the industry. Those who mechanically stuck to their existing skills and did not broaden their capacities found themselves ill-prepared to cope with the changing external environment and were made redundant. Instead of being able to shape their own destinies, Sennett's interviewees recognised that their conservatism left them unable to survive or prosper in a changing world. The crisis here involves social position and sense of self-identity, and can also, given the links between employment and well-being, implicate individual health.

There is a tradition of sociological writing that shares the pragmatist concern with how crises can threaten the continuity and coherence of the embodied subject. It includes Garfinkel's (1963, 1967) experiments with trust, Goffman's (1956, 1983) analyses of embarrassment and the interaction order, Berger's (1990 [1967]) discussion of 'marginal situations' and Giddens's (1991) analysis of 'fateful moments'. The works of Berger and Giddens highlight the existential crises that individuals can suffer when their entire habitual mode of orientation to the world is shown to be fragile and impermanent. This is exemplified by the experience of bereavement and serious illness. These can render ineffective our routinised ways of dealing with the environment, devastating the 'business as usual' attitude which characterises everyday life, and challenging the existence of even the most 'intelligent' of habits that are predicated on functioning effectively within the normal parameters of life (Berger, 1990 [1967]: 23, 43; Dewey, 2002 [1922]: 173; see also Bauman, 1992; Elias, 2001 [1985]). What is interesting about this example is that society has historically recognised this threat to the habitual actions on which its structures depend (Durkheim, 1995 [1912]). The confrontation with death has been managed via a number of contrasting strategies (e.g. the ritual containment of death in public, the sequestration of the dying in private, the domestication and 'rehabilitation' of the dying within the community), but each of these has sought to restrict its disruptive effects to the routine business of daily life (Giddens, 1991).

Crisis is not something that embodied subjects usually welcome or enjoy, and Peirce and Dewey argue that there exists a strong human impulse to escape the doubt that can attend blocked or failed habits. Crisis can be a prelude to 'new beginnings', though, encouraging people to rediscover the 'horizon of possibilities' that exists within every situation (Scheffler, 1974; Joas, 1996: 1). Robbed of their usual avenues for expression, impulses and desires push forward, and the embodied subjects seek to re-establish an effective, workable relationship with the world around them. In such cases, habits 'which were interfered with begin to get a new direction' (Dewey, 2002 [1922]: 126, 181).

Habits may exist at the centre of the pragmatist view of embodied action, but this additional concern with crisis offers us something sociologically distinctive. This is particularly clear if we compare the pragmatist view of action with Bourdieu's conception of *habitus*. Bourdieu is one of the few recent sociologists to have paid serious attention to the role of routinised action in social life. In contrast to his argument that there is a 'relative irreversibility' to the habitual orientation of the embodied subject (Bourdieu and Wacquant, 1992: 133), however, pragmatism maintains that all action is caught in the tension between 'unreflected habitual action' and the experience of disruption and crisis as circumstances change and habits become ineffective. This is because the relationship between the external and internal environments of action is ultimately unstable. Even in the most apparently static of situations, social, physical or biological factors such as aging and illness can change the demands made of people (Kilpinen, 2000: 334). The sense that pragmatism offers us something distinctive is reinforced when we take into account the third phase of action it identifies as an irreducible part of human life. In contrast to the apparent determination of action by social class factors that we see in Bourdieu's work, pragmatism identifies 'acts of creativity' as phases of action that re-establish a productive relationship of change between the embodied subject and the environment (Joas, 1996: 131).

Creativity

Classical writers such as Marx, Durkheim, Weber and Simmel attributed great significance to innovative action in their respective writings on revolution, the social and emotional force of collective effervescence, the transformative power of charismatic action, and the vitalism that provides an impetus for new social forms. Creativity tended to become removed from the sociological view, however, in the face of Parsons's enormously influential focus on social values and norms; a focus that derived social action from apparently intractable societal standards. Pragmatism, in contrast, established creative action as an integral part of the phases of social action. We have already seen how intelligent habits incorporate within them a creative response to the world. My focus in this section, however, is on the creativity that is performed within situations which call for solutions after habits have ceased to be effective.

Creativity is associated with actions that alter certain aspects of oneself and/or one's surroundings in order to repair or enhance one's embodied capacities for action. As such, creative action may result in the establishment of newly efficacious relations with the environment or, when carried out after a period of crisis inducing disruption to established habits, can resecure for the individual what Dewey (2002 [1922]: 15) refers to as the 'stability essential to living.' In resecuring such stability, creativity requires practical reflection, involving an engaged deliberation with one's surroundings. As Peirce (1878) argues, it may be accompanied by images that 'pass rapidly through consciousness, one incessantly melting into another, until at last, when all is over – it may be in a fraction of a second, an hour, or after long years – we find ourselves decided as to how we should act'. Creativity may involve memory and foresight, intelligent deliberation and a 'dramatic rehearsal' of 'various competing possible lines of action' in order 'to solve the problems of present behaviour in terms of its possible future consequences as implicated on the basis of past experience' (ibid.: 100; Dewey, 2002 [1922]: 191, 193). Such processes are not abstracted from our bodily feelings and experiences. As Dewey (2002 [1922]: 194) argues, creative choices do not constitute 'the emergence of preference out of indifference', but result from 'a sensitiveness' to the integrity of options, and a 'feeling' of having done 'justice to all facts'. If an individual succeeds in reorienting action through intelligent deliberation 'something new enters the world: a new mode of acting' for that person 'which can gradually take root' and become routinised as a habit. For Dewey (1980 [1934]: 15), as for Peirce, the creative overcoming of obstacles carries within it 'the germs of a consummation akin to the esthetic'; an aesthetic pleasure that replaces the irritation of practical doubt associated with crisis by the assurance of *belief.*

The emotional experience associated with creativity is at its height during sudden experiences of revelation or epiphany when someone is gripped by the realisation that their relationship with the environment could be radically different. This feeling is often associated with religious insight or conversion, and is clearly not understood adequately solely as a cognitive event. As James (1982 [1902]: 113) argues, revelation and epiphany emerge from specific situations and problems, and can strike the individual with a physically and emotionally palpable force. They can feel like a 'bolt of lightning', increasing an individual's heart rate and blood pressure, and making them unable to contain themselves. The recipients of such revelation suddenly realise how they can be fulfilled by circumstances or can undertake a radical readjustment to their social and material milieu which completely alters their outlook on life (James, 1982 [1902]: 48).

Revelation and epiphany are not exclusively religious phenomena, but can occur in virtually any situation. Musicians have talked of reaching a stage when they no longer struggled to perform a skill, but suddenly found themselves accomplished and at ease in what they were doing in a manner that was akin to becoming 'the instrument through which music flows' (James, 1982 [1902]: 206). Having laboured to acquire and execute techniques smoothly, sportspeople have awoken 'suddenly to an understanding of the fine points of the game and to a real enjoyment of it' (ibid.). The 'peak experiences' associated with feeling 'at one' with a demanding physical activity have been experienced as 'life changing events' in which a harmony is achieved between the participant, the activity and the environment (e.g. Baker and Moreno, 2001: 15–17). Irrespective of the particular form that such experiences of revelation have taken, however, they seem to share a sense of conviction that what one is doing is right, of perceiving previously obfuscated truths, and of reaching a new and higher relationship of equilibrium with the environment (James, 1982 [1902]: 250–4).

Embodiment, character and collective action

This account of the phases of embodied action illustrates the significance pragmatism attributes to the existence of, and interaction between, the external and internal environments of action. These concerns are also evident in pragmatism's writings on identity or *character*. Up to this point in the chapter, identity has been treated almost in passing as a cumulative effect of embodied action. One's sense of self emerges and develops on the basis of one's repeated interactions with the environment. The manner in which this is achieved, however, is a key issue for pragmatism and allows us to see how its analysis of embodied action is also connected to a deep concern with individual and social morality.

The sociological tradition has displayed a longstanding concern with the moral dimensions of identity. Max Weber and Georg Simmel are two of the best known sociological writers on this subject and proposed what Levine (1995: 320) refers to as an 'existentialist ethics in which the authentic personal decisions of each actor become the principle for directing action'. Individuals are seen here as seeking to organise their actions and experiences on a basis that is consistent with their self-identity by standing over, controlling and dominating their social and material surroundings.[1] This has been criticised as a masculinist conception of personality which ignores human interdependency (Bologh, 1990). Pragmatism's view of the *interconnectedness* of the embodied subject and this environment, furthermore, contains an additional warning against viewing embodied identity through the metric of *domination*. In place of this approach, pragmatism is more concerned with conceptualising human identity or character in terms of how individuals *adjust* to and achieve *integration* with their surroundings, accomplishments associated with the human capacity to engage in an intelligent responsiveness.

This adjustment and integration does not entail a masculine dominance or a passive subjugation to our social and physical surroundings, and is very different from Weber's conception of the heroic subject. Instead, it is concerned with people finding *coherence* between their internal and external environments, achieving some consistency between their actions and the raw materials of life that surround them (Siegfried, 1996: 35–6) and, in so doing, being able to express and develop the creative 'I' of their identity. This is crucial because, as Mead (1962 [1934]: 204) argues, the imaginative experiences of the 'I' belong to 'the most fascinating part of our experience' in which 'novelty arises' and where 'our most important values are located'. This can only occur, however, when there is some sort of alignment between the 'I', the possibilities afforded to the subject by the physical milieu, and the norms of identity central to the 'generalised other' within the social milieu. As such, while the development of identity and character may not require a domination of the environment, it is likely to require initiative, adventure, experiment and an intelligent engagement with, and evaluation of, the circumstances in which individuals find themselves (Dewey, 1958).

Within the context of this valuation of expression, adjustment and integration, pragmatism recognises a whole spectrum of character types. The extent of this range is highlighted in its explication of the 'integrated subject' and the 'fractured subject'. In the case of the *integrated subject*, the expressive and creative 'I' element of embodied identity is developed and enhanced, rather than being obstructed, through the individual's actions in the social and physical environment. This realisation can be associated with an extraordinary form of experience, involving an individual feeling that they have progressed to a richer and higher relationship with their surroundings (Dewey, 1980 [1934]: 35).

There are many different ways in which embodied subjects can achieve this type of integral being, and feminists have praised pragmatism for its capacity to recognise typically female modes of living within this formulation (Siegfried, 1996). A mother's relationship with a child, for example, is often characterised by the high degree of emotional integration analysed by Dewey. Nevertheless, it remains more difficult for oppressed and subordinated groups within society to achieve high levels of integration. Racist, patriarchal and other oppressive social relationships can make it especially difficult for those subjected to them to construct a positive, empowering identity which can be aligned with the wider environment. It is not impossible, however, and in contemporary global societies there are numerous bases on which diverse yet coherent identities can be forged by embodied subjects despite the existence of material inequalities and prejudicial norms.

At the other end of the spectrum from the integrated character lies the *fractured subject*. Here, there is no satisfactory alignment between the 'I' element of embodied identity and the external environment, and individuals find themselves 'broken off, discrete' and 'at odds' with their surroundings. As Dewey (1958: 245) notes, in cases such as these, people either surrender or conform to their surroundings, and for the sake of peace become 'a parasitical subordinate', or indulge 'in egotistical solitude'. For this type of identity existence is often 'little more than a series of zigzags, as now one tendency and now another gets the upper hand' and experience remains fragmented (James, 1982 [1902]: 169). In contrast to the more satisfactory form of 'Experience' that pragmatism associates with the integrated subject, the fractured self is more likely to encounter what Dewey (1980 [1934]: 260) refers to as 'the apathy, lassitude and stereotype' characteristic of 'ordinary experience'. The emotions associated with such experience may be intense or shallow, but without the integrative force of a unified character they are unlikely to be harnessed to individual growth or to result in a more productive and harmonic relationship with the environment (ibid.: 156).

The above depictions of integrated and fractured subjects are 'end points' on the pragmatist spectrum of character. Human identity and action are processual rather than static phenomena, and it is just as unlikely for the embodied subject to be characterised in reality by a totally unified character as it is for the individual's identity to be completely fragmented and condemned to 'the humdrum; slackness of loose ends; submission to convention in practice and intellectual procedure'

(Dewey, 1980 [1934]: 40). In line with its emphasis on intentionality and creativity, it is also important to note that pragmatism recognises that individuals can effect changes in their characters. James, for example, recommended to his students that they keep the 'faculty of effort alive' by 'a little gratuitous exercise every day' which involved them in being 'systematically ascetic or heroic in little unnecessary points' (Scheffler, 1974: 126–7). He recommended this on the basis that just as we 'become drunkards by so many separate drinks, so we become saints in the moral, and authorities and experts in the practical and scientific spheres, by so many separate acts and hours of work' (Scheffler, 1974: 127). The training into mystical insight via yoga that occurs in India is another example of a technique of the self mentioned in pragmatism. Yoga means the 'experimental union of the individual with the divine' and is based on a combination of diet, posture, breathing, intellectual concentration, movement and moral discipline that are designed ultimately to effect a complete readjustment between the embodied subject and their world (James, 1982 [1902]: 400). The end result of such training may be entry into a superconscious state accompanied by a revelation far higher than the 'truths' yielded by reason could ever bring, but the means of reaching this state centrally implicate the body. A similar point can be made about the techniques of breathing and exercise central to Taoism. These seek to harmonise the mind and body, and place the individual in a sympathetic relationship with the 'natural energies and order of the universe' (Graham, 1989).

This analysis anticipates Michel Foucault's (1988) writings on technologies of the self. Through an evaluation of texts of Greco-Roman philosophy and Christian spirituality, Foucault examined how individuals could work actively on themselves as ethical subjects. Instead of being the product of shifting circumstances, such technologies (be they religious tracts or secular regimes of care for the self) permitted the subject 'to effect by their own means or with the help of others a certain number of operations on their own bodies and souls, thoughts, conduct and way of being, so as to transform themselves in order to attain a certain state of happiness, wisdom, perfection, or immortality' (Foucault, 1988: 18). In the contemporary West, there exist an unprecedented number of operations, procedures, projects and regimes available to those seeking to maintain or enhance their health, or to alter their appearance in line with social norms (Shilling, 2003). When accomplished successfully, such changes readjust the embodied subject's relationship with at least part of their environment, and can result in an enhancement of their capacities for action.[2] Pragmatism warns us that such attempts usually involve a degree of resistance, however, even if only from the body's own limits and frailties. Furthermore, the results of such efforts are not known in advance: the embodied self that results from their labour depends 'on the unforeseeable results of an adventure' (Dewey, 1958: 246). As Dewey puts it, 'No one discovers a new world without forsaking an old one; and no one discovers a new world who puts the act of discovery under bonds with respect to what the new world shall do to him [or her] when it comes into vision' (ibid.).

If pragmatism is concerned with the moral consequences of individual identity or character, it is also committed to exploring the moral consequences of *collective action*, and its proponents have long been concerned with how practical inquiry, knowledge and dialogue can contribute towards the democratic management of the external environment in a manner which best assists the development and meeting of people's needs (Levine, 1995; Stuhr, 2002). Dewey's (1927) political writings take the process of collective action as their starting point, and are concerned with the conditions in which social problems are responded to through communication between all those concerned. This communication is seen as an essential condition for a healthy social order (Joas, 1993: 25). At its most effective, it can impart an aesthetic experience to the process of living and a sense of communion to the cementation of social relationships (Dewey, 1980 [1934]: 270; Shusterman, 1992: 6). Mead and Peirce also exhibited a strong concern with the social whole, viewing the 'social attitude' not from the vantage point of 'the interests of an isolated individual, group, community or nation', but from a concern with 'the future welfare of the human community-at-large' (Lewis and Smith, 1981). This perspective ascribes to the social sciences an enormous moral and political importance in seeking to 'aid human communities in improving their potential for collective action' (Joas, 1993: 25).

Conclusion

In examining the corporeal dimensions of action, pragmatism enables us to take account of the social consequentiality of the body's own needs and capacities whilst also travelling beyond the biological organism to the external environment. This enables us to recognise the dynamic interactions that occur between these environments, while avoiding the problems of conflation that hamper structuralist and individualist approaches to the body. The phases of action recognised by pragmatism – phases informed by interactions and processes that are constantly vulnerable to change – also allow us to avoid the reification of action that can occur when it is conceptualised in terms of ideal types or as a product of some rational choice preference schedule. Within this more dynamic conception of the phases of action, the predominance of habitual action is most likely to be associated with a period of relative stability in the external and internal environments, while the onset of crisis tends to precipitate changes in routinised actions. Pragmatism also recognises the various ways in which actions relate to the identities of embodied subjects in its concern with *character*. Eschewing the sociological view that individuals develop personality through the distance from, and the command they are able to exert over, the environment, pragmatism recognises and validates identity formation that develops through integration with, and adjustment to, the surroundings. In particular, its concern with techniques of the self (a concern which was developed long before Foucault's work on the subject) provides us with a useful way of approaching the myriad ways in which individuals seek to structure their lives amid the changing situations they encounter. Finally, the pragmatic approach outlined in this chapter acknowledges the importance of collective action as a means of altering the external environment in line with the evolving needs and capacities of embodied subjects.

By focusing on the situated actions and identities of embodied subjects, this chapter has been concerned with how pragmatism can assist theoretically sociological conceptions of embodied action. I have also suggested it has an important contribution to make to *substantive* sociological studies of the body, however, and it is to that issue I now turn.

Notes

1 In their analyses of modern society both Weber and Simmel argued that the realisation of such authenticity had become increasingly problematic. For Weber, this necessitated a heroic stance in the face of the amoral rationalisations of modernity. Through a process of existential struggle, heroic individuals were still able to reach a stage in which they settled on a passionate commitment to a set of values core to their identities. For Simmel, the fate of the individual in modernity has become a tragic one: we are surrounded by a world of social groups and objects that constrain and dominate us, making the pursuit of authenticity increasingly hopeless (Coser, 1971: 192).

2 The question of whether changing one's appearance in line with social norms enhances one's capacities will be discussed further in this book. There is little doubt, however, that the cultivation and achievement of slenderness and good looks is associated with social capital in contemporary consumer culture. Research suggests, for example, that women's attempts to conform to stereotypical ideals of beauty can be empowering for the individual subject even though they may have a detrimental effect for women as a whole (by reinforcing the legitimacy of such ideals). Similarly, studies suggest that children perceived as unattractive or physically disabled continue to be stigmatised from an early age, while people viewed as attractive tend to be classified as socially skilled (Newell, 2000).

3

Embodying Social Research

Introduction

Pragmatism imparted embodied subjects with emergent capacities and needs, and recognised that people were shaped and partially constituted by the social and the natural world. As such, it appeared to offer a highly suggestive resource for those interested in exploring *empirically* the reciprocal jostlings that occur between individuals and their surroundings. Yet most European sociologists remained unconvinced. Embedded in well-established traditions of thought, they tended to be hostile or indifferent to pragmatism (e.g. Durkheim, 1955; but see Baert and Turner, 2007). The fate of this tradition within its home nation, however, was quite different. Pragmatism was well-represented in the first American university to establish a Department of Sociology, the University of Chicago. Dewey and Mead taught at Chicago, while C.H. Cooley, W.I. Thomas and Robert Park (the three intellectually dominant figures of American sociology in the early decades of the twentieth century) studied under Dewey and had contacts with other major pragmatists (Joas, 1993: 32–3; Levine, 1995: 263). Cooley, Thomas and Park each translated pragmatist themes into ambitious writings on sociology and social psychology, and supervised a rich and diverse collection of related studies which had a lasting impact on sociology and social research (Rucker, 1969; Levine, 1995). Indeed, the Chicago School dominated sociology and political science in the United States between 1915 and 1940 (Bulmer, 1984).

As the Chicago School was influenced deeply by pragmatist themes and concerns, we should not be surprised that it included the bodily dimensions of human beings within its vision of sociology. Specifically, Chicago bequeathed to the discipline a legacy of sociological research concerned with the external and internal environments of the embodied subject, and with the importance of habit, crisis and creativity, in an age marked by rapid urbanisation, industrialisation and immigration. By the time the Chicago School's dominance came to an end in the 1940s, however, the presence of the body had faded within the discipline. The impact of this physical dematerialisation was lasting: much has been written about the legacy of the Chicago School in recent years, but this has usually been undertaken from the perspective of conventional subjects of sociological interest (e.g. urban studies, 'race' and research methods). Furthermore, while sociological studies have excavated 'secret traditions' of body-relevant writings, they are yet to explore the significance of the Chicago School for our understanding of embodiment.

There are three major reasons for this neglect. First, as the concern with embodiment often remained implicit within the Chicago studies, it was possible for subsequent generations of sociological commentators to underplay and even ignore its significance. Second, the writings of the most influential pragmatist, G.H. Mead, came to be defined and investigated mostly in terms of a focus on *symbolic* interaction. It was Mead's interest in the significance of symbols in interpersonal role-taking that came to have an enduring impact within what came to be known as 'symbolic interactionism', and in sociology's general interest in role theory and socialisation research. His concern with the *physical* dimensions and environments of interaction received much less interest. Third, in the course of exerting an unprecedented influence on sociology's view of its own heritage, Talcott Parsons marginalised pragmatism while also helping to establish a general sociological climate in which the boundaries between sociology and the biological and physical sciences were strengthened. While pragmatism provided the discipline with a promise of what it could achieve by adopting a flexible and more dynamic view of the relationship between the external and internal environments of action, Parsons reacted to this by reasserting the autonomy and primacy of 'the social'.

In examining how sociology was successively embodied and disembodied in the American context, this chapter provides some contextual background to the Chicago School and a brief introduction to the range of issues associated with its sociological research. It then illustrates in more detail how its bodily concerns were instantiated in empirical research by focusing on Nels Anderson's classic 1923 case study, *The Hobo*, and on fieldwork conducted into sexuality. The chapter concludes by analysing how it was that this pragmatist concern with embodiment was marginalised by later developments in sociology, before looking at those factors responsible for a recent revival in concern for the physical materiality of human being.

Pragmatism and the Chicago School

At the end of the nineteenth century, John Dewey and George Herbert Mead were appointed to the University of Chicago. Together with other first generation pragmatists (including Jane Addams who was not actually appointed to the University but who conducted influential research into urban sociology, ethnic relations and gendered knowledge [McDonald, 1997]), they and their graduate students embarked on inquiries that exerted an impact across the social sciences. The Chicago School of Sociology was characterised by a combination of pragmatist philosophy, a concern with the promotion of democracy within conditions of rapid urbanisation and industrialisation, and attempts to make sociology into an empirical science concerned centrally with experientially gained knowledge (Joas, 1993: 17). As Donald Levine (1995: 258) notes, it aspired 'to nothing less than a program to resolve all philosophical questions through analyses of practical action', analyses that remained sensitive to the external *and* internal environments of action. In so doing, it established a tradition in which sociological work that clarified people's understanding of social reality was seen as an important contribution to collective problem solving (Janowitz, 1991). The influence of this research programme produced an important immediate change in the direction of American sociology during the first third of the twentieth century. It was during this period that the speculative theoretical works of the first generation of American sociologists, figures such as Ward, Sumner, Ross and Giddings, were replaced by a more empirical turn (Shils, 1980; Bulmer, 1997: 243).

The environments of embodied action

The research programme undertaken at the Chicago School had at its centre the translation of pragmatism's general concern with the external and internal environments of action into *sociological* concepts; concepts that could be operationalised in empirical research. The main components of the *external environment* for these sociologists were clear. America had been going through a rapid phase of industrialisation, urbanisation and immigration. The physical parameters of the built environment and the physical conditions of work were being revolutionised, and so too was the social environment. As the nineteenth century wore on, Chicago became 'an ethnic melting pot of Germans, Scandinavians, Irish, Italians, Poles, Jews, Czechs, Lithuanians, and Croats', to be followed in the first few decades of the twentieth century by a steadily growing number of Afro-Caribbean immigrants (Bulmer, 1984: 13). This was the context in which the principal content of the external environment examined by the Chicago School involved the characteristics and problems of the *modern city*, especially the city of Chicago (Joas, 1993: 28). In Robert Park's words, it was the city that was to become the 'social laboratory' in which pragmatist themes were translated into sociological problems.

This research resulted in *The City* (1925), a collection edited by Park and Burgess, *The Urban Community* (1927) edited by Burgess, and a variety of other studies. It had an immediate social impact. As Robert Faris (1967: 57) points out, while the eugenics movement in the nineteenth century had been influential in suggesting that the problems of urban slums were a consequence 'of generations of selective breeding of defectives', the Chicago School provided a more convincing account of how 'human behaviour pathologies' were associated with 'the type of urban area and not with the particular ethnic group that inhabited it'. It did this by demonstrating that each new population that began their residence in the slum areas of the city usually 'experienced the same severe disorganisation', but that 'as each of these populations in time prospered and migrated outward into more settled residential districts, the symptoms of disorganisation declined' (ibid.). In the case of W.I. Thomas and Florian Znaniecki's 1918–20 *The Polish Peasant in Europe and America*, such findings were said to have had a significant impact on the treatment of Poles by social workers (Faris, 1967).

The varied features of the social and physical environments character-istic of urban life investigated by the Chicago School are hinted at in the well-known titles to appear during the 1920s under the supervision of Park and Burgess. These monographs included *The Hobo, The Gold Coast and the Slum, The Gang, The Taxi-Dance Hall*, and *The Pilgrims of Russian Town*. Further investigation into the external environments of embodied life in the city was detailed in a series of studies, with which Burgess was associ-ated, conducted at the Institute for Juvenile Research. These included the 1929 ecological study *Delinquency Areas*, written by Clifford Shaw and his colleagues, and John Ladesco's 1929 *Organised Crime in Chicago* (Bulmer, 1984: 4, 89). What is so impressive about these writings is their attention to the importance of the interaction between the social and physical envi-ronment for the phenomenon under investigation. In contrast to a later, mid-century tendency in sociology to ignore the social significance of the built and natural environment, the Chicago School was concerned with geographical locale, with the quality of people's concrete surroundings, with the proximity and situatedness of facilities and with evoking a strong sense of the 'feel' of the neighbourhoods that contextualised its studies.

The pragmatist heritage of the Chicago School was also evident in the concern exhibited by some of its most prominent members with the *internal environment* of human being. In exploring the needs and potentialities of the embodied subject, however, Chicago sociologists were performing something of a balancing act. On the one hand, they were determined to undermine biologically reductionist forms of instinct theory which had served as popular accounts of human behaviour. On the other hand, they were committed to retaining a concern with embodied capacities and needs so as not to fall into the trap of explaining everything on the basis of external 'social facts'. In a methodological note at the start of *The Polish Peasant*, for example, Thomas and Znaniecki oppose what they saw as Durkheim's dependence on social facts by insisting that explanation consist of a combination of social *and* individual factors. Indeed, Chicago sociologists accepted that a comprehensive understanding of social action required an appreciation of the integration of physiological organisms and conscious selves – selves founded on a bodily and sensory basis, albeit developed through a social process (Faris, 1967: 92–3).

This approach was exemplified by Cooley who explored not only the organised structural units of society, but the genesis of the individual person-ality and other aspects of human nature (Cooley, 1909, 1922 [1902]). At an early stage in his career Thomas attributed great importance to the pursuit of food and sex as motivating forces (Faris, 1967), and classified human motives through his analysis of the 'four wishes'; the supposedly general human wish for (1) new experience, (2) security, (3) response and (4) recognition. Park too, from a different perspective, was concerned with the internal environment of embodied action. In a rarely noted but vital aspect of his writings, Park pointed to the unique perspective afforded by the physical mobility of the embodied subject. As he put it, the individual experiences associated with the subject making their corporeal way through space and time impart to them a unique consciousness that makes it difficult for habits to become totally shared, assimilated and unconscious (Matthews, 1977: 153–4).

This determination to operationalise pragmatist concerns through social research was not confined to the formation of concepts that would assist the examination of urban space and embodied motivation, but extended to the development of research methods. Thomas and Park encouraged their students to immerse themselves 'in the field', mix with people of different social backgrounds, and collect first hand information via methods that later became known and developed as 'participant observation'. In order to investigate how people imagined their appearance to another, and how that appearance would be judged, Cooley promoted the idea of sympathetic introspection that encouraged empathy and identification with others. Similarly, in line with the importance he attributed to the embodied foundations of individuality and knowledge, Park (1941: 33) emphasised the importance of empathy and used to repeat something he had once heard James say, 'the most real thing is a thing that is most keenly felt rather than the thing that is most clearly conceived' (Matthews, 1977: 39). Thomas emphasised the importance of the actor's 'definition of the situation', and utilised all manner of personal documents (including life histories, letters and diaries) in building up a profile of individuals and communities. Thomas gave life histories a particularly high rating, and spoke of them as having the potential to constitute the 'perfect type of sociological material' (Bogardus, 1949: 46).

One of the most significant early developments of empirical research methods in Chicago sociology appears in Thomas and Znaniecki's *The Polish Peasant in Europe and America*. This was not the first American sociological monograph, 'but it was a landmark because it attempted to integrate theory and data in a way no American study had done before' (Bulmer, 1984: 45). Later Chicago studies continued to show the mark of such innovation. Life histories, for example, were used in studies such as Paul G. Cressey's *The Taxi Dance Hall* (1932) and Clifford Shaw's *The Jack Roller* (1930), while Nels Anderson's *The Hobo* (1923) and Pauline Young's research into a religious cult in Los Angeles used 'participant observation'. As Bulmer (1997: 252) notes, in their concern with this type and variety of research methods, the Chicago School carved out a distinctive vision of sociology which 'more resembled social anthropologists such as Bronislaw Malinowski and A.R. Radcliffe-Brown than they did some of their predecessors in the first generation of sociologists, such as E.A. Ross or William Graham Sumner'. It was through such empirical research that social action came to be explored as resulting from the interaction of the external social and physical milieu, and the capacities and needs of the embodied subject.

The phases of social action

Reflecting the importance pragmatism attributed to habitual action, Chicago sociologists explored how an individual's actions could become stabilised as a result of congruence between the organisation of the social and physical milieu and their own development. Cooley was most radical here. He viewed the individual and society as different aspects of the same thing, and developed James's conception of the 'Me' through his conception of the 'looking glass self' (Levine, 1995: 265). In gaining a sense of our actions, Cooley (1922 [1902]) suggests that we imagine how we appear to other people, imagine their assessment of that appearance and then experience some sort of self-feeling, such as pride or mortification, based on that judgement. 'Primary groups' (face-to-face associations based on cooperation like the family, the children's play group and community elders) were particularly important in this respect. They served as an intimate communicative mechanism through which people's actions and wider customs and institutions maintained their vitality (Cooley, 1909). In these circumstances, habitual actions served to consolidate the wider environment in which people lived. Similarly, Thomas and Znaniecki (1918) analysed the relationship between the individual and social in terms of 'attitude' or *disposition* to act in a certain way which was itself embedded within the collectivity. Thomas recognised that habitual actions could frequently be observed and were essential to the stability of institutions. Park also acknowledged the importance of habitual social action by linking self conception to the notion of social roles. People's actions, sense of self and knowledge of others are informed by these roles – roles which lend a stability to social life.

Habit was an important feature and phase of action, but its significance did not rule out alternative ways of responding to the environment or the occurrence of major changes in the social and physical organisation of the city. In terms of *crisis* and *creativity*, Cooley (1909) recognised the positive opportunities associated with the decline of traditions. Thomas's (1909) analysis of crisis was central to his theory of social organisation. He insisted that stable patterns of behaviour only emerged following an individual's definition of and adjustment to a situation, and remained contingent on an individual's expectations being satisfied (Thomas, 1909; 1937: 8). Crisis was something that disturbed this run of habit. It necessitated that an individual develop 'a new mode of behaviour', and became endemic when cultures failed to provide their members with values that were sufficiently consistent and vigorous (Thomas, 1909: 16–17). Here, society entered a period of 'social disorganisation', a phenomenon that Thomas and other Chicago sociologists witnessed among immigrant communities as their young came into contact with values and opportunities that differed radically from those experienced by their parents (ibid., see also Matthews, 1977). Thrasher's research into boy gangs, for example, shows how the organisation of the city results in a tendency for the children

Changing Bodies

of immigrants to escape parental control, with gangs acting as a substitute for morally effective institutions (Faris, 1967). Park identified spontaneous collective gatherings (in addition to the unique perspective provided by the embodied individual's movement through space) as an important and creative source of social change (Matthews, 1977: 153–4). Finally, Thomas even suggested that the existence of chronic crises provide the foundations for specialist occupations – such as those in medicine, law and government – dedicated to dealing with disturbances in the physical and social environment.

For each of these sociologists, the crises that made untenable traditional institutions and ways of acting paved the way for *creative* responses that could shape the environment anew and result in a new equilibrium between individuals and their social and physical contexts.

Embodiment and character

Chicago sociology also displayed its pragmatist credentials by exploring the moral consequences of character. This is particularly apparent in Thomas's analysis of how individuals developed contrasting personalities as a result of negotiating their own needs and capacities (especially the desire for new experiences) in the context of the social group's concern with promoting normative stability. Thomas identified three major personality types. The 'philistine' is characterised by a rigid and habitual orientation to life – with habits so fixed that they only respond to certain stimuli, those constituting the most stable part of their milieu – and manifests the dominance of the environment over the individual. Social traditions are taken as given, and the physical environment as unalterable. In direct contrast, the 'Bohemian' has no coherent character structure, reacts on the basis of temperament or an isolated character trait, and constantly changes his/her attitudes and actions. This personality type manifests the dominance of individual desires over collective norms. Finally, the creative personality is able systematically to guide his or her own development and find solutions to the tensions involved in balancing individual impulses with social opportunities. This personality displays a character which is both organised and open to further development on the basis of planned and productive activity.

Thomas treats these personalities as ideal types, and is careful to emphasise that none are realised completely by an individual in every aspect of his or her life, but he attributed the creative personality with an important role in facilitating progressive social change (Thomas and Znaniecki, 1918). Cooley's conception of personality, explored through his notion of a 'healthy' self, complements Thomas's concern with the creative character. For Cooley, the healthy self is neither dominated by, nor closed off from, its external environment. Instead, it

> requires the same cooperation of continuity with change that marks normal development everywhere; there must be variability, openness, freedom on the basis of organisation: too rigid organisation means fixity or death, and the

32

lack of it, weakness or anarchy. The self-respecting man values others' judgments and occupies his mind with them a great deal, but he keeps his head, he discriminates and selects, considers all suggestions with a view to his character, and will not submit to influences not in the line of his development. (Cooley, 1922 [1902]: 236)

Pragmatism's concern with moral character is, as this summary suggests, replicated in the Chicago School. Possessed of a fundamental need for 'reciprocal communication', embodied subjects are ideally 'trusting, truthful, and open in their displays of self. The social relations that ensue between such actors are communicative as well, displaying cooperation, mutual adaptation, and exchange' (Alexander, 1997: vii). Cooley, Park and Thomas also addressed pragmatism's wider concern for an intelligent, self-directing public by seeking to build a sociology that enhanced society's capacities for 'intelligent self-direction' (Levine, 1995: 267). For Park, this involved a critical engagement with the 'fear of the crowd' that had characterised European social psychology. Defining the difference between the crowd and the public in terms of the forms and effects of the interactions they incorporate, Park separates the 'milling' of the crowd from the informed dialogue of the public. While the former is conducive to the emergence of no more than a 'collective impulse', the latter involves a constructive meeting and modification of opinions based on knowledge and experience (Matthews, 1977: 55). In this context, the pragmatic moral project of sociology should be concerned with helping to '*create* the larger public Dewey and Mead advocated by enabling diverse sectors of the great society to learn about one another and to help inform the public by presenting dispassionately observed and analysed facts about the natural processes of social life' (Levine, 1995: 268). For Levine (1995: 263), the challenge that pragmatism had set sociology, to conceive of disorder and flux as natural occurrences that provided opportunities for adaptive innovation, had been addressed with 'extraordinary creativity' by the central figures of the Chicago School.

Empirical studies

The Hobo

One of the best examples of a Chicago study that translated the pragmatist concern with embodied social action into empirical sociological research is Nels Anderson's (1961 [1923]) *The Hobo.* The subjects of Anderson's study are 'homeless men' ('few women are ever found on the road') who are migratory workers. Hobos survived by working in and moving between such areas as agriculture, building and construction, fishing, sheep shearing, ice harvesting and lumbering (Anderson, 1961 [1923]: 91, 137). They differed from tramps, 'who don't work', and 'bums' who 'seldom wander or work', although changing social conditions or motivations could cause individuals to pass from one group to another (ibid.: 90–6).

For Anderson, Chicago was an ideal place for his study. It was a popular location for hobos – with trains leaving every day to forty-four states across the country – and from 300,000 to 500,000 passed through the city during the course of an average year. However, Anderson's study was not the choice of an established academic deciding to involve himself in what later became known as 'participant observation'. It was a means, as Anderson (1961 [1923]: xii) himself notes, of 'getting by', of 'earning a living while exit [from the hobo life] was under way.' It is this immersion in hobo life that helps make Anderson's study such a rich and palpable account of human activity.

Anderson was born in 1889 in Chicago. His family moved around in search of a better life, like many American families of that time, and his early years were spent 'in covered wagons in the West, in tenements in Chicago, and on farms in Michigan' (Rauty, 1988: 1). Anderson left home in his mid-teens and took up a series of migrant jobs. 'Beating' his way across the country on freight trains, he worked as a skinner, laboured in a lumber camp and a metal mine, and took jobs on farms. When money ran out, he acquired another form of hobo experience, 'panhandling' from passers-by and begging for food at the back doors of houses. Eventually, he was hired on a Utah ranch and was subsequently taken in by the family and persuaded to return to education. The journey to study sociology at the University of Chicago was, as Anderson (1961 [1923]: xi) put it, 'my final effort at riding freight trains'.

Anderson's decision to study the hobo emerged after he wrote term papers on the subject, and received encouragement from the Department. Referring to his Masters' viva, an exam in which he struggled, Anderson (1961 [1923]: xii) remembers how Albion Small (then Head of Department) pointed to the street and said to him '"You know your sociology out there better than we do, but you don't know it in here. We have decided to take a chance and approve you" for your degree.' Later, once Anderson had written up his research into a report, Robert Park interested the university in publishing his study. Later still, after the book had been published, Ernest Burgess helped Anderson secure employment by putting him in touch with the Juvenile Protection Agency (JPA) who had decided to commission a related research project.

Social scientists have talked in recent years about the need to develop embodied research methods in order to put the corporeal actor back into the discipline (Ness, 2004). What strikes one immediately upon reading *The Hobo*, however, is the acute sensitivity with which Anderson describes the interactions that take place between the physical and social environment, and the embodied actor. In terms of the external physical environment, he describes how tens of thousands of men were concentrated into Chicago's 'Hobohemia', a lodging house area and the place where the hobo 'spent or lost his earnings and started again on the road' (Anderson, 1961 [1923]: xvi, 129–34). Conditions were not good.

Accommodation ranged from a bed in a single room for fifty cents to a space on the floor of a cockroach infested loft for a dime. Cheap hotels could have as little as two toilets for one hundred and eighty men, while some had no outside ventilation and opened direct onto sleeping rooms, causing 'foul and nauseating odors' (Anderson, 1961 [1923]: 129–34).

Hobohemia contained a range of other 'characteristic institutions' including 'eating joints, outfitting shops, employment agencies, missions, radical bookstores, welfare agencies … to minister to the needs, physical and spiritual, of the homeless man' (Anderson, 1961 [1923]: 14–15). Cinemas provided somewhere warm for a few hours, while apprentice barbers offered cheap haircuts. Anderson's description of the hobohemian restaurants is characteristically visceral.

> The waiters work like madmen during the rush hours, speeding in with orders, out with dirty dishes. During the course of this hour a waiter becomes literally plastered with splashes of coffee, gravy, and soup. The uncleanliness is revolting and the waiters are no less shocking than the cooks and dishwashers. In the kitchens uncleanliness reaches its limit. (Anderson, 1961 [1923]: 35)

In contrast to the urban centre of hobohemia, 'the jungles', were places where hobos passed their leisure time. Characterised by proximity to the railroad, located in a 'dry and shady place that permits sleeping on the ground', and having access to 'plenty of water for cooking and bathing and wood enough to keep the pot boiling', 'the jungle' is an institution fitted for bodily rest and recuperation in which 'the hobo is his own housewife' (Anderson, 1961 [1923]: 17). It is against this finely drawn evocation of the physical milieu that the social milieu of the hobo emerges in Anderson's study. The bootlegger and the dope peddler find homes here, the professional gambler works here and so too does the 'jack roller' ('the man who robs his fellows while they are drunk or asleep'). Within the reciprocal development of the physical and social surroundings, 'these and others of their kind find in the anonymity of the changing population that freedom and security that only the crowded city offers' (ibid.: 5).

Anderson's depiction of the external environment provided by hobohemia is counterbalanced by a concern with the embodied motives and needs of its inhabitants. Hobos struggle to cater for their basic biological needs. Many men end up in hobohemia because of industrial or other accidents resulting in 'bent and twisted bodies' and even 'missing limbs' (ibid.: 56, 129). More generally, poor food, bad accommodation, and the effects of the hobo lifestyle mean that many others 'are not physically able to do eight or ten hours hard labor without suffering' (ibid.: 129). Some choose this lifestyle as a way of satisfying a 'wanderlust', for example, yet may end up having to beg to survive and having to 'walk the streets all night' in order to avoid freezing to death (Anderson, 1961 [1923]: 49–56). In these conditions, ill-health is a constant danger and there is little incentive for the hobo to plan and think long-term: when money is accumulated through a period of work, it is often spent in a hedonistic binge involving alcohol and prostitutes.

For all its varieties and contingencies, the hobo lifestyle was associated with certain habits. The habit of moving from place to place, according to the availability of work and a decent climate, the habit of working and resting in periods of extreme contrast, of enjoying comfort when it was possible, and of sometimes having to survive by begging or stealing, could serve these men well. However, the hobo lifestyle was one that also presented its occupants with crises. Liable 'when not at work to arrest for vagrancy and trespassing', hobos also experienced the fact that virtually 'every home-less man "goes broke" at times' (Anderson, 1961 [1923]: 49, 167).

It might appear misplaced to talk about the moral character of the hobo in terms of this figure's capacity to integrate his/her inner and outer environments in a manner which contributes to the well-being of a larger group, but Anderson's study suggests otherwise. Anderson argues that hobos played a vital role in American history, despite their transitory status and whatever their weaknesses. While the 'first frontier' involved a movement of land settlement and a rush to appropriate natu-ral resources, a 'second frontier' began two decades later, once railways were established, and consisted of the founding of towns and cities, and the establishment of major industries (ibid.: xvii–xviii). It was with the work of the hobo that 'the railroads were built, out-of-the-way mines were developed, and outpost towns were established' (Anderson, 1961 [1923]: xxi). By providing the considerable workforce that was required in these industries before the second frontier had established a perma-nent and local supply of labour, hobos were essential to the development of modern America (ibid.).

Sexuality

If *The Hobo* exemplified the Chicago School's capacity to translate prag-matist themes into empirical research, it is also worth examining its research into sexuality. This had, until relatively recent times, been an underreported aspect of the Chicago School but provides us with more evidence of how a number of its studies sought to place the body at the centre of the discipline long before this became fashionable. Chad Heap's (2003) analysis of the city of Chicago as a 'sexual laboratory' for socio-logical research is particularly useful in this respect. As he notes, this research resulted in a 'characterisation of non-normative sexualities as *social*, rather than personal, pathologies' which produced 'a remarkably rich map of the dynamic sexual order of early C20th Chicago' (Heap, 2003: 459).

This 'map' included a range of studies from graduate students. Anderson's *The Hobo* is once again relevant, containing a whole chapter on the 'Sex life of the homeless man' and detailing how the nearly all-male content and high mobility of the area contributed to casualised and commercialised heterosexual relations, and commonplace homosexual relations. The physical geography of that area also meant that night time parks and alleyways, as well as crowded lodgings, provided ready spaces for sexual activity (Anderson, 1961 [1923]; 1923/24). Paul Cressey's (1929) study of Chicago's taxi-dance halls explored the sexual double-life made possible by the city's sex-oriented public amusements (see also Zorbaugh, 1929; Reckless, 1933). This was complemented by an unpublished student collection of life-histories characterised by a wealth of information about the sexual lives of its subjects (Heap, 2003: 475).

Research on sexuality was also conducted and promoted by the major figures in the Chicago School. Thomas's essays on the subject, later published as *Sex and Society* in 1907, argued that changing social conditions produced changes in sexual norms and practices, while his *The Polish Peasant in Europe and America* charted the supplementation of monogamous marital norms with other sexual expectations and practices as marriage became less essential for economic survival. In this context, individuals were able to effect a realignment between social constraints and personal desires. Park also contributed to research on sexuality by suggesting that students study the impact of newer and more widespread forms of communication on twentieth century urban sexual relations. Burgess's (1925) model of urban ecology encouraged researchers to associate non-normative sexualities with transitional zones in urban space, an approach that was developed in E. Franklin Frazier's *The Negro Family* (1932). In a radical argument that anticipates much later work on sexuality and gender identity, Burgess (1934: 147) concluded that Chicago research demonstrated that even normative heterosexuality, despite its apparent biological necessity 'can only be fully understood as a cultural phenomen[on]' (Heap, 2003: 477). This assertion of the importance of the external environment for sexual practices did not ignore people's impulses and desires, but emphasised the significance of society to an audience used to thinking of sex in purely biological terms.

The Chicago School's concern with the pragmatist emphasis on character and morality was also replicated in these studies on sexuality. They explored how leading a sexual dual life (involving compartmentalisation, concealment and being 'different people' during distinctive parts of one's day/week) could not only lead to a reorganised and revitalised self-identity, but to personal disorganisation and demoralisation stemming from an inadequate alignment between the embodied self and its surroundings (Reckless, 1925; Cressey, 1929). These findings were not, though, associated with a conservative assertion of traditional sexual mores or living arrangements. As we have seen, there was instead a concern to recognise the effects that social and physical surroundings had on sexual practices and norms. Chicago research fed into Vice Commission reports, for example, that recognised the exploitation of female prostitutes and encouraged a movement away from their criminal prosecution (Vice Commission, 1911; Heap, 2003).

The fading body

Given the prominence of physicality within Chicago's concern with the environments of social action, it might seem surprising that anyone could talk in later decades about the 'disembodied' discipline of sociology or the need to put the body 'back into' sociological research. However, a series of events and developments revealed another side to Chicago's apparent embrace of embodiment. To begin with, while Chicago scholars never lost sight of the significance of embodiment at a general level, there was a certain ambivalence among the broader sociological community about research involving 'low status' issues that concerned itself with bodily needs. Nels Anderson was warned by his mentors at Chicago about the attitude of others towards his chosen specialism, for example, and did not secure his first permanent academic job until he was in his seventies. The stigma associated with his involvement in begging and other aspects of street life may well have been a contributory factor to this situation.

More generally, the climate in which Chicago research into sexuality was conducted changed when W.I. Thomas was dismissed following his arrest in 1918 on a disorderly conduct charge after falsely registering at a Chicago hotel as the husband of the young wife of an army officer. As Thomas (1918: 16) cautioned, sexuality is 'a dangerous subject of study' because it has 'not been opened up freely to scientific investigation' (Heap, 2003: 463). As if to confirm these sentiments, there was increased public regulation of non-normative sexualities in Chicago towards the close of the 1930s in response to local and national sex crime panics in the press (Terry, 1999). In their crusade to remove the city of sex criminals, the Chicago authorities rounded up gay men in their cruising grounds. It was against this background that at least two members of faculty at Chicago University were dismissed, while a third 'was forced to resign' after being arrested for a second time (Heap, 2003: 481). As Heap concludes, 'Such dismissals undoubtedly had a chilling effect on the study of homosexuality and other non-normative sexualities at the University of Chicago by forcing potential researchers to worry about the possibility of becoming too closely identified with such research' (ibid.).

There were other reasons which help explain why the prominence of the body faded within Chicago sociology. To start with, there was a diminution in the cultural authority of sociologists to study sexuality and other bodily issues as psychologists managed to position themselves as dominant 'experts' on such matters (Heap, 2003: 482). In addition, there were features of the work of Chicago sociologists themselves which sometimes colluded in marginalising the significance of the physical body. Cooley's conception of the 'looking glass self', for example, focuses on imagination, and has been seen as reducing the structural complexities of society to the individual mind. Mead himself criticised Cooley on these grounds (Jandy, 1969: 115–18). If Cooley overemphasised one aspect of people's capacities in analysing the interaction between the external and internal environment, the urban and communication studies of Burgess, Park and others could push the embodied subject to one side in their focus on the external environment. In this respect, the main direction of their work provided a basis on which subsequent interpreters of the Chicago tradition of research could marginalise the significance of the body. Another reason for the fading prominence of the body in sociology was that the pre-eminence of the Chicago School of Sociology was not to last. Chicago's dominance in the sociological community ended by the early 1940s and its influence in the discipline faded (Joas, 1993).

Finally, two very contrasting developments in American sociology accelerated the general eclipse of the body from the discipline. Herbert Blumer portrayed his writings as a faithful exposition of Mead's position and as a distillation of core ideas formulated by other prominent first-generation Chicago thinkers (Collins, 1988; Colomy and Brown, 1995). Although Blumer's development of symbolic interactionism did much to keep alive interest in Mead, his appropriation of Mead's work was partial and ignored many of its pragmatist themes (Shibutani, 1997). In short, Blumer reified the interactions of the external and internal environments of human being into an all pervading concern with symbolism. As Rochberg-Halton (1987: 195) argues, 'Symbolic interactionism as practised today and as originally set forth by Herbert Blumer, is largely an act of selective forgetting of pragmatism ... in which the lively interest by Mead and the other pragmatists in forging a socialised conception of nature and human biology for social theory has been purged.' Blumer's focus on *symbolic* interaction not only tends to gloss the distinctive properties of the social and physical environments, and the capacities and needs of the embodied subject, but makes it difficult to sustain the material basis on which pragmatism based its moral concerns. Reinforcing this development was the emergence of a quite distinctive Iowa School of symbolic interactionism committed to quantifiable positivist research methods and focused on the ways in which people internalised rules rather than on how the internal environment of embodied subjects was itself partly responsible for the *emergence* of rules (Swingewood, 2000).

The second development internal to American sociology that was involved in the general erasure of the body from the discipline is even more significant. It is difficult to overestimate the significance of Talcott Parsons for the heritage of sociology. Not only did Parsons play a major role in naming and detailing a tradition of sociology which remains of enormous influence to this day, but he bequeathed to the discipline a series of concepts and approaches to social life that have become central to the stock of sociological knowledge. His influence continues to permeate the writings of even those who understand themselves as having rejected his legacy (Shilling and Mellor, 2001). Parsons (1968 [1937]: 768) drew on the likes of Durkheim and Weber in defining the discipline as 'the science which attempts to develop an analytical theory of social action systems insofar as these systems can be understood in terms of the property of common value integration'. Sociology should be the study of 'voluntary' action that was defined and analysed as such because it took place *in relation to* the dominant norms of society. Parsons was interested in the subjective understandings of the actor and the extent to which norms enter into that understanding. Action itself was no longer directed by the natural environment and the material capacities and needs of the embodied subject, but concerned 'those aspects of human behaviour ... involved in or controlled by culturally structured symbolic codes' (Levine, 1991: 192). Sociology should concern itself with culturally patterned actions, egos and selves, while the physical organism should be left to other disciplines. The body is almost invisible in this formulation. It is confined to being part of the hereditary conditions of action, and is made residual in relation to Parsons's key concern with normative action.

Parsons's definition of and approach to sociology differed radically from pragmatism's concerns and priorities, and this is reflected in his treatment of pragmatism. As Joas (1993: 14) notes, his review, assessment and proposals for sociology 'literally did not devote a single word to the accomplishments of John Dewey's and George Herbert Mead's pragmatist social philosophy, or to the pioneering methodological achievements of the Chicago School ... and the theoretical implications of their large-scale empirical investigations.' Parsons may not have completely destroyed the sociological influence of pragmatism, but he helped ensure that it enjoyed a long period on the sidelines. At the same time, he also did much to put the body to sleep within sociology.

As the twentieth century wore on, then, the physical, biological and material components of human being were increasingly marginalised in favour of a focus on the human capacity for symbolism, in the case of symbolic interactionism, or defined as being the province of the physical sciences, in the case of Parsonian inspired structural-functionalism. Parsons (1991 [1951]: 541–2) acknowledged that the body was important, but his definition of sociology, his aversion to pragmatism and his analysis of social action, precluded him from pursuing the full implications of this recognition.[1] This eclipse of the body was not limited to the discipline of sociology, moreover, but is a manifestation of what Rochberg-Halton (1987: 194) has referred to as a far greater 'pervasive rationalism in contemporary life'.

The resurgence of pragmatism and the recovery of the body

Hans Joas's (1993: 17) assessment of the Chicago School suggests that it only ever effected a 'partial realization ... of the possibilities inherent in the social philosophy of pragmatism'. Nevertheless, elements of the pragmatist tradition such as Mead's conceptions of the self and of role-taking, Thomas's interest in the material consequences of people's definitions of situations and the significance accorded to the biographical method, 'all belong to the standard stock of sociological knowledge' (Joas, 1993: 15). What faded from any shared knowledge and method after the period of Chicago's greatest influence was the centrality of the embodied subject to the discipline's concerns with the external and internal environment.

The body was not lost entirely to the sociological scene, however, and neither was the influence of the Chicago School. The writings of the cohort that has come to be known as the 'Second Chicago School' were published and became influential from the late 1950s through to the 1970s. They included the likes of Goffman's *The Presentation of Self in Everyday Life* (1959), Becker et al.'s *Boys in White* (1961), Becker's *Outsiders* (1963), Gusfield's *Symbolic Crusade* (1963) and Freidson's *Profession of Medicine* (1970) (Fine, 1995). Dealing with the fine grained details of subjects and their environments, these and other studies were relevant to an appreciation of the body within sociology and also contained within them important pragmatist themes. Stone's 1962 article on appearance, for example, draws on Mead's work in examining the importance of clothing to self-identity. Fred Davis' 1963 monograph *Passage through Crisis* was characterised by a pragmatist concern with the various phases of embodied action. Subtitled 'Polio victims and their families', this study traced reactions to illness from its onset and analysed the interactions occurring between hospital and home. In so doing, it examined the interplay between crisis and habitual action as family members struggled to retain some sense of stability in their lives while also trying to gain some rational control over the definitions of the hospital and the disease itself (Davis, 1963).

Various factors were responsible for the marginalisation of pragmatism and for the eclipse of the body within sociology but, as the continuing significance of the Chicago School suggests, this was not the end of the story. Two factors were of particular significance in helping to reverse this situation. The first involved the philosophical renaissance of pragmatism, a renaissance that Joas (1996) dates as starting in about 1979 (various elements of which have become known as neo-pragmatism, The New Pragmatism, or post-analytical pragmatism). One of the events that helped spark this revival was the publication of Richard Rorty's highly influential *Philosophy and the Mirror of Nature*, a book that identified Dewey as standing alongside Heidegger and Wittgenstein as one of the most important philosophers of the twentieth century. While the pragmatist pedigree of Rorty's own work has been questioned (Halton, 1995), there is no doubt that it contributed to a climate in which the work of the original pragmatists was re-examined and in which it became acceptable to develop theories which placed the external and internal environments of the embodied subject at their centre (e.g. Shusterman, 1992; Joas, 1993, 1996).

The second factor that helped reverse this situation involved a general cultural and intellectual interest in the body that developed and accelerated during the last few decades of the twentieth century. Analysts of consumer culture highlighted the commercialised body as increasingly central to people's sense of self-identity (Featherstone, 1982). During the same period, feminists emphasised through a critical interrogation of the biological sex/cultural gender divide that there was nothing natural about women's corporeality that justified their public subordination (e.g. Oakley, 1972). Analysts of governmentality highlighted the significance of physicality as an object of social control (e.g. Foucault, 1970; 1979a,b). Finally, technological developments involving transplant surgery, *in vitro* fertilisation, genetic engineering and stem cell research increased debate about the body's malleability. These factors raised very different issues about, and dimensions of, the embodied subject's external and internal environment, and were pursued initially through a series of theoretical perspectives that had little in common with pragmatism. Nevertheless, this general interest in embodiment also resulted in a renewed interest in empirical studies on body-subjects which drew, often unknowingly, on the agendas of pragmatism and on many of the methods developed by the Chicago School. This heritage was often unacknowledged, but was no less relevant for that.

Having explicated a tradition of sociological writings that sought to deploy in empirical research pragmatism's concern with the external and internal conditions of social action, I now seek to show how this approach can illuminate issues that have been key to contemporary empirically oriented work that has focused on bodies-in-their-social-contexts. The introductory chapter outlined and provided the rationale for these chapters: they explore the phases of action and development of character in very different areas of human life, and also provide us with contrasting examples of how the environments of embodied life interact and shape each other. I will not repeat this summary here, but it is worth noting that the diverse chapters share a similar structure which reflects the analytical framework laid out in the book thus far. After an introduction to the subject under discussion, each of these case studies focuses on the relevant external environments that provide the context for embodied action. The initial effect of these environments on the identity of individuals exposed to them is then analysed, before exploring the modalities of action employed by embodied subjects confronted with these circumstances. It is by examining these actions that the internal environment of human needs and capacities becomes evident. Finally, each chapter explores how individuals have developed their characters as a result of interacting with the external environment, and explores the consequences of this for the capacity of social groups to engage in collective action that can effect changes to this context. Starting with how the external environment shapes the individuals subject to it, then, each chapter progresses by exploring how these embodied subjects respond to, and subsequently impact upon, this wider context. In this way, the body is viewed as not only a location for the effects of society, but as possessed of emergent properties which enable it to be a *source* of social relations and processes.

Note

1 Parsons's (1978) late writings do reverse this situation somewhat, identifying the body as central to the human condition and providing a set of fascinating analysis of how the body was related to cultural norms, but these were produced well after his influence on the discipline declined.

4

Competing

Introduction

Sport is a highly significant part of contemporary culture, has flourished in benign and virulent political orders (Kruger and Murray, 2003; Rippon, 2006) and provides a good illustration of how the external and internal environments combine to inform particular types of embodied action. Sport, furthermore, requires the existence of a *surplus* of energy on the part of its participants, is predicated upon the *cultivation* rather than the denigration of at least a selection of human potentialities and is associated in the public mind with *health* and *fitness*. If sports cultivate human potential, however, they have over the centuries been associated with a broad range of social goals and physical locations which develop people's capacities in different directions. 'Natural sports' are associated with societal attempts to survive in the face of both social and physical threats. 'Socialised sports' are infused with a much wider range of normative ideals that may retain a link to, but are increasingly distanced from, society's immediate need for survival. Finally, 'performative sports' have cut themselves adrift from short-term necessities and are shaped by a global emphasis on instrumental rationality that supersedes the norms of any single society or nation-state. These notions of natural, socialised and performative sports are ideal type constructs, implicit within the literature, but they provide us with a useful sense of how sports have developed historically.

This chapter proceeds by elaborating on these typifications before focusing on the phases of habitual and creative action involved in the acquisition of contemporary sporting skills. Sports provide an interesting case-study of how embodied actions are culturally learnt. The techniques required to participate in them are more rule-bound than many other competencies people acquire, and hence easier to explicate, yet sports also provide for the possibility of creative adaptation within a structured framework. The chapter then extends this analysis by comparing performative sporting identity and culture with the rise of 'alternative' sports and the increasing popularity of longstanding Eastern traditions of exercise. Sports are not identical, and have the capacity to promote very different relationships between the external and internal environments of human action. As participants choose to practise and submerge their bodies in the routines and cultures associated with specific sports, they not only acquire distinctive skills and abilities, but become different people. In this context, sport is far from being of marginal significance to societies or to human being in general. Furthermore, given the contemporary emphasis placed upon performativity, the production of elite sporting bodies seems to exemplify more general tendencies within technological culture; tendencies which are thrown into sharp relief when compared with alternative traditions of sport and exercise.

The external environments of action

The social milieu: from survival to performativity

Natural sports is a term used by Brasch (1990) to describe competitive, game-like activities that evolved from early religious rites, hunting, and training for warfare. What defines a sport as 'natural' is that it is used to increase a social group's capacity to survive in its wider social and physical environment. Such sports constitute a 'survival mechanism'. This is evident in Lukas's (1969) argument that the first sport was spear throwing and in the invention of such sports as karate and other martial arts (Brasch, 1990; Birley, 1993: 2). Training for self-defence, engaging in ceremonial or mock hunting or participating in games played as a rite to bring rain, employs people's energies in sporting activities linked inextricably with the maintenance of a social and physical environment conducive to the reproduction of the social group.

Natural sports were evident in the very earliest forms of human society. Their influence later pervaded medieval society, and was still evident across much of Europe in the seventeenth and eighteenth centuries. One of the problems associated with natural sports, though, was that in order to function as an effective survival mechanism they often involved dangerous and violent contests. Indeed, the frequency with which jousting and related tournaments spilled over into fatal combat in the Middle Ages has led commentators to suggest that this form of sport was 'too much like the real thing' to be useful for training purposes (Birley, 1993: 28).

Socialised sports were characterised by a greater distance from necessity and developed in association with a growth in state monopolies over the means of violence, with the increased reliability of crop production, and with the division of labour reaching a stage when most people were not involved directly in procuring food or defending territories. There was no absolute start or end point to these 'civilizing processes', but they became increasingly evident from the seventeenth and eighteenth centuries, initially in England (Elias and Dunning, 1986). Here, the institutionalisation of peaceable means of settling political conflict provided a wider impetus for sports such as cricket, boxing and horse racing to become transformed into highly regulated and recognisably modern sports which curbed levels of violence previously deemed acceptable in competition (Elias and Dunning, 1986: 26). These tendencies reached a high point in the nineteenth century in sports such as rugby, soccer, tennis, track and field events, and boxing (e.g. Queensbury rules were introduced in boxing in 1867 in order to reduce bodily injury and increase levels of skill) (Maguire, 1999). Socialised sports continued to possess important continuities with their antecedents (e.g. they were often still justified on the basis of making the population fit for purposes of military defence (Bailey, 1978; Eisenberg, 1990; Guttman, 1994)), but were increasingly overlaid with other normative considerations. Three of these were of particular significance.

First, sport became increasingly important *symbolically* as 'a medium for and barometer of national identification and competitive community struggle' (Maguire et al., 2002). This symbolic function existed in the past for tribal and other groups, but the scale and purposes for which sporting symbolism was used grew enormously from the eighteenth century – an era littered with examples of sport being used to legitimise social inequalities and colonial enterprises (Dunning and Sheard, 1979; Goodger and Goodger, 1989). As Mangan (1992) argues in the case of Britain, imperial sport served as a moral metaphor, a political symbol and a cultural bond used to enhance national power across the globe. Britain used sports to promote imperial values and cultivated a hierarchy of body types corresponding to those values (Mills and Dimeo, 2003).

Second, from the 'athletics craze' to the 'games cult' and 'muscular Christianity', sport developed on *masculine* terms, creating a 'male preserve' from which women were marginalised and in which gender differences were magnified and celebrated (Whitson, 1990: 21; Maguire et al., 2002: 14). Natural sports may have been male dominated, but this period of socialised sports saw a steep accentuation of gender inequalities. By the end of the nineteenth century, sport had become a prime arena in which the culturally prized 'man of character' could make his mark (Mangan and Walvin, 1987). Women participated in their own exercises and sports, but they had a restricted range of identities on offer to them based on their roles as (future) wives and mothers, and very often aligned to 'national efficiency' movements concerned with the health of the nation (Hargreaves, 1994).

Third, instrumentally rational economic norms came increasingly to shape the socialisation of sport. In the United States, this occurred initially when the Protestant work ethic became incorporated into the sports ethos through an emphasis on rationalisation, hard work, goal directedness, moral asceticism, individualism, achieved status and competitiveness (Overman, 1997: 160). The development of these values continued apace in the late nineteenth and early twentieth centuries when they became associated increasingly with the economy. There was, for example, a close parallel between the scientific management movement's attempts to maximise the efficiency of work through calculation and the compartmentalisation of tasks, and the attempts of sports coaches to 'time and measure every aspect of [athletes'] performance: speed, stamina, power, agility and mental factors' (Sage, 1978).

Socialised sports may have increased their distance from the imperatives of defence and subsistence, but they did not break all links with these needs. Their associations with nationhood and the market involve at the very least a symbolic affinity with the goals of natural sports. Furthermore, at times of societal crisis – such as war, economic depression, political conflict or rapid cultural change – sport still has the capacity to express sentiments associated with the very survival of a social system (Douglas, 1970). It is also important to note that sports became socialised at different times across different societies. The sporting and leisure activities of early American settlers, for example, maintained strong links with the rhythms and needs of agriculture well into the nineteenth century (Struna, 1994). Despite these caveats, though, it remains the case that socialised sports possess a relative autonomy from *basic* societal existence which is both greater than that evident in natural sports, and allows them to be shaped by and linked to all manner of other norms and goals.

During the twentieth century, sports underwent a further autonomisation from the basic needs of subsistence and safety. While they have long required participants to perform efficiently within the rules of the game, the emphasis placed on the rationalisation of bodily display appears to have taken on a domineering logic of its own and it has been suggested that we are now living in an era of *performative sport* (Hoberman, 1992: 5). The decline of amateurism in England is a good example of this, with the imperative of winning having eroded the value that used to be placed on 'fair play' (Perkins, 1989; Birley, 1993: 239). Similarly, while coaches developed from the early 1800s as low-status, working class assistants to gentlemen amateurs, they now draw on the very latest sports science in securing for their charges any competitive edge (Lyle, 2002). More generally, sports are increasingly structured on 'the fierce temporal-spatial disciplines of measurement and record-breaking, in the course of which time-space becomes minutely calibrated'; a tendency exemplified by the 'quintessential' modern sport of track and field 'with its emphasis on linear motion, speed and timekeeping' (Eichberg, 1990: 131; Bale and Philo, 1998). As Weber (1968) anticipated with regard to society as a whole, the dominance of instrumental rationality in sport reached a stage in the twentieth century when its influence transcended (and, indeed, started to erode) other societal values with which it had previously been associated.

This relative distancing of sports from the norms of specific societies is linked in part with the institutionalisation of sport on a global level (decreasing the influence that any one country can exert over the normative meanings associated with sport) and with the difficulties associated with maintaining homogenous national sentiments in an increasingly post-colonial world (a world in which former colonies made much political capital out of beating the colonists at their own sports) (Perkins, 1989). Traditional values may continue to exert an influence within certain sporting institutions (Horne et al., 1999), but it is performance and success that count above all else in the contemporary era for both men *and* women (Cashmore, 2000; Connell, 1990: 91).

The physical milieu: the elemental forms of sporting life

The physical as well as the social environment exerts an inescapable impact on the forms sport takes, and this is most immediately illustrated in the case of *natural sports*. Natural sports made much use of pre-existing land-scapes, and people accommodated themselves to these places and spaces in developing trials and contests. Tribes would designate as ritual sporting spaces particular regions of their hunting grounds, the distance between two sacred landmarks associated with divine good fortune would mark the length of races, and canoeing and swimming contests took place over strategic stretches of local rivers.

The physical environments in which *socialised sports* occurred remained of vital importance, and this was evident in the state use of sport to manage domestic populations and pursue strategies of imperial domination. In terms of the former, the nineteenth century witnessed a huge growth in govern-mental attempts to compact games and exercise into spaces and times suited to the disciplining of the workforce (Foucault, 1979a and b). The promotion of 'rational recreation' in England during the mid- to late-nineteenth century, for example, sought to regulate and control the 'undisciplined' sites and spaces in which the working-classes engaged in sports and leisure (see Holt, 1989; Horne et al., 1999). For Eichberg, the cumulative effect of these developments replaced the season-informed sporting metric of the medieval era with an ordering of land which removed the body from 'the peculiarities of the natural environment', 'suited to creativity and the expression of difference', and relocated it to 'the uniform geometries' of the gymnasium and the running track, and the 'straightened, right-angled, sealed up and segmented' blocks of the sports stadium (Bale and Philo, 1998: 12; Eichberg, 1998: 71). In addition to using sport as a means of managing domestic populations, states also used it in pursuance of imperialist objectives. Imperialism and sport have been intimately linked, and the Cold War sporting competition that took place between the Communist East and the Capitalist West reflected in substantial part the aim of geographical domination shared by these regimes (Mangan, 1992; Cashmore, 2000).

The physical environment in which sport is played in the contemporary era may not be removed completely from societal norms, and the goals of specific social groups, but it has become structured by a general imperative of *performativity*. Arenas, stadiums, grounds, pitches, halls and equipment are now expected to deliver uniformity in terms of the sporting accom-plishments they facilitate: nothing from the natural environment should interfere with athletic accomplishments (Eichberg, 1998: 71; Gaffney and Bale, 2004). For Eichberg (1998: 152) these developments constitute a performative effacement of space. In place of the 'noble exercises' of courteous dance, rapier fencing, figure riding, horse vaulting and court tennis, space has tended to 'disappear', becoming 'a blurred horizon' and 'a standardised channel for the streamlined body projectile' and the 'time-dynamic production of results' (ibid.). The materials out of which running tracks are built, for example, have been optimised to maximise speed (while also seeking to reduce injuries), while footwear and ground surfaces for throwing competitions have changed in line with the need to maximise velocity of approach. Above all else, the places and spaces in which sports are played should enable athletes to *perform* as effectively they can within the rules of the game.

This 'effacement' of natural space and place has been pursued at great cost to the environment. As Maguire et al. (2002) note, concerns about the destructive effects of leisure activities on land and water vegetation, and on wildlife, led to the development of national park areas in the United States, while the rapid expansion of golf courses poses a threat to biodiversity. The environmental damage caused by the growth of sporting infrastructure is such that bids to host the Olympic Games now routinely address this problem, while there is an increasing acceptance that many contemporary sports developments are ecologically unsustainable (Maguire et al., 2002: 88). There is another problem with imposing performative sport on a natural environment that is neither infinite nor immune to damage. As Heidegger (1993 [1954]) argues, one of the problems with treating nature as a 'standing reserve' is that *humans* come to be seen in the same way, as a resource for technological colonisation in line with the demands of performativity.

The phases of embodied action

Sporting identities and sporting needs

It could be inferred from this brief overview of sporting forms that the external social and physical environment has come to dominate human needs and capacities. In being treated as a performative resource, the contemporary sporting body is defined increasingly on the basis of quantifiable measurements, while the boundaries of sporting identity are moving away from traditional conceptions of masculinity, femininity, class or 'race', and towards the cellular and molecular factors that sports scientists associate with athletic capacity (Blake, 1996; Gilroy, 2000: 36, 47). Research has reached a stage where 'there is now a search not just for sport-appropriate physiques but also for "performance genes"' (Parry, 2004: 6). Genetic tests are already being offered in Australia and elsewhere with the aim of identifying athletic ability in young children. Still more invasive is the growing interest that has been shown in muscle gene transfer as a means of increasing athletic performance. Drugs and supplements are hardly new in sports, but developments such as these mean that sporting identities may soon become associated with radical genetic modifications (Mottram, 1996; Miah, 2004).

To leave analysis here, however, would be partial. It suggests that sports develop human identities only insofar as they can be harnessed to the imperatives of performance, and are not associated with fostering the creative expression of physical capacities. This is one tendency that can be, and has been, extrapolated from performative and socialised forms of sport (e.g. Huizinga, 1970 [1938]), but it implies that the external environment has developed in contradiction to, and almost without reference to, the internal environment of human being. In complete contrast to this evaluation, Elias and Dunning (1986) argue that participating in sports is linked to the fulfilment of quite basic human needs. As they suggest, in an ordered, rational society which has made daily life increasingly predictable and which requires from its citizens a levelling and dampening of affects in comparison with times past, it is plausible that humans need opportunities to experience forms of motility, intense sociable 'we-feelings', and a mimetic 'controlled decontrolling' of emotions that are increasingly marginalised from public life (Elias and Dunning, 1986: 3, 29, 49, 89).[1] The result of such experiences involves a building and release of emotional tension; a controlled decontrolling of emotional controls which humans may both want and need on a regular basis.

If Max Weber's (1991 [1904–05]) description of the 'iron cage' of modernity still has much to say about the structures of sport, Elias and Dunning illustrate how sports can, at least potentially and at certain levels, fulfil other functions. How is it, though, that sport can appear to both ignore *and* fulfil human needs? In exploring this paradox I shall now examine the actual processes, mechanisms and stages involved in acquiring sporting skills. These are often ignored in sociological accounts of sport, but the habits, creativities and crises associated with acquiring such skills provide part of the 'raw materials' out of which grow particular sporting identities and cultures. They are also important to the question of whether sport is conducive to the general expansion of human potentialities, or a practice which more usually facilitates a damagingly one-sided development of a very limited selection of abilities.

(Creative) sporting habits

Performative sport may have become dominant during the contemporary era, but sporting activities have *always* been predicated on the need for participants to acquire a certain level of competence and skill. Sociologists and anthropologists have not ignored the processes involved here (e.g. Mauss, 1973 [1934]; Bourdieu, 1984, 1986), but they have been investigated in more detail by those sports scientists concerned with motor learning, physiology, psychology and biomechanics (e.g. Bartlett, 1999). Sports sociologists have generally been highly critical of these specialisms – because of their focus on technical considerations and marginalisation of social factors – but this work can help us understand how skills involve creative as well as habitual components which, in their various combinations, provide a foundation for quite different forms of sport.

Sporting skills are enormously varied, but Guthrie's (1952: 136) definition of skill as 'the ability to bring about some end result with maximum certainty and minimum outlay of … time and energy' remains widely used. The processes involved in acquiring sports skills have been simplified into three distinct stages which involve the novice in imitation, in attaining motor competence and finally in autonomous proficiency. In the *imitative* stage, the beginner applies existing competencies to new tasks – even if their actions are usually only 'jerky, uncertain and poorly timed to the external environment' (Schmidt, 1991) – in order to gain a 'feel' for the activities, the technologies and the environments used by a sport. A prerequisite of learning to swim, for example, is 'feeling at ease in the water' (Meredith et al., 2001: 4), whereas windsurfers must get used to the experience and tensions of the board as it sits on and travels through water (Baker and Moreno, 2001: 33). Similarly, skiers need to 'get the feel' of their equipment (Bartelski and Neillands, 1993: 25), whereas rock climbers must physically accustom themselves to the touch and response of rock to hands and feet (Johnston, 1995: 17).

Coaching is often associated with elite sports training, but novices usually receive formal or informal guidance or teaching at this imitative stage. Parents, competent friends or qualified instructors will physically demonstrate, physically guide and verbally instruct or encourage the learner to adjust their movements, reduce mistakes and gain confidence. The body positioning and actions involved in new sports often feel awkward and unnatural, and novices in sports such as skiing must also struggle to bring nerves and fears under control in order that effective technique is not impeded. There is an emotional as well as a physical acclimatisation to new sports. This imitative stage of skill acquisition may be basic and elementary, but repeated practice provides a platform for subsequent advance. As imitation becomes less awkward, and results in successful outcomes, the novice is able to work towards the second stage of skill acquisition.

The *motor competence* stage of learning presupposes a basic physical, emotional and cognitive familiarity with a competence, and works towards building effective movement patterns that habitualise routines and allow attention to begin to be focused on the acquisition of higher and more complicated skills. We are well past gross imitation here, having achieved a degree of mechanical efficiency which allows participants to focus on improving their performance. Wacquant (2004) provides us with an example of this in the case of boxing. Having endured the different phases of his training 'infinitely repeated day after day, week after week, with only barely perceptible variations', Wacquant relates how his 'field of vision clears up, expands, and gets reorganised' as his body becomes acclimatised to sparring (Wacquant, 2004: 87). This mechanical state of efficiency probably best describes the vast majority of participants who would view themselves, and be viewed by others, as proficient in a sport. Here, basic techniques, patterns, movements and plays have been assimilated, and there is at least a reasonable degree of match between the participant and the environment of a sport. It is no small feat to reach this stage of skill acquisition, and becoming even remotely motor competent at a sport such as boxing or soccer can require a long apprenticeship involving 'monastic devotion' and a subordination of the self (Wacquant, 2004: 60; see also Matthews, 2000: 75).

Finally, the stage of *autonomous proficiency* is associated with the advanced acquisition of sporting skills. It involves the ability to acquire, process and respond highly efficiently to exteroceptive information (stimuli that comes from the external environment) and proprioceptive or kinaesthetic information (deriving from the internal environment through 'relative joint positions and movement, muscular tensions and orientation in space') (Schmidt, 1991: 46–7). Having reached this stage, individuals have acquired a plurality of automatic responses that regulate and steer their actions and enable them to redirect energy, expended previously on controlling bodily and environmental stimuli, towards more complex problems and challenges (Schmidt, 1991). The individual can now focus on 'higher level' skills in a sport, and seek to improve his/her performance by employing creative variations on routines. In the case of boxing, for example, the body is in the long run turned into 'a virtual punching machine, but an *intelligent* and *creative* machine capable of self-regulation while innovating within a fixed and relatively restricted panoply of moves' reflecting the thinking and reasoning in the ring of an 'undivided organism' (Wacquant, 2004: 95–6; emphasis added). Reaching this stage of autonomous proficiency is an essential prerequisite for elite sports participants: they could simply not function in the upper echelons of a sport by wasting energy on basic tasks. As the racing driver Ayrton Senna noted, judgements that have to be made in a split second on the track must be made in a calm and natural manner so that they become part of the routine of the driver (Henry, 1991: 70).

This analysis of skill acquisition is only a rough guide to the multiple, overlapping and uneven processes that occur when an individual becomes proficient in a sport. Nevertheless, as the learner gains proficiency in the acquisition and execution of skills, they generally experience a number of related changes. These involve the rate of improvement, coordination of movement, changes in the muscles used to perform the skill, alterations in the amount of conscious attention devoted to the tasks and the selectivity with which the senses engage with relevant stimuli, improvements in error detection and correction capability, and greater probability and efficiency of successfully executing the skill (Magill, 2003). Competence, efficiency and the capacity for creative variation become incorporated into the very fibres and neurological responses of body-subjects who have accomplished 'relatively permanent changes in the capability for skilled performance' (Schmidt, 1991: 153).

If we take stock of what is going on here, it is clearly unreasonable to make simple distinctions between habit and creativity. The body is being steered and rationalised in a particular direction as actions become habitualised, but competent participants are also creatively assimilating themselves to a sport associated with a new form of experience. Merleau-Ponty (1965) talks about how the body schema of the accomplished soccer player, for example, is so assimilated into the structures and affordances of the game that they feel and see what is going on in a manner that is totally different to the lay person. The player does not wait for an opportunity to emerge before thinking about how to respond, but is 'called into action' through a process of automatic adjustment in which their body feels the game just as clearly as it does its own vertical and horizontal planes (Merleau-Ponty, 1965: 168–9).

This mutual accommodation of sport and participant is borne out in a variety of experiential accounts. Soccer players talk of not needing to look to see where the ball is in relation to their feet and legs (e.g. Matthews, 2000: 68). Climbers discuss how the rock they are ascending becomes part of them (Lewis, 2000). Expert skiers detail how they 'read' the slopes the same way that a good motorist is subconsciously aware of everything around them (Evans et al., 1978: 232). Athletes comment on how their world narrows and becomes harmonised with the track that lies between them and the finishing line (e.g. Gunnell, 1994). Motor racing drivers describe entering a state of 'secondary consciousness' in which they are 'so fully in tune' with their surroundings that they can completely feel their environment through their car and its 'balance of sensitivities' (Blundell, quoted in Hilton, 2003). At its most advanced, the experience of this attunement has been referred to as a sense of 'flow' characterised by a transcendence of the ordinary parameters of daily life. As Jackson and Csikszentmihalyi (1999: 73) put it, there is a 'sense of calm, of assurance, of mastery and of intense involvement here' when the 'merging of action and awareness has almost a mystical feeling'. This sense of affinity with a sport can, indeed, possess a religious dimension. William James (1982 [1902]) suggests that athletes sometimes reach a stage where they feel they are taken over and 'played' by a sport in the same way that a convert is taken over by religion, with both experiencing an incomparable sense of fullness and inspiration.

Performative sports are often criticised for being prescribed and mechanised, but the possibility of athletic immersion in flow qualifies such a conclusion. As Victor Turner (1982: 79) suggests, the 'flow' associated with even highly structured actions and interactions can result in innovative experiences and meanings that can be incorporated into subsequent performances. Few people reach this level of command and attunement, though, especially in sports involving open environments characterised by unpredictable variables such as the moves of opposing players. In an extensive study of experts from diverse fields, for example, Ericsson et al. (1993) argue that expertise across a variety of fields is the result of intense practice (involving hours of work a day informed by optimal instruction) for a *minimum* of ten years. Nonetheless, it is clear that the acquisition of sporting skills is based firmly in the acquisition of particular habits of practice, movement, anticipation and response that can facilitate performative capacity, creativity *and* an experiential transformation. Habit and creative actions are not opposites in the search for maximum performance, but can combine to effect a fundamental change in the capacities and experiences of the sporting subject.

Sporting crises (and creative responses)

If the rationalisation of the sporting body can sometimes facilitate a transcendent sense of 'flow', it is also important to recognise that performative sporting cultures can be deeply constraining. There are costs and even crises associated with sports participation, and prominent examples include a general devitalisation of experience, injuries and the damage done by the consumption of performance-enhancing drugs.

First, while performative sports may occasionally result in transcendent experiences, they nevertheless involve a loss of the 'play element' that Huizinga (1970 [1938]) identified as a key feature of human experience. The suggestion here is that the emphasis on rules and regulations, on training and competition, on being the *best*, has emptied sport of its spirit of spontaneity. In this context, an occasional sense of sporting 'flow' may not compensate for a more general denigration of human experience. Furthermore, there is no guarantee that the sporting proficiency associated with peak performance will stay with the athlete. While elite training and competition may provide the platform on which excellence is maintained, there arise occasions when it breaks down and has to be reconstructed. One common example of this can be found in golf, when a player's swing no longer works and has to be rebuilt. The English golfer Nick Faldo went through two years of reconstructing his swing – involving new arm, body and leg actions as well as 'countless small adjustments to establish a whole new sensation of feel and consistency' prior to enjoying a period of major success between 1987 and 1990 (Faldo and Saunders, 1989).

Second, intense, disciplined and rationally ordered training can lead to physical breakdown. It is interesting to note that the sports science literature overflows with details of the connections between sports and injuries, and that sports biomechanics has been described as having contradictory aims, 'the reduction of injury and the improvement of performance' (Bartlett, 1999). The basic problem, as Kreider et al. (1998) note, is that the athlete's formula for success 'hard training, may also, unfortunately, be the formula for demise'. Intense (over)training has been associated with physical, psychological and emotional changes resulting in a 'chronically depressed athletic performance' (Bartlett, 1999), and is on the rise among children as well as adults.

As organised children's sport has increased in the past few decades, so too has there been a growth in overuse injuries at ever younger ages (Russell, 1986; Aldridge, 1993). Performative sports have reached a stage where it is not unusual for children to be pushed into training at three or four years old, and where the term 'battered child athlete' has become commonplace (Wilkinson, 1984; Hargreaves, 1994). There have even been cases of parents in America asking paediatricians to administer human growth hormone to their children in order to make them into 'more imposing athletes' (Hoberman, 1992). Physical injury and risk is just one consequence of children's performative involvement in sports. A number of studies have pointed out that many young people grow to resent being robbed of those social maturational experiences experienced by most of their age group. Research has shown that the 'tedious, routinised work, [and] the anti-social training hours' associated with sports such as swimming, for example, prevents children from participating in a normal range of friendship patterns. More damning still are the judgements of those elite gymnasts who felt they had been robbed of the developmental experiences they needed to be able to even survive at the end of their sporting careers (Dacyshyn, 1999). If early involvement in performative sports can damage children, however, it is not irrational in its own terms. Tiger Woods swung his first golf club when he was three years old and was a competent player by age six, while Venus and Serena Williams were introduced to tennis by their father at the age of four. Top sports professionals start *young*. Yet, as Bee (2003: 8) observes, 'For every Serena and Tiger there are thousands upon thousands who crumble under the pressure of being asked to do too much too soon.'

A third form of cost and potential crisis associated with sport involves the consumption of performance-enhancing drugs linked to the revolution in the pharmacological industry in the 1960s. While there have been documented cases of athletes taking supplements and stimulants since Ancient Greece (Mottram, 1996), the 1960s was witness to a massive increase in the consumption of powerful drugs. One of the first reported drug-related deaths was that of a cyclist in 1968, but a host of dangerous side effects also accompany this trend. Anabolic steroid consumption among men is associated with heart disease, hypertension and liver toxicity. Diuretics can lead to dehydration, fainting, muscle cramps, headaches, nausea, and kidney and heart problems (Verroken, 1996), and blood doping can induce metabolic shock. Deaths of prominent athletes do not, however, seem to have deterred people from taking drugs.

In recent years there have been widespread concerns about increases in dangerous drug use. During the late 1980s and early 1990s, studies reported that up to twenty per cent of intercollegiate athletes reported using anabolic steroids, while the percentage of non-college athletes taking such drugs was much higher (George, 1996). One third of US power lift- ers used the drug, while research in the United Kingdom reported that up to forty per cent of weight trainers used steroids in a single private gym (ibid.). Despite the efforts of sports's international governing bodies, drug use remains rife and retains a strong affinity with the culture of winning and maximising performance that is so prevalent within contemporary sports. More generally, there is also the issue of the medical treatment that players receive in order to recover from injuries sustained as a result of their training and competition schedules. The ex-Liverpool player,

Alan Hanson (1999), for example, is just one of the many retired footballers who report being pressured to play when injured, and of suffering from 'chronic arthritis and joint problems after their retirement from the game' because of the number of pain killing injections they had during their careers.

When experience is devitalised and the physical well-being of sports participants damaged, it is reasonable to conclude that sporting regimes are developing human potentialities in line with the logics of performativity rather than in line with embodied needs or constraints. Phases of creativity and crisis are not completely separate, however, but can appear and disappear periodically throughout a sports career. Michael Watson's near death in his 1991 boxing rematch with Chris Eubank, for example, led not only to six major operations and the end of his career, but twenty-one months of gruelling physiotherapy involving 'tortuous pain' during which time he was eventually able to stand with the aid of three carers. Watson struggled with depression as 'a full grown man' who 'had to ask for everything and have everything done for me', but found strength from his religious belief and was eventually able to walk and even complete a marathon course (Watson, 2005: 148). What is clear in his story is that while many of the habits and skills he had acquired as a boxer were suddenly, and quite literally, knocked out of him, the determination he used to employ when training for a fight 'inspired' him to 'push harder and harder' in his battle to walk.

These phases of sporting action outlined above do not manifest themselves identically in different sports, and I want to explore some of these variations in this final section by comparing the sporting identities associated with performative body cultures with those associated with 'alternative' sports and traditional Eastern forms of exercise. These sporting cultures are less influential than those of performative sports, but they have become increasingly popular in recent years and illustrate how the acquisition of sporting skills can still be associated with quite different orderings of the external and internal environment of human being.

Sporting characters, cultures and moralities

Elite performative sports have promoted a clearly identifiable and powerful form of *rationalised body culture* which values a disciplined lifestyle. Whatever moments of transcendence or excitement occur in these sports, they appear to be centred around a personal and institutional culture that treats the body as a machine. This has five related elements to it.

First, treating the body this way involves *ceding control* of one's self to appointed 'experts' or authorised 'programmes'. As Rintala (1995: 69) notes this 'submissiveness to training and unquestioned acceptance of authority (be it science or the coach or perhaps both) typifies the lives of many athletes. Sport in many countries, including the United States, is replete with examples of athletes who go through a tightly controlled sports system without ever making decisions.'

Second, it involves *subjecting the body to strict regimes* that take over the athlete's life as they ascend the sporting hierarchy, and allow little room for physical contingency or frailty. Diet, rest, sleep and practice, are all carefully specified in an attempt to maximise the individual's perform-ance. As one 'iron man' triathlete commented, 'You're up at 4:30 to go training ... most of the day. And you are too tired to go out anyway and you've got to get your rest. It is a pretty disciplined sort of life. It's like being in jail' (Connell, 1990: 85). This is also reflected in the training regimes that members of elite team sports are increasingly subjected to (e.g. Woodward, 2004: 355–6). Coping with the effects of such regimes requires a normalisation of hard work, exhaustion, self-denial and pain for men and women (Coakley, 1994; Young and White, 1999: 212).

Third, it is predicated on a peculiarly Cartesian approach to the self. The willingness to train and compete while injured, commonplace in elite sports, reflects a detachment from certain aspects of the flesh. As Hoffman (1992: 282) argues, injured athletes phenomenologically remove themselves from their body and rationalise it into functioning and non-functioning parts in need of extra attention. Athletes are here involved in assisting the production of themselves as 'the quintessential body object' (Willis, 1991: 69).

Fourth, the body-as-a machine culture of elite performative sports involves a *commodification* of the body: athletes' bodies are traded between teams, assessed on the basis of their market appeal, and required to perform on the basis of commercial considerations.

Fifth, this culture has associated with it a specific form of sporting ethics. We have already seen how performative sports treat the physical environment and the body as a 'standing reserve', a raw material to be consumed according to its own logics and needs. Another implication of prioritising the maximisation of performance is that winning overrides any other value. Whatever undesirable traits or behaviours a sports star may have, these can apparently all be forgiven if they are successful. Compulsiveness, brashness, egocentricity, vanity, ruthlessness and so on, may not be valued in many a philosophical treatise on morals, but they become part of the ethics necessary to survive in the 'dog-eat-dog' world that is performative sport in the contemporary era (e.g. Bollettieri and Schaap, 1997; McEnroe, 2002: 108).

The pervasiveness of this rationalised body culture is perhaps why Jean-Marie Brohm's conception of sport as a form of 'Taylorisation of the body' remains relevant. As Goldman and Papson (1998: 161) suggest, being an Olympic calibre athlete involves internalising some of the most rational-ised regimes ever associated with capitalism. This does not mean that performative sports can be reduced to issues of rationality, or that success and achievement do not involve participants in moments of effervescent transcendence. It is commonplace for retired athletes to talk about how nothing matches the feelings they experienced at the height of their career during an unprecedented performance or victory. Nevertheless, such extraordinary experiences do need to be analysed in terms of their wider context, and it has been suggested that they are moments of 'extended social control in which the individual demonstrates he/she is willing to sacrifice his/her body for the good of the society or the corporation that sponsors the team'.

This highly rationalised, performative body culture may be increasingly pervasive, but it remains informed by previous sporting cultures. Current rituals – from the totemic flags carried by athletes during the Opening Ceremony of the Olympic Games, to the national anthems sung before international soccer matches – continue to incorporate the nationalistic sentiments and affiliations that have driven socialised sport so strongly. Similarly, the long-standing link between religion and sport still plays a role in performative sport. American athletes often pray prior to sports events and cross themselves while preparing for, or running onto, the field of play, while there is also an affinity between those athletes who embrace their ascetic training regimes as a vocation and the Protestant ethical devotion to long hours of ceaseless work analysed so persuasively by Weber (1991 [1904–05]). The athletes Hoffman (1992: 275) studied, for example, experienced their sporting lives as 'religious experiences, opportunities for worship in which an omniscient and understanding God recognises the spirit in which they train and perform ... as reflecting glory on his divinity'. Magdalinski and Chandler (2002: 1) have even suggested that 'sports arenas function as substitute places of worship, as "cathedrals".' It would be wrong to think that religion informed sports in a manner which had not changed since the era of natural sports, however, as these links are often *reinvented* in order to impart a sport with an 'authentic' image (e.g. see Light and Kinnaird, 2002).

If the body culture of performative sports has yet to disavow religion, neither is it fully disassociated from traditional conceptions of gender identity. Performativity is increasingly pervasive amongst athletes irrespective of their sex, but sex testing continues to be used as a device to divide and separate athletes. Sports clubs and associations have prevented girls and women from competing with boys and men (Kane, 1995), while there remains a strong culture of heterosexuality in some sports which pressurises women to construct a feminine appearance and to 'fear the stigma of masculinisation' (Hargreaves, 1994: 261). Financial rewards for sporting success remain much higher in traditionally male sports, while it is still wives who perform the bulk of (often difficult and lonely) unpaid labour involved in supporting professional sports players' moves to new clubs (e.g. Thompson, 1999). More generally, at lower levels of the sporting hierarchy, there remains much evidence that men use sport as a means of bolstering their identities vis-à-vis women (Birrell and Theberge, 1994). These features of sport may be anachronistic, running against the logic of performativity which is based on a general recognition of success and efficiency, but it would be wrong to think they had been eliminated.

The performative body culture is increasingly influential and pervasive (even if it continues to be mediated by other influences), but there exists a growing 'alternative' sporting body character and culture which appears to place much greater emphasis on the creative elements of sporting skills. This is linked to activities known variously as 'lifestyle', 'extreme', 'whizz' and 'action' sports, and is also associated with new forms of sporting communities and a 'creolisation of sports culture' which have been viewed as presenting a radical challenge to the dominant 'western sports model' (Bale, 1994; Maguire, 1999; Wheaton, 2004). The diverse sports in this category include snowboarding, skateboarding, BMX biking, Parkour and BASE jumping. What seems to unite these activities, however, is that they utilise the 'unruly' properties of the elements to escape from the constraints placed on movement in, and interaction with, the domesticated environment (Rinehart and Sydnor, 2003). Even when use is made of the 'built environment', skateboarders and BMX bikers are among those who subvert its functional design and make creative use of the affordances embedded in handrails, steps and slopes (e.g. Borden, 2001). There is also a quite conscious and related emphasis on the deliberate pursuit of *experience*, on the search for excitement, risk, creativity and extraordinary sensations that contrasts with performative sport. Elite performative sports may sometimes result in such experiences, but lifestyle sports often have them as their primary *goal* rather than as just a possible outcome.

The significance of such experiences is apparent in numerous participants' accounts. Drawing on Simmel's comments on mountaineering, Lewis (2000) contrasts the climbing body with the metropolitan body and refers to how the former engages with the world through touch in an unmediated manner. Walter's (1991: 85) account of climbing talks of 'the excitement, the camaraderie, and the unique adrenaline buzz of a successful ascent' as well as the possibility of sensing 'a fleeting unity with your surroundings as you watch the sunset from the top of an inaccessible pinnacle'. In the case of white-water canoeing, Orlick (1990: 4–5) talks of discovering how 'the challenge of running a river is not a conflict between human and nature, it is a melting of the two. You do not conquer a river, you experience it.' Similarly, surfers and windsurfers talk about the excitement of immersion in a different elemental milieu: there is something transcendent about returning home 'after a day at the beach, sunburned and tired and sore from a day's sailing amongst giant, windswept waves, eyelids caked with salt crystals, and to be happy in the knowledge that you know something the rest of the world is quietly oblivious to' (Baker and Moreno, 2001: 17). Surfers have compared their experiences on the waves with 'the heights of orgasmic pleasure', and have talked about dancing 'for Krishna' or 'supporting the revolution' when they surfed (Booth, 1995: 205). Others refer to surfing as 'a spiritual experience' which involves a re-formation of identity 'on a higher plane' (Sheehan, 1992: 84–5). These experiences of excitement or transcendence may range from the pleasurable to the exceptional, and from the unexpected to the consciously sought after thrills associated with what Lyng (1990) refers to as 'edgework', but they are not incidental to such activities. Indeed, the frequency with which 'alternative' sports have been associated with such experiences has led Heywood (1994: 185) to conclude that there exist ready body cultural alternatives to 'the outlook and values belonging to the process of rationalization' in this field of activity.

Before drawing too great a contrast between the body, identities and cultures associated with elite performative sports and so-called alternative sports, three qualifications need to be made. The first concerns how these sports are played. While my comments about performative sports have focused on elite level competition, it is possible to play just about any sport in a competitive, perfectionist, 'high octane' manner. Participants in 'lifestyle' sports frequently vie with each other to execute new moves, climb faster or higher, and increasingly take part in competitions. Surfing, for example, has become more competition oriented over the last few decades (Booth, 1995). The emphasis on setting records also has its own (performative) dangers of injury and even death. Audre Mestre, for example, died in 2002 during an attempt on the world record for depth freediving. Lifestyle sports cannot, then, be separated completely from those dimensions of competition, commercialism and injury often associated with elite mainstream sports. In this context, it should also be noted that performative sports can be engaged in playfully (if not usually by elite competitors). School children will sometimes be introduced to sports in this way, and many of them continue (often to the chagrin of their teachers) to exhibit a playful, lighthearted and less than serious attitude to compulsory sports at school.

The second qualification concerns the continuation of more traditional divisions and inequalities within these sports – a feature which suggests their development is not as 'alternative' from 'conventional' sports as is sometimes assumed. Kusz identifies 'extreme-sports' participants as overwhelmingly white and middle class, and engaged in activities that reassert traditional identities.

> Extreme sports are ... implicitly figured through the absence of women and people of colour – as a racially and gender exclusive place ... a homosocial preserve, where (white) men can unapologetically perform an ideal masculinity which they covet by taking death-defying risks, ensuring the pain of participation, and displaying an unwavering confidence and coolness in the face of apparent danger. (Kusz, 2004: 205)

Loy (1995) makes a similar point by arguing that lifestyle sports provide new opportunities for the performance of aggressive young male identities that have become unacceptable elsewhere in the sporting world. Wheaton (2004) adds to this picture by reporting how male windsurfers objectify women as sexual objects, while also viewing certain risky moves as specifically male activities and becoming irate when women tried to emulate them. Similar attitudes were reported in Beal's (1999) study of skateboarders. Furthermore, most of these sports have done little or nothing to overcome social class inequalities in participation. Sports such as windsurfing require expensive equipment, coaching and the capacity to travel, yet most people living in cities simply do not have access to the finances or spaces required to participate in sports that take place outside of the built, urban environment.

Finally, while certain lifestyle sports may have developed as non-commercial alternatives to performative sports, they have not been immune from commodification. As Rinehart (2000) points out, 'the "alternative sportscape" is increasingly controlled and defined by transnational media corporations like ESPN's X-Games and NBCs Gravity Games, as well as an ever-expanding range of international and transnational commercial images and interests' (see also Wheaton, 2004). The tourist industry has also made strides increasingly into the alternative or lifestyle sports market (Downer, 2004).

Despite these similarities, it would be wrong to conclude that the culture associated with 'alternative' sports is not distinctive from its performative and socialised counterparts. This distinction exists in terms of a predominant focus on experience, and informs the ethical approaches towards the environment developed by some of these sports. Many guides to, and participants' accounts of, outdoor activities emphasise the importance of *looking after* the environment. Manuals concerned with rock climbing and skiing stress the need to treat the environment with respect, not only for one's own safety but for reasons of preserving it for other participants and future generations. These considerations are often codified into rules contained in such guidelines as the 'Climber's Code' (Creasey et al., 2000: 90). Certain sports such as windsurfing, moreover, run their own campaigns for, or are associated with, environmentalist efforts to improve the quality of their physical surroundings.

The contemporary sporting field is not exhausted by the contrast between performative and 'lifestyle' sports. Within the West, certain national traditions of exercise, such as the Turnen tradition of German gymnastics, continue to exert an influence on the physical activities in which people participate. These may not be immune from competitive pressures, but neither do they simply replicate the instrumental, domineering ethos so frequently found in contemporary sports. More generally, there is the enormously important set of Eastern traditions towards exercise which cultivate a very different relationship to the body, character and, indeed, to the environment than is the case with dominant Western sports. Yoga, tai chi chuan and other exercises (often mixed with elements of Oriental spirituality such as Zen, Taoism or Tantra) have histories that can sometimes be traced back hundreds of years, and are practised by growing numbers of people in the West increasingly disillusioned with rationalised forms of sports, exercise and leisure (Eichberg, 1998: 105). On a worldwide level, the numbers of people participating in these exercises are also often much greater than is the case with many

Western sports (tai chi chuan is the most practised form of structured exercise in the world). In explicating the body culture associated with these exercises, Levine (1994: 214) starts with yoga:

> Two thousand years ago the Sanskrit classic Bhagavad Gita represented a state of human joy and fulfillment brought about by a practice that calms the mind and the passions. This practice of unification – of 'yoking' or yoga – the body with the soul, the individual self with the universal spirit – involves a complex of methods that are not only moral and meditative but physical as well. They include asan, a discipline of holding carefully designed postures, and pranayama, exercises in the rhythmic control of the breath.

The diet, posture, breathing, intellectual concentration and moral discipline of yoga in India has long involved 'an experimental union of the individual with the divine' involving a 'oneness' that eschews the rationalisation characteristic of the modern world (James 1982 [1902]: 400). Aikido follows a similar path. Harmonising the bodily system through a focus on its centre of gravity, Aikido was conceived by its founder as 'the way of unifying the mind, body and spirit' (Levine, 1994). Again, the martial art of tai chi chuan seeks to develop a union and harmony between the mental and physical energies of the practitioner and wider cosmic forces (Liao, 2000).

These Eastern forms of exercise may be associated with a body culture other than that evident in performative or even many 'lifestyle' sports, but the *experiences* associated with them do possess certain parallels. Indeed, in discussing the concept of 'flow' in performative sports, Jackson and Csikszentmihalyi (1999: 123) explain the sense of transcendence that is possible to achieve in terms of the Taoist philosophy which is integrally related to tai chi chuan.

> When the experience is so intense that it requires every bit of attention, the person can no longer process information even about his or her existence. She loses her sense of identity, like an automaton proceeding in a trance. In such movements flow resembles those states of ecstasy that religious disciplines reach through ritual, prayer or meditation. For instance, the floating sensation described by athletes is reminiscent of the concept of yu, which the Chinese Taoists prescribed as the 'right way to live'. Yu has been translated to mean 'floating', 'flowing' or 'walking without touching the ground'. At such levels of intensity concentration is not only effortless, but it also achieves a pure, spiritual dimension beyond the body whose efforts made it possible in the first place.

These Eastern forms of exercise do not, however, link this experience to sports which dominate the self or the elements. In contrast to performative sport, for example, the philosophy of tai chi chuan disassociates exercise and health from 'work', an approach which it views as wearing the body out (Graham, 1989; Tzu, 1996: 149), and emphasises an intelligent responsive adjustment to the environment and the capacities of the individual.

Such exercises have proved increasingly popular with young and old in the West and can be practised outside of rationalised sporting environments at home, in the park or by the beach. These activities are not immune from commercialisation and performativity (there have, for example, been attempts to make yoga into an Olympic Sport), while there exist numerous tai chi chuan competitions in and outside of China. Furthermore, reaching the stage of autonomous proficiency in such activities as tai chi chuan and yoga can take far longer than is the case for conventional Western sports. Nevertheless, what distinguishes this category of Eastern exercises from Western sports is that they seek to cultivate a very different relationship between the external and internal environments of embodied action. In so doing, they encourage the development of very different forms of character and exhibit a very different ethical relationship with the natural world.

Conclusion

Contemporary sports cultures may continue to share certain features with each other and even with historically distant forms of sporting activity. It is for these reasons that feminists, for example, can talk quite validly about the unequal sporting opportunities available to men and women as longstanding and cross-cultural phenomena. Different forms of sports also appear to share in common the phases or modalities of action required to attain a degree of competence and expertise. Sports are not identical, however, and have the capacity to promote very different relationships between the external and internal environments of human action. As participants practise and submerge their bodies in the routines and cultures associated with specific sports, they not only acquire distinctive skills and abilities, but in an important sense become different people equipped with a different orientation to the world around them. This requires a significant degree of dedication, of course, and is by no means an automatic outcome of becoming involved in sports at a lower level, or of playing sports casually. Indeed, the various levels at which sports can be played and enjoyed (as well as the different types of sports) helps explain why they can be seen both as an exemplification of Weber's 'iron cage' and as a means of fulfilling important human needs. Nevertheless, elite sport in the West provides an important example of the effects that an increasingly performative, technologically oriented culture can have on embodied subjects who choose to dedicate their lives to a single activity.

Note

1 *Motility* involves the pleasure and loss of self that can sometimes result from being immersed in movement. This movement may itself be rationalised but this does not prevent it from being an activity that individuals rarely experience in most contemporary jobs. *Sociability* brings satisfactions derived from playful interaction that occurs for its own sake, outside the rationalised environs of work (Simmel, 1971 [1910]). Finally, *mimesis* involves the enjoyable arousal of strong affects in safe contexts; affects that are not usually prized in the contemporary workplace (Dunning, 1999: 26–7).

5

Presenting

Introduction

The manner in which people *present* their bodies to others has been viewed sociologically as key to the constitution of identities, cultures and societies. Thus, presentational concerns were central to Cooley's (1922 [1902]) notion of the 'looking glass self' (in which self-identity was formed and re-formed in the reflected gaze of others), Park and Burgess's (1969 [1921]: 341) contention that society 'reduces to social interaction', Mead's (1962 [1934]) 'Me' and 'I', and Goffman's (1963b) analysis of people's 'actual' and 'virtual' social identities. These and other writings established a close connection between the manner in which individuals presented themselves in public, prevalent forms of self-identity, and the ethos and operation of the social system. Conforming to the presentational norms of a social group generally signified membership of that collectivity and acceptance of its values, allowing individuals to develop a subjectively experienced sense of self validated by the community. Deliberate transgression of such norms, in contrast, constituted a sign of protest, and was often associated with periods of cultural change in which individuals sought to develop identities divergent from those sanctioned by the status quo (Douglas, 1970).

In recent years, however, presentational issues have become increasingly complex. Individuals now confront a proliferation of commercialised styles and fashions that have blurred previous markers of cultural belonging *alongside* the resurgence of traditional modes of dress and behaviour among religious groups.[1] This has led certain cultural commentators to suggest that we live in an era of almost limitless choice in which there no longer exist widely shared presentational norms. Sociologists, though, are generally more circumspect about the existence of such freedom and diversity, and have explored how the external environment continues to require careful presentational navigation. In particular, the pressures associated with work and consumer culture have increased the time during which people are 'on show' and judged according to marketable ideals of efficiency and success (Turner, 1984: 110–11; Lasch, 1991 [1979]). The conditions intrinsic to the staging of 'smooth' social encounters in daily life (such as turn-taking, respecting personal space and trusting the identities that others present to us are sincere) provide another set of presentational constraints

(Goffman, 1983), while gendered and 'racial' norms have also been identified as limiting *which* identities may legitimately be presented in public, *how* people can present themselves to others, and *whether* individuals are able to experience as positive their subjective sense of self.

Presentational constraints such as these are clearly interrelated (as evident in the strategies of negotiation that have to be undertaken by a female executive who must conform to the demanding expectations of corporate culture while also displaying the expected traits of a feminine persona in her work and social encounters). Furthermore, while they do not physically *compel* people to act in a certain way, they constitute a massive incentive to conform to normative expectations. Goffman (1983: 2–8) typifies the reasoning of sociologists here when suggesting that the motive to conform is derived from the fact that our ability to experience ourselves in a positive light is strongly affected by the responses of *others*. If we receive social validation from others, we are more likely to be able to appraise our own self in a positive light. If we transgress presentational norms, in contrast, our behaviour tends to be interpreted as 'evidence of weakness, inferiority, low status, [and] moral guilt', and the feedback we receive makes it difficult for us to see our self-identity in anything other than a negative light (Goffman, 1956: 266; 1963). Our self-respect and sense of self-worth can be destroyed as a result of becoming stigmatised within and excluded from the 'order' of respectful interaction, and we can become 'discredited' individuals facing 'an unaccepting world' (Goffman, 1963a: 31, 43, 112).

The importance of such presentational pressures is particularly well illustrated in the case of those who risk breaching norms pertaining to gender and sexuality. The rich heritage of work on marginalised sexualities conducted by the Chicago School, for example, detailed how gays and lesbians sought to present themselves as 'straight' in their public interactions because of the devastating consequences of being discovered in breach of gendered norms (Heap, 2003; see Chapter 3). In what follows, though, I want to extend this focus by concentrating on presentational issues related to transgenderism and transsexuality. 'Transgender' refers to those who transgress gender norms (e.g. through dress and appearance or via surgery) and/or are oppressed due to their difference from social norms of gendered embodiment. It is broader than 'transsexual', a term that was popularised in the 1950s by Dr Harry Benjamin, which refers exclusively to someone who is either seeking to change, or has already changed, their genitals in order to 'claim membership in a gender other than the one assigned at birth' (Stryker, 2006: 4). Finally, individuals belonging to either category are often referred to by the generic term 'transpeople'.

While the stigma associated with sexual orientation may have been mitigated in recent decades, transgressions of ascribed sexual identity continue to breach fundamental social taboos. Indeed, there is perhaps no other category of individuals who stir such strong feelings of incomprehension and revulsion among 'conventional' interactants, or who illustrate as effectively the difficulties that 'outsiders' face in gaining a sense of acceptability for a self that is often discriminated against and censored. The reasons for this are associated with the fact that one of the first things that individuals attribute to others in an encounter is the status of being *male* or *female*, and this attribution plays an important part in informing subsequent judgements about the acceptability of the self presented during interaction (Kessler and McKenna, 1978).[2] Dominant Western norms admit of *two* sexes and two only, while both Western and non-Western societies have constructed on this basis whole gendered systems of exchange, taboo, apprenticeship into adulthood and social stratification (Rubin, 1975; de Beauvoir, 1993 [1949]). In this context, the experiences of transpeople highlight particularly effectively what is involved and at stake in passing as 'acceptably normal'. They continue to face ridicule, harassment, a lack of protection from laws that others take for granted and even (in extreme cases) forcible incarceration in mental institutions.

This chapter begins by examining how the gendered norms that permeate modern society are grounded in a 'two-sex model' – a model that has been reinterpreted by science in a manner that treats the topography of the sexed body as an *external* physical environment in which people's 'real' identities are encased. It then focuses on how transpeople have sought to align their internal and external environments so as to achieve a consistency between the identities they present to others and their own sense of self. Their struggles are complex and varied, but they illustrate clearly that while the body does not determine identity, it is vital to people's sense of self. In analysing these issues, I use the term 'sex' to refer to the biologically ascribed status of an individual, and 'gender' as the cultural expression of what is masculine or feminine.[3] When discussing male-to-female or female-to-male transsexuals, I use the term 'he' or 'she' to refer to the individual's self-ascribed identity as a woman or man.

The external environments of action

The social environment, the 'two-sex' model and the threat of transsexualism

In order to appreciate the potency of the gendered norms governing sexed identity in the contemporary West, it is useful to understand the conditions surrounding the emergence of the two-sex model that underpins them. The idea that there are just two, biologically opposite, sexes has not always been taken for granted. It emerged during the eighteenth century when science decided that the categories of 'male' and 'female' rested on radical physical differences (Laqueur, 1987; Duroche, 1990). This two-sex model replaced its more malleable antecedent, which suggested that male and female constituted a continuum rather than opposites, and suggested that biology rendered men fit for the public sphere and women for the private sphere.[4] It proved enormously influential as well, being highly convenient for the political authorities of the time. This was because proponents of Enlightenment egalitarianism could continue to hold that all citizens were formally equal, while acknowledging in practice that women's biology rendered them less capable than men. Social reforms were not needed to address women's disadvantaged position because it was biology rather than society that destined this outcome.

The strength and durability of the contemporary two-sex model, then, is associated with a system of gender inequalities which became incorporated into the modern Western social order. Yet this model is not and never has been a comprehensive categorisation of sexual identity. Aside from its antecedent in the West (Laqueur, 1987), there exist other ways of classifying sex and gender identity. In Mesopotamian mythology, for example, there are references to people who are neither men nor women, while in Babylonia, Sumer and Assyria, individuals who performed particular religious duties have been described as belonging to a 'third gender' or 'third sex'. Since the sixteenth century, transvestite shamans have been reported among the Araucanians, a large tribe living in southern Chile and parts of Argentina, while cross-dressing also used to be practised by shamans in the Vietnamese countryside, in Burma, in India among the Pardhi – a hunting people – and also in Korea (Feinberg, 2006: 214). The Hijra of India, Pakistan and Bangladesh are the best known and largest such group in the modern world (estimating around 5–6 million). They see themselves as neither male nor female and, in 2005, Indian passport forms reflected this by being issued with three gender options. Other cultural groups referred to as a 'third sex' or 'third gender' include the kathoeys or 'ladyboys' of Thailand, and the berdache of the indigenous cultures of North America.

Even before the full development of the two-sex model, however, transgendered identities went beyond the boundaries of acceptability established by the less rigid one-sex model, and were generally regarded as constituting an 'abnormal' assault on the civilized Western social order. These flagrant displays of difference appeared to constitute a transgression of social hierarchy and a wilful disregard of natural sexual identity. Sexual identity may have been viewed as a continuum within the framework of the one-sex model, but it was seen as being based *in* the body rather than being something that was *added* and apparently in *opposition* to the body. In this context, history provides us with many examples of how European colonisers vanquished or massacred the 'third sexes' they encountered abroad (Stryker, 2006: 13). Attempts to impose such 'regimes of normalisation' were also common before the eighteenth century in the West itself, as the authorities sought to regulate homosexuality, hermaphroditism, gender inversion and other forms of 'social monstrosity' (Foucault, 1981). The consequences of being caught flouting interactional norms and seeking to 'pass' as a man or woman were severe. At the end of the seventeenth century, transvestites were placed in stocks and paraded through the streets in an open cart in England, and were burnt to death in France as late as the 1760s (Feinberg, 2006).

The scientifically grounded view of sexual opposition developed in the eighteenth century provided an additional justification for stigmatising and persecuting sexual transgression. Forms of 'rational dress' adopted in the 1880s by 'new women' in England and France, for example, were condemned by *The Lancet* as being 'detrimental to the health and morals' of women (Rudacille, 2006: 42). Cross-dressing certainly did prove bad for the health of those mid-twentieth century male 'transvestites' subjected to aversion therapies using electric shock treatment and nausea-inducing drugs (Hausman, 1995: 131). Irrespective of the means used, attempts to normalise sexual identity continued apace. In the sphere of sport, for example, chromosomal sex testing for athletes was carried out in 1958, and has since 1966 become a major means of segregating individuals into two sexes in major sporting events (Kessler and McKenna, 1978; Dyer, 1982).

As the twentieth century wore on, the price for those caught transgressing gender norms remained high. In the United States, men appearing in women's clothes on the street risked arrest (Newton, 1979: 36), while transsexuals faced daily battles against discrimination and violence. Alyn Liebman, for example, remembers how failing to look and act like a girl resulted in a school career characterised by bullying, violence and being blamed by the school authorities for 'being different' (Rudacille, 2006: 201–2). Problems such as these seem to have increased during the era of social conservatism which has characterised recent American history. Risking physical violence if exposed, transgendered individuals could not even be guaranteed emergency treatment in hospitals. In 1995, Tyra Hunter, a black male transvestite, was struck by a car. The emergency medical technician at the scene stopped treatment after reportedly exclaiming 'this bitch ain't no girl … it's a nigger, he's got a dick!' (Juang, 2006: 712). Hunter later died of the injuries sustained in the accident. Recent murders of transgendered individuals include the case of Gwen Aruajo, whose killers alleged in their retrial that they were so sickened on discovering that she was biologically male that they 'bludgeoned and strangled her in a passionate rage', and that of Joel Robles, whose killer used a similar argument to defend his multiple stabbing (Rudacille, 2006: 304). In 2002 alone, twenty-three people were murdered in the United States as a result of what appear to have been transgender hate crimes (ibid.: xxii; Namaste, 2006). Furthermore, the stigma and discrimination faced by transgendered people exacerbates other social problems. A recent survey in Washington DC, for example, estimated that the median life-expectancy of a transgendered person in the capital of the United States was only thirty-seven years. Inadequate health care, poverty, substance abuse, employment discrimination, HIV infection and the risks facing those who work or have worked in the sex industry have contributed to this statistic (Rudacille, 2006: 12). Even those who manage to escape such a fate have to deal with being categorised as suffering from 'gender identity disorder' as listed in the 'bible' of psychiatry, the *Diagnostic and Statistical Manual of Mental Disorders*.

The desires and actions of transpeople violate the social norm that those born to a sex should quite naturally develop identities commensurate with that sex. It is on this basis that they have been identified as members of Gunnar Myrdal's (1962) category of '*unassimiliables*' (including communists, blacks, Jews and homosexuals) who will never be accepted as full citizens and who suffer as a consequence in terms of their status, prestige and honour (Newton, 1979). Despite such penalties and dangers, however, the transgression of gender norms has often been employed as a form of protest against the status quo (Kane-Demaios and Bullough, 2006). Joan of Arc's refusal to wear women's clothing, for example, was associated with her rejection of the authority of the Church and of the English. Throughout the Middle Ages and into early industrial capitalism, cross-dressing played an important role in militant struggles against landlords, taxation and other manifestations of class rule (Feinberg, 2006).

The overt transgression of gender norms has historically been accompanied by less open ways of attempting to live as a member of another sex. 'Passing' has a long history and has been engaged in for a variety of purposes. During the seventeenth and eighteenth centuries it was common enough to be the theme of novels, fictionalised biographies and memoirs, art, plays, operas and popular songs. Women passed as men throughout Europe and most notably in Holland, England and Germany in the nineteenth century (Feinberg, 2006). More recently, the 1960s was characterised by a period of sexual experimentation and liberalism regarding sexual identity in which there was a certain blurring of gender appearance associated with the promotion of alternative lifestyles and political protest. Nowadays, transgender traditions persist in the Mardi Gras and other festivities across the world which display a carnivalesque inversion of traditional categories and a ridiculing of established authorities (ibid.). At the same time, passing has become an increasingly common theme in popular culture from the late twentieth century onwards, and has featured in a growing number of mainstream films.

If passing has historically been persecuted as deviant and more overt displays of gender transgression associated with political protest and alternative lifestyles, there is another, perhaps more surprising, dimension to the recent history of transgenderism. The twentieth century witnessed a limited alliance between medical science and transsexuals. Science first took direct note of transpeople in the early twentieth century. Much of this involved research in the socially diverse setting of Berlin at the Institute of Sexual Science founded in 1919 by the pioneering physician and liberal activist Magnus Hirschfeld (and met its end at the hands of the Nazis). Hirschfeld began referring patients for sex reassignment surgery in 1920. As the twentieth century wore on, the numbers seeking and getting access to hormonal treatment and sex-change surgery across Europe and America grew. While there remain important national differences, surgical advances have gone hand in hand with a hard-fought, if limited, degree of acceptance and access to medical services. During the 1960s, the judiciary in the United States took decisions that recognised sex change at a legal level (Meyerowitz, 2002). In 1966, John Hopkins Hospital (an institution which had for decades served as a centre for the study and treatment of intersexed conditions) announced a programme to perform sex-change operations, while it is now possible in exceptional cases for people to claim on their medical insurance for sex reassignment surgery (Meyerowitz, 2002: 247). These developments have resulted in a situation whereby the idea of transsexuality in the contemporary West is tied inextricably to the practice of hormonal and surgical intervention.

Given the general social unacceptability of transgender phenomena, how did science become so heavily involved in issues of sex reassignment? What seems especially interesting about this situation is that it marks a convergence between the wishes of transsexuals seeking to surgically alter their bodies in line with their sense of self *and* society's expectation that there should exist a continuity between a sexed body and its gendered behaviour. Yet the search for radical physical alterations has not always been on the agenda of those who reject the continuity between biological sex and gendered identity. As we have seen, the notion of a third sex or gender describes individuals considered *neither* men *nor* women in certain cultures, while the aboriginal North American berdache are just one of many groups who employed ritual means to mark the passing of a child or an adult to the status of an alternate sex without believing it necessary to alter the genitals. In this context, the 'alliance' of science and transsexuals can be seen as operating to *support* the norms of a system that validates two sexes and two sexes only (Hausman, 1995: 197). Although the idea of 'transgressing' or 'mocking' the binary oppositions of male and female still carries with it considerable stigma and risk, the wholesale *transfer* of an individual from one sex to the other in terms of their bodily being and public presentation at least upholds the idea that there exist just two sexes. Without necessarily undermining the two-sex model, then, science began to suggest that the biological sex of male and female could be *reassigned*. By undertaking these interventions, furthermore, science also became instrumental in promoting the view that the body itself constituted part of the external physical environment of human identity and action.

The physical milieu: the body as a container for the sexual self

The dynamic relationship and shifting parameters that exist within and between the external and internal environments of human being are especially well illustrated in the case of transpeople who undergo sex reassignment surgery. This is not only because transsexuals and the medics who treat them tend to view the body as a *container* that encompasses within its parameters a more essential kernel of sexual identity, but because surgery demonstrates that this 'container' is subject to alteration. Thus, while transsexuals have to struggle with the phenomenological sense that they have been placed in the wrong flesh, medical interventions make possible the partial reconstruction of the organs, orifices and topography of the body. In examining how medics came to view the sexual body as part of the external physical environment of identity, it is useful to start with those newborns labelled 'hermaphrodites' or 'intersexuals'.

According to the Intersex Society of North America, about one in a hundred births exhibits some anomaly in sex differentiation, while about one in one thousand is different enough to render problematic the question 'Is it a boy or a girl?' (Green, 2004: 3; see also Chase, 2006 [1998]). Instead of accepting these babies as biological variations who do not match social norms, but who are usually physically healthy, the medical authorities have in recent decades altered the bodies of these infants to make them 'fit' as closely as possible to an acceptable sexed appearance. Since the early 1960s in the United States, nearly every major city has had a hospital 'with a standing team of medical experts who intervene in these cases to assign – through drastic surgical means – a male or female status to intersex infants' (ibid.: 300). Such surgical intervention is governed by a logic of physical determinism: the body of an infant is altered to correspond as closely as possible to male or female status, and it is assumed that this provides a physical platform on which an appropriate gender identity can be developed. This logic was problematised, however, by those individuals who continued to express the 'wrong' gender identity despite medical interventions, a situation which resulted in some psychiatrists and biologists reasoning that sex must be fixed at some deep level within the interiors of the body (Hausman, 1995). In seeking to account for this possibility, two explanations proved influential.

First, advances in endocrinology (the study of hormones) during the early to mid-twentieth century were drawn on by medics seeking a new view of the relationship between the location of sex, the individual's sense of gendered identity and the body. As Hausman (1995: 42–3) explains, endocrinology proposed that: (1) sex differences could be reduced to the chemicals that produced them, (2) there was actually a continuum of sex that ran from 'ideal' to 'defective' male and female, and (3) the endocrine function exerted a determining influence on identity, behaviour and social role. By proposing the idea of a *continuum* of sex, endocrinology challenged certain features of the two-sex model of biological incommensurability (as well as echoing certain aspects of the earlier one-sex model). It rejected the idea that there existed a *necessary* continuity between sex, identity and the body, and gave scientific credibility to transsexuality.

The second explanation focused on *post-natal*, rather than ante-natal, factors by suggesting that 'abnormal' features of early infant socialisation were responsible for mismatches between the body and sexual identity. This explanation was associated with the work of John Money, a psychologist working at John Hopkins. During the 1950s, Money published a series of papers arguing that an individual's sense of identity as male or female was formed largely *after* birth. For a strictly limited period in infancy the brain was receptive to being imprinted with a particular sexual identity, an identity that need not necessarily match the biological sex of the individual's body. This theory was interpreted as a social constructionist theory of gender and adopted enthusiastically by feminists who interpreted it as providing proof that women had been socialised during childhood to be a 'second sex'. Money was not a proponent of androgyny or the existence of 'multiple sexes', however, and insisted that psychological health 'was entirely dependent on the development of an unambiguous identity as either a man or a woman' (Rudacille, 2006: 103). Money also argued for the necessity of surgical intervention and a strongly gendered socialisation to ensure that an infant's body and sense of self corresponded as closely as possible to being either male and masculine *or* female and feminine. Scientists and physicians often adopted this theory in justifying the extensive surgical and hormonal manipulation they visited upon intersexual infants and children.

These contrasting accounts led to what Meyerowitz (2002) has described as 'turf wars' between medical, scientific and psychiatric authorities as each sought to establish its own view as the legitimate 'truth' of sex. This is far less important, though, than the cumulative effect of the general recognition they promoted that there could be a gap between the sex of an individual's identity and that of their body, and that this could and should be rectified through hormonal and surgical intervention.[5] The two-sex model may have been modified as a result of these scientific theories, in that there now existed a recognition that bodies and identities could be anomalous in relation to its categories, but it retained its essential influence in recognising that there could be two authentic *physical* sexes only and in informing the medical view that the bodies of intersex infants should be *changed* to resemble that of a 'normal' boy or girl. The biological notions of 'male' and 'female' were thus essentialised and naturalised at a level beneath that of the visible body. 'Sex' was no longer defined by external markers of the body and its genitalia, but existed at a deeper level within the hormones or the psyche. In one stroke, this solved the dilemma for those who held that there were only two sexes or genders and whose views were being challenged by the increasing numbers of transsexuals seeking to have their genitals surgically transformed (Kessler and McKenna, 1978: 108–9). By locating sex in the hormones and/or in the mind, *the body became an external physical environment which did not necessarily correspond to the 'true' sex of the individual*. It was in this context that doctors and others could legitimise the surgical procedures that would transform 'the sex of the body to correspond with the sex of the mind' (Meyerowitz, 2002: 113).

The social and physical environments in which transsexuals in the West seek to achieve a body they can be happy with eschew those ritual means and markings evident in other cultures that facilitate the liminal transformation from one sex to another, and also reject the category of a 'third gender'. Instead, the two-sex model continues to be honoured by legitimating surgery as *the* rite of passage enabling one to change from male to female or from female to male. This is not in itself without limitations. Surgeons have made great strides in changing bodies (to the extent that some have compared sex reassignment procedures to other forms of body modification such as tattooing, piercing and branding (Sullivan, 2006)), but these remain approximations. The problem of how to create a fully functioning penis has yet to be overcome and there are health risks associated with breast implants and other features of sex reassignment surgery. Furthermore, sex change is not an automatic right for individuals. Transsexuals have to demonstrate to the relevant medical authorities that their gender identity is coherent, stable and opposite to that which would ordinarily be expected of someone inhabiting their body (Hausman, 1995). Even the graduated approach towards sex reassignment recommended by the widely respected Harry Benjamin Gender Dysphoria Association Standards of Care exposes the individual to traditional conceptions of masculinity and femininity based on the two-sex model. Nevertheless, from a period in the 1960s when 'the sex reassignment of genitally normal adults was still taboo' in the United States (despite some well-publicised cases of its occurrence such as Christine Jorgensen's, involving male-to-female surgery in Denmark during 1951–52), this surgery has become easier to obtain and more common (Rudacille, 2006: 113).

A major problem with the external environment confronted by transsexuals, however, is that while the modern, medical reinterpretation of the two-sex model may have helped create the conditions in which sex reassignment surgery became feasible, it has not mitigated the gendered norms that continue to suffuse social interaction. One of the first things that individuals assign to others in an encounter remains the status of being either *male* or *female*: it is on the basis of this attribution that subsequent judgements are made about the acceptability of the self presented during interaction. Transsexuals face enormous pressures in this respect. Cosmetic surgery and other forms of body modification may now be common, but sex reassignment surgery goes beyond most people's tolerance of what is normal. As Stryker (2006: 245) argues, the transsexual's body is seen as *radically* unnatural, constituting a technological construction of 'flesh torn apart and sewn back together again in a shape other than that in which it was born'.

The phases of embodied action

Identity and crisis: the dys-eased body

Transsexuals waiting for, or who have undergone, sex reassignment surgery may provoke revulsion and raise the spectre of monstrous technology incarnate, but there is nothing normal about the profound phenomenological sense of being born into the wrong body. Leder (1990) assumes that the body in its usual state 'fades away' from our consciousness when we are 'at ease' with it, and only 'reappears' to us in pain or malfunctioning. On these occasions, it makes us feel ill at ease or *dys-eased*. Transpeople, in contrast, experience a chronic sense of dys-ease with the original sex of their bodies. This manifests itself as a deep sense of alienation with the body into which they were born, which is frequently accompanied by an equally strong desire to inhabit a body of the 'other' sex (Hausman, 1995). In this context, Rubin (2003) draws on Sarte in talking about the transsexual body as an alienated body which is coerced into taking the viewpoint of the other, while Green (2004: 13) refers to the common 'trans' experience of being separated from the body. The autobiographical writings of Christine Jorgensen (1967), for example, describe how she was unable to identify with the male body with which she had been born. Brad, one of Rudacille's (2006: 11) interviewees, talks about how it was possible to be a tomboy when very young but that subsequent social expectations regarding femininity added to a growing sense of inhabiting the wrong body, of 'waking up in this nightmare'. Ben Barres, a female-to-male transsexual Professor at Stanford, judges these experiences of bodily dys-ease to be so common among transsexuals as to become almost 'boring' in their repetitiveness. Barres himself remembers thinking that he was a boy as early as he could remember, being jealous of the 'boys toys' given to his brother, and experiencing the growth of breasts as 'foreign objects', feeling 'incredibly uncomfortable' wearing dresses, and being unable to contemplate applying make-up (Rudacille, 2006: 23). Green (2004: 22), another female-to-male transsexual, reflects on his life by stating that he had been unable to grow up fully because he felt he had been a 'failed child', and was never going to be an 'adult woman': the only way he could become mature was to balance his body and psyche by becoming a man. It may be unfashionable amongst academics to speak of a 'core' identity, but 'transsexuals, like most people' have 'a deeply rooted sense' of who they are (Meyerowitz, 2002: 367).

Irrespective of the precise manifestation of this bodily dys-ease, it is common for transsexuals to report a growing crisis of identity alongside an ever greater mismatch between their body and their sense of self. This tends to reach critical proportions with the onset of sexual maturity; a time which represents an accentuation of physical maleness or femaleness and a heightening of social norms regarding appropriate gendered behaviour. Rubin (2003: 96) talks of the extreme discomfort experienced by those 'trapped' in the bodies of girls when they begin to receive sexual attention, and of how puberty and adolescence 'disfigured their essential male selves'. The onset of menarche in particular was an event that forced them to realise 'that they were not the boys they thought they were' (ibid.: 102). These are examples of how female-to-male transsexuals frequently suffer from 'agnosia' – a term used by Merleau-Ponty to designate the rejection from the body schema of a part of the actually existing physical body. Such experiences have led many to self-harm and even suicide. More commonly, however, this crisis results in one of three responses to a sense of self shot through with rupture and discontinuity.

First, transsexuals have sought to realign their identities with their bodies by engaging in stereotypically masculine or feminine pursuits and behaviours in the hope that this will stop them feeling a dissonance between their identities and their bodies. This is evident in Brown's (1988) explanation of the concentration of male-to-female transsexuals who enlisted in the military at some point in their lives. He argues that such individuals pursued a hypermasculine career in the hope that this would enable them to achieve a reintegrated sense of being a man. Similar engagements in hyperfeminine activities can be found within the writings of female-to-male transsexuals, although these often occurred in childhood and ceased when puberty and adolescence resulted in an overwhelming sense of inhabiting the wrong body.

Second, transsexuals aware of the possibility of sex reassignment surgery, yet unable to access it, have taken steps to alter their bodies themselves. Some visited back-street abortionists, in the belief that they would undertake any operation in return for the appropriate payment, while others have eaten 'female hormone facial cream', attempted to push their testes back inside their bodies, and tried to create breasts by injecting 'air, hand cream, mother's milk and water' into their chest (Meyerowitz, 2002: 143). Male-to-female transsexuals have even cut off their genitals. As Meyerowitz (2002) notes, according to one review of the medical literature published in 1965, eighteen out of one hundred male-to-female transsexuals had attempted to remove their own testicles or penises and nine had succeeded. At the age of forty-three, for example, Caren Ecker 'gave herself a local anesthetic, removed her testicles and in her own words "almost bled to death" ' (ibid.: 145). Doctors eventually recommended additional surgery in order to remove the penis. Ecker's case was not the only one in which doctors agreed to operate after the botched attempts of the layperson. As in the case of self-induced abortions, doctors were far happier undertaking 'cleaning up' operations than they were in initiating surgery (and this was often at least partly due to legal restrictions).

The third manner in which the crisis of living in a dys-eased body manifested itself among transsexuals involved the psychiatric services. Over the past few decades, psychiatrists have recommended therapy (in order to eliminate inappropriately masculine or feminine 'inclinations'), incarceration (as transgendered behaviour was seen as part of a wider personality disorder) and have insisted that only officially sanctioned motives constituted adequate grounds for seeking sex reassignment (Meyerowitz, 2002; Spade, 2006). Furthermore, individuals seeking sex reassignment surgery not only have to confront the considerable pain, difficulties and risks of failure involved in such procedures, but a consensus among the psychiatric service that the best candidates for such surgery are those who can demonstrate most convincingly that they have had since birth an invariant gender identity corresponding to that of the 'opposite sex' (Kessler and McKenna, 1978: 118).

Each of these manifestations of crisis raises the issue of *passing* in the external social environment. For those who seek to realign their identities with their bodies by engaging in hypermasculine or hyperfeminine pursuits, there is the need to pass in terms of their bodily appearance and behaviours as a member of the masculine or feminine gender of which they do not feel part. Jorgensen (1967) discusses this during her time in the military, while Dana Beyer (a male-to-female transsexual) describes just how difficult this can be: 'All that energy needed to be a man in this society when you're not. You can't imagine ... You're constantly on guard, constantly aware that you are who you know you are but you can't let it slip' (quoted in Rudacille, 2006: 226–7). For those who seek to pursue the route of authorised sex reassignment, there is the issue of passing as suitable candidates for surgery in the eyes of the medical authorities. For these transsexuals, and also for those individuals who decide to alter their own bodies or cross-dress, there is in addition the considerable challenge of passing as a member of a gender different from that ascribed them during their upbringing. This is no small task. Passing as a man or woman involves acquiring an entire 'body pedagogics' of appearances, behaviours, skills and capacities that are usually the product of years of gendered socialisation. Rudacille provides us with a sense of this in pointing to the myriad ways in which a woman is recognised as such on the street in even the most fleeting of encounters.

> My identity as a woman is clearly visible in 100s of small and large ways. When you pass me on the street, your brain registers my long hair, make up, skirt, pocketbook, and painted nails, and renders the verdict 'female'. Even if I cut my hair short, skipped makeup and wore jeans and T-shirt, you would still identify me as a woman by my physique, by my gait, and by the way I related to you, my fellow pedestrian, as I walked by. (Rudacille, 2006:8)

The problems of passing and the risks involved in failing to pass are considerable, but they do present opportunities for individuals and possible resolutions to the crisis in which they find themselves. There is little evidence, however, that immersion in hypermasculine or hyperfeminine roles and activities experienced as alien works as a way to reduce the dissonance between body and identity. Brown's findings concerning the high numbers of male-to-female transsexuals who had spent part of their lives in the military, for example, was only possible because their sense of inhabiting the wrong body persisted and they were prepared to report this. Nevertheless, other strategies employed by those who seek to cultivate the bodies and gendered habits required to pass as a man or a woman have at times been more successful.

Creative transitions

Towards the end of the twentieth century, when surgery was more accessible, transsexuals seeking sex reassignment had to navigate the views of the psychiatric profession that candidates most suited for such physical alterations should conform to a specific gendered identity. In addition to the challenge of having to pass as a different gender in public, then, transsexuals were also having to pass as appropriate 'patients' in medical settings. Candidates responded creatively to these norms and did all they could to exploit them in order to be approved for surgery. Male-to-female transsexuals presented themselves 'as demure heterosexuals who wanted nothing more than a good man and a stable home, with lots of delightful children running around' (Rudacille, 2006: 130). Once significant numbers of candidates encountered the psychiatric services as gatekeepers to sex reassignment, moreover, a 'grape-vine' emerged through which patients informed each other of the best ways to pass the necessary approval process that gave them access to surgery. Transsexuals suppressed information concerning homosexuality, and the enjoyment of sex with their unaltered body, that would disrupt the version of normative femininity or masculinity they were presenting to the doctors, and there were even stories of post-operative transsexuals posing as the mothers of pre-operatives in order to add credibility to their testimonies (Hausman, 1995). The narratives of those who had gained access to surgery began to exert a 'discursive hegemony' among transsexuals. Collecting the autobiographies of successful transsexuals – either through personal contact or by print – became common as candidates for sex reassignment responded creatively to their situation by modelling themselves on those who had acquired the surgery they so desperately sought (Stone, 1991; Hausman, 1995).[6] This is exemplified in Feinberg's acknowledgement of the tactical importance of accepting medical terms and definitions 'in order to obtain access to the hormones and chest surgery necessary to manifest my spirit in the material world' (cited in Spade, 2006). The medical authorities did not remain unaware of these issues. Billings and Urban (1982: 273) describe how physicians during the 1970s began recognising that candidates for surgery 'had routinely and systematically lied' and complained that the task of diagnosing transsexualism had been made more difficult as 'most patients who request sex reassignment are in complete command of the literature and know the answers before the questions are asked'.

The best known case of transsexuality dealt with in the sociological literature is the story of 'Agnes', related in Garfinkel's (1967) ethnomethodological study of how gender is a managed achievement involving a learnt presentation of identity. Agnes sought surgery before the widespread knowledge about medically acceptable transsexual narratives was available, but exemplifies the creativity that people can exhibit in dealing with the social and physical environment in which they live. Agnes presented herself at the Gender Identity Clinic at the University of California, Los Angeles, as a physically and socially feminine woman with male genitals who had spontaneously begun to feminise at puberty. Diagnosed with testicular feminisation syndrome, medical staff arranged genital transformation surgery for her in order to equip her with a vagina that would reduce the intersexuality of her body and help harmonise her physicality with her sense of self-identity. Garfinkel (2006 [1967]: 60) describes Agnes's appearance as 'convincingly female' and notes that she was a nineteen-year-old girl raised as a boy whose fully developed penis and scrotum sat in tension with her 'female measurements of 38-25-38'.

Garfinkel's analysis recognises much of the creative project that Agnes embarked upon in order to pass as a woman and be accepted as a suitable candidate for surgery. Agnes demonstrated a 'preoccupation with competent female sexuality' to the extent that she became a 'practical methodologist' who undertook a 'secret apprenticeship' in behaving 'like a lady' (Garfinkel, 2006 [1967]: 61, 87). However, Garfinkel remained unaware of just how inventive Agnes had been. Years after Garfinkel's study, Agnes revealed that, far from spontaneously feminising at puberty, she had started taking female hormones before she was a teenager (stealing from her mother's prescription and then getting that prescription filled on her own). Agnes lied to the medical team about these events on the not unreasonable assumption that she would otherwise have been denied the surgery she wanted. What was of most significance about this case was completely missed not only by the medical authorities, but by the sociological investigation reporting on Agnes. Agnes's biggest challenge in securing access to surgery was not any general ability to pass as a woman, but the success she achieved in passing to the medical authorities as an intersexual case whose natural hormonal development resulted in her inhabiting an 'abnormal' body.

Securing access to sex reassignment surgery is not the only obstacle confronting transsexuals. Surgically altered or not, the challenge of becoming accepted as a man or a woman in the social environment is dependent on the ability to pass as a member of one's chosen sex in inter-actional situations. This requires not just the ability to pass in a one-off situation, but the cultivation and adoption of mannerisms, appearances and behaviours as *habits*. Creative strategies are important, but these need to be transformed into routinised displays of *who one is* as an embodied subject. This takes us away from questions associated exclusively with *becoming* to those also linked with *being* a changed person.

Naturalising sex: confronting and learning the habits of gender

Judith Butler (1994) argues that gender is a *performance* that has to be reiterated in order to give the impression of being natural. The norms governing feminine identity, appearance and actions are not biologically rooted, but have to be enacted repeatedly by those subject to them if they are to appear part of the essence of an individual's identity. In seeking to validate her theory, Butler illustrates it with reference to Newton's (1979) study of drag artists. Drag artists are acutely aware of the performative elements of feminine behaviour and must reflect upon and manage, rather than simply take for granted, the stylistic, theatrical and role-based features of their work. This process is relevant to transsexuals, but they must also take it further. Agnes's case, for example, exemplifies the painstaking process involved in developing the capacity to engage in *habitual* performances. The apprenticeship that would help her pass as, and become, a woman began with a prolonged period of silence and withdrawal. Agnes's High School career was apparently dominated by her attempts to remain inconspicuous: she avoided communal eating places and school clubs, sat in the back of classrooms, and restricted her movements and conversations as much as possible. As Agnes put it 'whole days would pass and I wouldn't say a word' (cited in Garfinkel, 2006 [1967]: 74). Agnes's apprenticeship also involved learning ad hoc lessons about being a woman. She learnt from her boyfriend – when he berated her for sunbathing in front of other men – and acquired knowledge about cooking, dress making and home management from her boyfriend's mother. Similarly, many of the transsexuals interviewed by Kessler and McKenna (1978) talk about learning how to act as a member of the opposite sex by 'picking things up' as they went along and of gradually learning the 'rules' of behaviour as one would learn a foreign language. Friends, belonging to the sex they were transferring to, also frequently acted as guides in helping them gather the information and practice required to execute convincing performances. As one of Rudacille's (2006: 185) respondents noted, 'One of my best friends is a gay man, who taught me how to shave, took me to men's bars, showing me what it was like to be a man.'

During this period of apprenticeship, the presentations of identity made by transsexuals are often guarded and display a heightened sensitivity to all nuances in relationships, as if acutely aware that 'a single note off key can disrupt the tone of an entire performance' (Goffman, 1969 [1959]: 60, 81; Kessler and McKenna, 1978). They display a 'sensitivity to devices of talk', a 'skill in detecting and managing "tests"', a 'mastery of trivial but necessary social tasks', and an ability to treat 'the "natural facts of life" of socially recognised, socially managed sexuality as a managed production' that is necessary 'to secure ordinary rights to live' as a normal member of the interaction order (Garfinkel, 2006 [1967]: 87). An essential part of this process involves the readiness to move beyond one's own judgement as to the success of one's learning, and assess one's efforts on the basis of the feedback provided by 'the mirror of the audience' in interactional encounters (Newton, 1979: 37).

This concern with 'getting things right' and monitoring social feedback is often exacerbated by the challenge of getting used to a new body. New clothes, new hairstyle, new facial hair, new breasts, newly removed breasts and so on, may all feel more natural than their antecedents for the transsexual who has for years clamoured for a different body. Nevertheless, each alteration involves a change in the body schema that takes some getting used to. So too can the changes in mood that accompany hormone treatment. Califia, who changed sex from female to male aged forty-five years, notes how well-established appetites became more intense during the first six months of taking testosterone. Citing a friend's description of these changes, Califia (2006: 437) observes that

> When I had to eat I had to eat right fucking now. If I was horny, I had to come immediately. If I needed to shit, I couldn't wait. If I was pissed off the words came right out of my mouth. If I was bored, I had to leave. My body and all the physical sensations that spring from it have acquired a piquancy and an immediacy that is both entertaining and occasionally inconvenient. Moving through the world is even more fun, involves more stimulation that it used to; life is more here-and-now, more about bodies and objects, less about thoughts and feelings.

Of course, it is possible that such changes are as much or even more about the *license* individuals feel to cultivate and act on certain inclinations once they are taking hormones, rather than the actual effects of the hormones themselves. Nevertheless, any such changes in orientation have to be integrated into new presentations of self that convince in encounters.

As suggested in the introduction to this section, however, the essential element to a convincing presentation of identity in social interaction goes beyond the simple learning of rules, or acquiring of techniques, or even feeling at ease in a changed body, to the state where all of these things become habitualised. Above all, as Kessler and McKenna (1978) argue, it is the sense of the *naturalness* of gender that must be sustained as a habit. Given the continued pervasiveness of the two-sex model, people will generally assume that one is of the sex to which one lays claim through one's dress, manner and actions, *unless* there is strong evidence to the contrary. The crucial factor here is having the *self-confidence* to be one's new self and to present one's new self in public. As the Erikson Educational Foundation *Guidelines for Transsexuals* (1974: 6, 12) notes, 'Most people will take you at face value ... if you are not apologetic in your manner ... The key to being accepted by others is your own self-acceptance ... An attitude of quiet self-confidence will get the best results.' In this context, the 'transsexual gradually acquires a comfort and spontaneity ... that smooths the rough edges off his (*sic*) manner and makes it unremarkable and convincing' (Erikson, nd. cited in Kessler and McKenna, 1978: 135). The most important word here is 'unremarkable'. Several of the trans-sexuals in Kessler and McKenna's (1978: 135–6) study 'mentioned "not overdoing it." One talked about the need to be "cool," not to react without first thinking. Another suggested that if you really are confident, then you do not worry about the "small stuff." ' In this respect, the 'background stories' that transsexuals often develop in order to account for their past life need to be 'owned' rather than simply narrated, and so too do the accounts used by transsexuals to explain their current behaviour. These need to be owned, furthermore, in relation to the individual's new body. This is the case with 'Mike', a female-to-male transsexual, who tells people he did not serve in the army because of a 'bad back'. This same reason excuses him from lifting heavy objects. Similarly, while 'Robert' was self-conscious about the ears he had pierced as a woman, he is now at ease accounting for them as identity markers for a street gang he belonged to in his youth. This story also worked to support his biography of having a 'real boy's' child-hood (Kessler and McKenna, 1978: 134). Confidence will not work with-out the presentational skills required to 'sustain the standards of conduct and appearance' common to one's social grouping (Goffman, 1969 [1959]: 81), but it is the habitual ease with which one is able to sustain an initial gender attribution which really marks the shift from 'trying out' to 'comfortably wearing' a new gender identity in public.

Transsexuality and character

Reaching a stage of being 'at ease' with a changed sexual identity is in itself a considerable accomplishment, given what remains at stake in passing as a male or female, but it does not by itself tell us everything there is to know about the relationship between transsexuality and identity or character. The idea of character as a coherent ordering of one's desires, preferences, actions and relationships in relation to self-identified priorities has long been recognised as a difficult task in today's fast-changing world, but it takes on a new dimension in the case of those who have crossed genders or changed sex. The US female-to-male transsexual activist Green (2006: 501) puts the problem in a nutshell. Irrespective of whether transsexuals reach a point at which they feel 'at ease' with themselves, they continue to face a situation in which exposure in encounters remains a risk:

> [I]n order to be a good – or successful – transsexual person, one is not supposed to be a transsexual person at all. This puts a massive burden of secrecy on the transsexual individual: the most intimate and human aspects of our lives are constantly at risk of disclosure. Every time a transsexual man goes into a public (or even private) toilet he is aware of his history; every time he makes love with a partner; every time he seeks medical care; whenever he is at the mercy of a governmental body or social service agency, he is aware of his history – or aware of anomalies in his body – and must consciously be on guard against discovery. And this is supposed to be the optimal ground of being for a successful person? I think not. (Green 2006: 501)

This is one side of the 'visibility dilemma' experienced by transsexuals, but Green (2004) also highlights the other side of this problem. When transsexuals do manage to pass as normal in relation to their subjective sense of gender, they render their own histories and biographies invisible. This can in itself be quite damaging to the achievement of an integrated and comprehensive sense of personal character. For Stone (1991), it runs the risk of contributing to the development of a two-dimensional character and of damaging the creation of 'authentic relationships'. In contrast, if they chose to reveal their life course to others, transsexuals risk undermin-ing their achieved gender status. As Green (2004) concludes, 'the closet' can induce a heavy burden on transsexual people. Stephen Whittle (2006: xiv) goes to the crux of this matter by arguing that the 'labels "man" and "woman" are inadequate to describe the trans experience, as the transperson's history and knowledge of the world is so different from that of "men born men" or "women born women".' Despite Califia's (2006: 436) enjoyment of inhabiting the world with 'male appetites', for instance, he notes that 'In a world where women are supposed to feel and men are supposed to act, I stand in the middle and comprehend what both of them are doing and why. But I remain a stranger in each of these territories.'

The problem of achieving an integrated character is a common one in transsexual writings and research on transsexuals. One of the respondents in Rudacille's study, for example, talks about how he still struggles with many aspects of being male, such as being perceived as a potential threat to children and having to cope with an increased social distance between him and women. Some transsexuals find that their struggle with incoherence diminishes as their preoccupation with transsexuality is gradually replaced with other issues. Many of Rubin's respondents, for example, note how what might appear to be a wholesale transformation is more accurately described as a transition which enables them to repair 'the link between their bodies and gender identity'. These transitions are simply 'a means of making their core identities visible and recognizable to the public' (Rubin, 2003: 144). Kessler and McKenna (1978: 214) remark on just this process in their detailed study of one transsexual in which they comment on how 'gender has become an integrated feature of her life as it is for all women. No longer is she preoccupied with being seen as a woman, but she is concerned now with what kind of woman she should spend her life being.' Similarly, one of Rudacille's (2006: 143) respondents simply noted that 'Transsexuality is the least weird thing about me. I happen to be a transsexual. Aside from that, I'm way the fuck out there.' Another male-to-female transsexual expresses this sense of integration in reflecting on how her own body reflects her sense of having achieved a coherence between her life priorities and her physical self: 'I'm really happy with this body – it's sagging, it's failing, it's all of that but it's me' (ibid.: 99). These responses do not constitute a *denial* of transsexuality, but can be seen as an *exploration of its possibilities* (see also Cromwell, 2006: 517).

Transsexuals may continue to define and experience themselves in terms of embodied *changes*, investing sometimes in the politically transgressive creation of a subjective space that exists outside of that made available to people within the two-sex model (Whittle, 2006: xiv), or they may seek to develop their character on the basis of the options that become available to them *after* their transition. What is common to each option, however, is a refusal to continue having their identity defined on the basis of social stigmatism. Goffman (1963a) insisted that the process of stigmatisation involved social relationships and norms and could not be reduced to some physical or behavioural 'essence'. He also recognised the importance of the internal environment, though, in arguing that 'the stigmatised individual can come to feel that he should be above passing' (ibid.: 125). This can take several forms, but the achievement of a certain transcendence in relation to passing, a determination to cultivate a character outside the negative stereotypes of conventional society, appears to be an essential element among transsexuals who have achieved a degree of success in constructing a self-identity with which they feel at ease.

Sexual character and morality

Transsexuality raises important moral issues about the types of identity or character that may be presented legitimately in contemporary society. Feminists have long argued that 'biology is not destiny', in insisting that there is no reason why the sex to which we are ascribed at birth should determine our behaviour, but transsexuality suggests that our biological sex at birth is no longer completely fixed. Along with other radical forms of body modification, to which it has been compared, it provides an example of how the body with which we were born no longer has to be the body with which we live (Sullivan, 2006).

That transsexuality provokes strong responses from those who have invested heavily in the status quo within society should not be surprising, but negative reaction to sex reassignment extends beyond traditionally conservative sections of society. One of the most infamous manifestations of this hostility, for example, was Janice Raymond's 1979 book *The Transsexual Empire*, an extended diatribe against transsexuals from a radical feminist viewpoint. Raymond argued that males who undergo sex reassignment remain deviant men, using the appropriated appearance of the female body to invade women's spaces in order to exercise male dominance and aggression over women. Raymond claims that this is tantamount to rape and argues that all male-to-female transsexuals are, by definition, rapists. Such views are extreme, but there has been a history of troubled relations between feminist groups and transsexuals (Rubin, 2006: 477). This is also evident to some degree with the gay and lesbian movements. Transgendered protestors played an important role in the Stonewall riots of 1969 that were so important in advancing gay rights in the United States, yet their actions have been marginalised in radical histories of these events, while those campaigning for anti-discrimination and equal opportunities legislation that would protect homosexuals have often stopped short of including transsexual and transgender rights in their proposals.

In recent years, however, an increasing number of activists have sought to forge common ground between transsexuals, feminists and others who find themselves restricted or oppressed by the two-sex model and its related gender stereotypes. As a contribution to this, Rubin (2006: 479) highlights the 'imperfect, historical, temporary and arbitrary' status of all identity categories, while Feinberg (2006) has called for a 'pan-gender' movement of the sexually oppressed to make common cause with each other in the name of social justice, and Spade (2006: 321) seeks to undermine all gender categories in an effort to rid individuals of their oppressive and restricting consequences. Calls such as these illustrate the broader moral issues raised by transsexualism as a phenomenon that is relevant to 'anyone who does not feel comfortable in the gender role they were attributed to at birth' (Whittle, 2006: xi). They also illustrate the potential for embodied action to respond creatively to even the most rigid features of the external environment.

Notes

1 The importance of presentational concerns was not unique to the nineteenth or twentieth centuries, but in earlier ages people's identities were bound up with marks of status and insignia that were *external* to any specific interaction. During the feudal era, for example, it was the shield that indicated status, while attributions of honour were dependent upon people's occupation of institutional roles (Turner, 1984). This was explored in detail by Elias's (1983) analyses of those court societies that played an important part in European 'civilizing processes' from the fourteenth century. In these settings an individual's presentational skills remained a vital resource in power struggles, but were deployed within a system of monarchical power in which the occupation of roles was often the overriding determinant of prestige and power. Widely recognised marks of status *overdetermined* the identity of the self presented by an individual within an interaction.

2 Different and unequal expectations follow from these attributions (Goffman, 1977: 320–9) and it is in this context that feminists like Simone de Beauvoir (1993 [1949]) examine how women are expected to put on 'a show' for men, and to allow men to 'steer' their social encounters (see also Bartky, 1988: 68). Men are also constrained in terms of gendered expectations, however, and for *anyone* to break the interactional norms that follow from the initial attribution of maleness or femaleness is to risk transgressing one of *the* most fundamental grounds on which encounters are based (Kessler and McKenna, 1978).

3 Butler and others have encouraged an increasing tendency to view sex as well as gender as socially constructed, but such a view effaces the ontological differences that exist between the biological body and social behaviour and would ill serve an analysis of the complexities of trangenderism.

4 During this period, while the male body was considered the norm, the female body was interpreted as being in possession of all the parts of the male even if they were rearranged in an inverted and inferior pattern (Duroche, 1990). Bodies were important – and they were certainly open to the interpretive demands of male-dominated cultures – but the essential identities or capacities of men and women did not inhere in any specific, permanent way in their flesh (Laqueur, 1990: 601).

5 In the case of infants this view led to some tragic consequences. As Rudacille (2006: 110) notes, very few genital anomalies were 'fixed' by a single surgery. Instead, children often endured repeated operations, physical pain and scarring and 'emotional torment as the secret of their births was withheld from them by parents trying desperately to adhere to the facade of normalcy'. While the West has long condemned the practice of female genital mutilation in Senegal, Somalia and elsewhere, it views as normalising painful and sometimes permanently debilitating surgery on intersexual infants. Ninety per cent of anatomically ambiguous infants are assigned to the female sex by the cutting and removal of genital tissue, a form of destructive surgery that can leave the individual without the ability to orgasm (see Chase, 2006 [1998]).

6 This creates an obvious difficulty in assessing the authenticity of transsexual autobiographies and this is why I have drawn on these resources sparingly and utilised cases such as Agnes's that yield data prior to the widespread assumption that there exist 'viable' and 'authorised' transsexual biographies that are most acceptable to the medical profession.

6

Moving

Introduction

Movement is essential for the maintenance of human life. It is integral to the walking, digging, cultivating and building involved in acquiring the food and shelter necessary for survival, while social relationships are established, maintained and transformed through the flux of locomotion that brings us into, and takes us out of, contact with different experiences and people (Simmel, 1971 [1908, 1911]). Yet sociological discussions of the global flows of commodities and digitalised information that characterise our current age, the virtual travels of those who traverse the world through the internet, and the multiple 'gazes' of Western tourists feasting on the spectacles of 'exotic others', often fail to provide any real sense that it is breathing, sweating, talking, *embodied* subjects who engage in these movements.

Pragmatism provides an antidote to these somewhat disembodied images of movement and travel as it assumes that the normal condition of healthy, waking humans involves active engagement with the environment through processes of motility. People are not kinaesthetically passive decision-makers, who calculate the relative satisfactions they will gain from alternative modes of action *prior* to engaging in physical movement, but make choices and engage in behaviours that are grounded in, and moulded by, the ongoing stream of activity through which they engage with the external environment. The capacity to shape or control such movement is, moreover, a hugely consequential element in the exercise of power. States across the world are concerned with population flows and the policing of borders (Moorehead, 2006), for example, while schools have traditionally been involved in regulating and disciplining the activities of pupils while seeking to transmit to them culturally sanctioned norms and habits (Shilling, 2004). More dramatically, Nazi attempts to turn those imprisoned Jews they did not gas immediately into spiritless automatons had at their centre concentration camp disciplinary regimes that prescribed in detail when, where and how movement should occur (see Chapter 8).

The significance of movement cannot be reduced to judgements regarding its enabling or constraining conditions and consequences, however, as daily locomotion and travel involves for the vast majority of people a *mutual accommodation* between, and a reciprocal *shaping of*, the external environment and our embodied selves. Mutual accommodation between individuals and the *physical environment* is evident in the ordinary activity of walking. As people make a pathway or route familiar, through repeatedly traversing a terrain, they do not simply become aware of its bends, bumps and directions, but actually *assimilate* these into their bodily capacities of movement and anticipation. Bachelard (1964: 11) refers to these processes as contributing to the development of our 'muscular consciousness'. Simultaneously, such repeated travellings leave their imprint on the grass, earth and even concrete that is walked on, carving out grooves, affecting where plants can grow and gradually wearing down hard material surfaces (Tilley, 1994; Ingold, 2004). Human movement also assimilates itself to, and is affected by, tools and other technologies. Computer keyboards, tennis racquets, saws and hammers can all become extensions of the 'arm in motion' for those practised in their use, while also shaping the bodily sensations, postures and musculatures of their operatives. Thus, while movements in the physical environment may be more or less constraining or enabling, they also shape humans and the milieu in which they move in ways which alter how they 'fit' or 'attune' themselves to each other.

Mutual accommodation between embodied subjects and the *social environment* can also be illustrated via the example of walking. The evolutionary development of bipedalism was shaped not only by the actions of individuals seeking to combine movement with tool use, but as a result of *group* pressures for survival. These collective influences stimulated the 'physiological division of labour' through which the feet and hands came to be perfected for different but complementary functions, 'of support and locomotion on the one hand, and of grasping and manipulation on the other' (Ingold, 2004: 317). Once accomplished, bipedalism also impacted upon the character of social groups by increasing the distances over which people could travel to hunt, fight or join with others. The writings of Bourdieu and others on the habits and *habitus* of embodied subjects reveal other ways in which there develops a mutual accommodation between people and the customary movements of a social group. On the one hand, the skills learnt by musicians or sports competitors are not simply technical accomplishments, but constitute socially accepted ways in which body techniques should be executed according to the customs of a profession (Mauss, 1973 [1934]). Similarly, the notion of an *esprit de corps* signifies the sense of ritual, physically expressive solidarity that develops in social groups encompassing not only an 'attitude of mind' but an 'attitude of *movement*' (Blumer, 1969). On the other hand, this accommodation is not one way. The changes that occur in how groups interact over time, and the innovations that occur in specific body techniques, show how the creativity of individuals to improvise and initiate new physical movements shapes the particular configurations assumed by the social milieu. Again, movement does not just enable or constrain, but can alter the capacities and identities of individuals as well as the environment they inhabit.

Movement may be regarded by some as marginal to the concerns of sociology: it was never considered a 'unit idea' of the discipline in its formation (Nisbet, 1993 [1966]), and interest was further depressed as a result of relatively static Parsonian conceptions of social systems in the mid-twentieth century. If we are interested in how individuals both shape and are shaped by their environment, however, and in how travel has impinged on the formation and transformation of social interactions and societies, it is clearly an important issue. This was recognised by some of the most important studies of the Chicago School which explored the relationship between physical and social mobility, and identity and community, and pre-figured sociology's recent attempts to come to grips with the accelerated pace of urban life and the central characteristics of globalisation (Faris, 1967). Nowadays, forms of movement (from the bygone figure of the *flaneur* in nineteenth-century Paris, to the 'post-modern nomad' that Bauman uses to evoke the spirit of the current era) and modes of movement (such as the car central to recent analyses of 'automobilities') increasingly exercise the sociological imagination.

In exploring these themes further, I focus initially on how the external environment provides a context in which the elite have privileged access to the fast-paced life of global existence, while the 'dispossessed' are limited to joining the underbelly of human flows across the world. The second half of this chapter then explores in more detail this underside of global life by examining how the actions and identities of refugees, asylum seekers, disadvantaged migrant workers and others excluded from global wealth, are forged through the travels in which they engage. Theoretical accounts of globalisation frequently concentrate on the lives of professionals whose work and leisure exemplifies the relative effacement of time and space that high-technology life has made possible. In contrast, I focus on how both the forced flows of slave labour in times past, and the pragmatic responses of dispossessed travellers in times present, provide an essential prerequisite and foundation for such developments.

The external environments of action

The social constitution of modern travel

Travel may not have been central to classical sociology, but Georg Simmel's (1971 [1903]; 1990 [1907]) writings on the metropolis and the money economy do much to capture how commercial urban milieu changed the character of movement in modernity. According to Simmel, the city stimulated a highly specialised social division of labour in which human interactions became multiple, varied and fleeting; conditions which heightened individuality, accelerated the pace of daily life and allowed people unprecedented opportunites for travel within and across the urban landscape. These conditions stood in stark contrast to rural, pre-modern contexts where the mobility and circulation of people was strictly limited and tied to ritual patterns involving predictable transfers of goods between clearly identifiable collectivities (Mauss, 1954 [1950]).

Simmel's writings identify much that remains of relevance about the social milieu that has shaped modern movement, but recent discussions of globalisation have focused on the extension and intensification of these trends on the international stage. Multinational corporations, electronic markets and telecommunications media, such as the mobile phone and the internet, have been viewed as compressing time and space and accelerating the pace at which transnational flows of commodities and people circulate the globe (Sassen, 2002: 254). There have even been attempts to reformulate the subject matter of sociology on the basis of such 'new forms of mobilities' that are arguably more suited to life in the twenty-first century (e.g. Urry, 2000). These visions of unconstrained movement emphasise just how much has changed in modernity, but they tend to focus on the social environment inhabited by the *established*; those with the resources enabling them to exploit this milieu. What they do not portray are the social boundaries separating the established from the *outsiders*; those on the receiving end of the negative consequences of these global processes or those stigmatised and barred from participating in the global travels of the affluent on the basis of such characteristics as 'race', religion or length of residence (Elias and Scotson, 1994 [1965]). Travel may increasingly flow through 'smooth spaces' for highly skilled, privileged classes, but globalisation has not resulted in a world without borders to security and well-being. There are several reasons for this.

First, globalisation has contributed towards the consolidation of deep-rooted inequalities. The ability of highly skilled professionals to jet around the world and forge rewarding careers in the 24/7 'global society' is itself dependent on the migration of millions of workers from poor countries to rich ones in order to undertake the personal 'body work' these professionals are no longer willing to do (Shilling, 1993, 2005a). What Ehrenreich and Hochschild (2002: 2–3) refer to as the 'female underside' of globalisation, for example, involves large numbers of women from the South migrating to do 'the "women's work"' of the North where they serve as nannies, maids and sex workers. The scale of this population movement is massive. Of the nearly 800,000 household workers employed legally in the United States at the turn of the twenty-first century, for example, forty per cent were born abroad (Hochschild, 2002). Neither is this trend confined to the affluent West. In Taiwan, for example, more than 120,000 foreigners are employed legally as domestic workers, with ninety-three per cent of them coming from the Philippines and Indonesia (Lan, 2002). This circulation of migrants is not confined to the least popular forms of work, moreover, but extends into the constitution of families. There are a growing number of adoption programmes that take young children from impoverished or less affluent parts of the world to the West, while there is a booming business in 'mail order' brides stimulated by Westerners seeking young and compliant wives, and by immigrant men seeking wives from their countries of origin (Thai, 2002; Dorow, 2004). These movements of women and children are, again, based in large part on global inequalities.

Second, and despite these major flows of migrants, affluent nation-states have jealously guarded their powers of border control. Migration has been characterised as 'the unfinished business of globalisation', and is an emotive and contentious issue for politicians 'because it challenges the last defining national characteristic: the ability of a country to say who comes in and who goes out' (Moorehead, 2006: 288). For every individual able to enjoy the fruits of increased travel, there are hundreds who remain in countries marked by poverty and conflict, and whose only hope of escape is based on often dangerous attempts to evade border controls and cross into other regions. Illegal immigration has become a major political issue since the early 1980s when Europe 'embarked with a new zeal on its project of seclusion' by making it increasingly difficult for unauthorised travellers to gain entry to its borders (Harding, 2000). Elsewhere, the dangers facing those seeking to cross the Mexican/US border have become much greater since the 1990s, when reducing immigration was made a priority, and there has even been a proposal to electrify the fences that mark this border (Moorehead, 2006). More generally, the political focus placed on immigration control in the West has stimulated a burgeoning business of illegal human trafficking. With an estimated annual worth of between $5 and $7 billion dollars, migrants often pay traffickers all they possess, yet run the risk of being cheated, killed or sold into the sex industry (Harding, 2000: 20). Wars, environmental catastrophes and market forces continue to uproot people, moreover, and while the countries of Western Europe complain most vociferously about the social and economic costs of asylum seekers, it is actually the world's poorest countries in Africa, Asia and the Middle East who bear by far the largest burden of these displaced travellers. Ninety per cent of refugees actually remain in the region from which they originate (Moorehead, 2006: 39).

Third, it needs to be recognised that contemporary dimensions of globalisation are built on a long history of population flows, controls, immigrant labour and slavery that have structured the wealth and the poverty of nations and continents. In terms of the sheer amount of travel, the years between 1850 and 1914 are notable, being characterised by mass migrations between Europe and North and South America and Australasia. During this period around fifty-five million Europeans embarked on new lives in places short of labour and rich in raw materials (Hatton and Williamson, 1998: 3), while over 125 million people were internationally mobile throughout the world as a whole at the end of the nineteenth century (Hoerder, 2002; Gabaccia and Leach, 2004). In terms of the use of migrant labour, the wave of post-war immigration from the West Indies to Britain was stimulated by an acute shortage of labour in low-paid service and manual jobs. Another notable example involves the US–Mexico Bracero Programme. This ran between 1942 and 1964, involved migrants toiling on the bottom rungs of agricultural and industrial work in the

United States, and employed at its peak in the late 1950s over 400,000 Mexicans (Mize, 2004; see also Brown and Shue, 1983). More consequential still for the inequalities embedded in contemporary global movements, however, has been the scale and longevity of the slave trade. It was the Islamic slave routes within Africa that first alerted Europeans to the potential of developing their own slave-trading systems on the West African coast in the late fifteenth century. This led to a system of Atlantic slavery that developed up until the late nineteenth century, involved Europe, Africa and America, and 'brought great material well-being to the West' while spreading 'impoverishment and misery throughout Africa' (Walvin, 2006: xiii).[1] Between 1662 and 1807, for example, British ships alone transported three and a quarter million enslaved Africans across the Atlantic (Walvin, 2006: 46). Indeed, it was not until the 1840s that annual voluntary European migration to the Americas exceeded the numbers involved in forced slavery from Africa (Hatton and Williamson, 1998: 7). While the anti-slavery movement appeared to be 'universally triumphant' by the end of the nineteenth century, slave labour was a characteristic of both Nazi and Stalinist regimes in the twentieth century (see Chapter 8) and is even today a 'flourishing business' in some parts of the world (Engerman et al., 2001). The organisation Anti-Slavery International has estimated that there are some twenty million bonded labourers around the world (adults and children having to work off debts, often involving massive interest rates, through forced labour), and some 800,000 people sold against their will each year (Walvin, 2006: 132). The victims of these practices range from children forced to work in the brick kilns of South Asia, to Burmese girls sold into prostitution in Thailand (Engerman et al., 2001). UNICEF estimates that there are one million children involved in the sea trade in South East Asia alone. Slavery, in short, has been a massive industry which lubricated world trade, and left a legacy that continues to shape international patterns of economic growth, trade and stagnation, and blights the lives of millions.

These dimensions of the social environment reveal that while globalisation may have contributed to a social milieu offering certain groups of people unprecedented opportunities for travel, there are other modalities of movement that need to be highlighted if we are to appreciate the less glamorous 'underbelly' of this phenomenon.

The physical milieu of modern travel

The social milieu in which travel occurs is, of course, informed by and bound up intimately with the physical environment. Thus, while movement in and through the urban milieu is shaped by the social division of labour and the multiple interactions that typify city life, so too is it structured by a built environment characterised by a noise, smell and visual overload that encourages people to concentrate on the instrumental task of reaching their destination (Simmel, 1971 [1903]). If cities have become spaces in which rational goals are facilitated – rather than being places for the leisurely aesthetic curiosity of the *flaneur* – city planners have consolidated this by increasing the potential *speed* of bodily travel into and out of cities.[2] In revolutionary Paris and nineteenth-century London, for example, traffic systems were modelled on the basis of efficient circulation (a model which appeared to project onto the urban body William Harvey's early-seventeenth-century understanding of the healthy biological body) (Sennett, 1994: 255, 264, 325). Freedom and ease of movement through the city subsequently became increasingly important considerations, alongside the emphasis ascribed to the free flow of commodities. The 'ideal' modern city allowed individuals to travel through this milieu, without having to engage with it.

Urry's (2000, 2002) discussions of contemporary global mobilities extend this picture of how urban milieu have been structured to facilitate the progressive liberation of the body from its physical environment. In terms of land-based transport, recent discussions of 'automobility' reflect the extent to which large areas of cities and, indeed, 'large areas of the globe now consist of car-only environments' (Urry, 2000: 193; Featherstone et al., 2005). Approximately one-quarter of the land in London and nearly one-half of that in Los Angeles, for example, is devoted to such car spaces (Urry, 2000: 193). Traffic jams and parking problems have increased the personal costs associated with driving, however, and many of those with the resources to do so (and those whose jobs require them to do so) not only seek to pass quickly through cities but increasingly jet into and out of them while travelling minimally within them. By the start of the twenty-first century there were nearly 700 million international passenger arrivals each year, while two million air passengers flew each day in the United States alone. International travel now accounts for over one-twelfth of world trade (Gottdiener, 2001; Urry, 2000: 50, 2002: 5).

Flying still involves expenditures of time, energy and effort associated with getting to and hanging around airports, and sitting in the cramped conditions and breathing the stale, recycled air in aeroplanes. In contrast, one of the most characteristic forms of contemporary global mobilities involves electronic forms of communication that minimise bodily movement. The ability to participate in virtual travel by communicating through conference calls, email and so on, enables people to avoid engaging with any physical milieu whatsoever (save that provided by the environment in which technology is used and that of the technology that facilitates this communication) while the importance of computer access/use to employment and social capital opportunities is such that analysts have judged the 'digital divide' to be one of the most important determinants of class, regional, national and international inequalities.

These observations should not allow us to overlook the continued importance of *local places*, especially for less privileged groups. Park et al.'s (1967 [1925]) classic *The City*, for example, may be dated in certain respects, but it identified an intimate relationship between physical and social mobility still relevant today. Cities were typically marked by 'zones' that exhibited a close link between length of immigrant settlement on the one hand and poverty and social disorganisation on the other (Park et al., 1967 [1925]: 54–5; see Chapter 3). Rex and Moore also found a strong correlation between the physical zones of a city, poverty and social disorganisation, and the relative establishment of different immigrant groups. In contrast to the 'zones of transition' referred to by Park et al., however, Rex and Moore (1973 [1967]) found that the relationship between immigrant group, social mobility and physical space could sometimes be captured more adequately by the term 'zones of stagnation'. Wilson's (1978, 1987) studies of the black underclass reinforce the importance of place further in their suggestion that processes of uneven urban development which bypass certain locales contribute to the erosion of family life, social opportunities and community coherence (see also Wilson and Taub, 2007).

Most of these studies took place before the most recent manifestations of globalisation, but MacLeod's (2004) ethnography of life in the Chicago projects reinforces the importance of the relationship between physical and social mobility. Revisiting the disadvantaged subjects of his study in the projects of Clarendon Heights eight years since his initial research, MacLeod (2004: xvii) remarks:

> If I had studied middle class boys I would have had to criss-cross the country to catch up with them as twenty-four year olds. But my own transatlantic travels contrasted sharply with the limited mobility of my subjects. The Clarendon Heights men, constrained geographically as well as socioeconomically, still lived nearby. Only those in prison resided far from the city.

Some sociologists have suggested that the physical environment in these studies is no more than a reflection of more important *social* processes, yet Elias's (1994) work demonstrates the significance of the physical environment to inequality, prejudice and discrimination. Among other factors, it is the particular characteristics of physical environments that allow them to be protected, travelled through or avoided altogether, that helps enable established groups maintain their privilege at the expense of outsider groups (see also Baumgartner, 1988).

These studies illustrate how the contemporary era is characterised by centripetal processes which tend to restrict physical travel, as well as centrifugal processes which enhance and accelerate travel, and also suggest that physical mobility is linked to social mobility. It is not only the affluent, however, who embark on international travel. At the turn of the twenty-first century, wars, famine, drought, flooding and other aspects of the external environment contributed to a situation where there were thought to be over thirty million refugees in the world as a whole (Urry, 2002: 5). The journeys of these refugees are often filled with hardship, danger and suffering, and frequently last for weeks and months. Often separated from family and friends, they can involve placing their lives in the hands of unscrupulous human traffickers, long treks on foot through inhospitable terrain, hiding in trucks and trains in attempting to evade border controls and beatings by police when they are apprehended (Taghmaian, 2005). Crossings undertaken at sea are often made in hazardous circumstances, in unseaworthy vessels, with insufficient food and water. Harding (2000) reports that of the 3,000 *known* deaths of people trying to enter Europe in the last decade, many drowned seeking to cross from North Africa to Italy and Spain. Estimated deaths resulting from these hazardous journeys are far higher and during 2006 alone 6,000 refugees are calculated to have perished seeking to reach Europe by boat (Campbell, 2007).

The phases of embodied action

The social and physical environment provides the external milieu in which travel occurs, but movement is also central to the needs and evolutionarily developed capacities of humans and it is the *interrelationship* of these factors that is crucial to the shaping of our actions and identities. Thus, planes, trains and automobiles have not only 'shrunk' physical space for some, but have increased the potential for people to choose to disengage phenomenologically from their surroundings. This may be comforting to those seeking to minimise the risks that encountering 'otherness' can bring, but may also create a blandness and emptiness in people (Sennett, 1994). Instead of focusing on how the privileged may be alienated in their comfort, however, I want to concentrate in the remainder of this chapter on the travellings of the 'dispossessed'.

By using the term the 'dispossessed', I am referring to three types of travellers. The first includes refugees and asylum seekers who have fled or been driven from a nation or an area as a result of some social or natural disaster, and who may face persecution if they return home. The second are those sold forcibly into slavery or bonded labour, taken from their homes to endure life in another area or country. The third are legal or illegal economic migrants who have left their country of origin in search of a better life elsewhere. While these migrant workers may not have been displaced in the same forcible and often violent way as others I discuss in this category, I include them here because of the frequency with which poverty and a prospectless future drives these people away from their home.

Identity and crisis: departing, arriving and changing

Matters of life and death loom large in accounts of refugees/migrants fleeing for their lives and/or desperate to make a new life in a new country. Layered on top of these narratives is a strong sense of how such journeys impact on people's identities. While the conditions that prompt dispossessed travellers to leave their place of residence can prove highly traumatic in and of themselves, the journeys they embark upon subsequently are often dangerous, leaving the individuals involved deprived of those social relationships which previously sustained their sense of selfhood. Those who successfully reach their destination, moreover, can find themselves imprisoned prior to being sent back home, or kept in holding camps while their applications for asylum are processed (Fassin, 2005).

The effects of these experiences on migrants already traumatised by their flight from home can be devastating. Moorehead (2006) details the plight of the 'lost boys of Africa' who had been separated from their families during their flight from the civil wars of the 1990s and made their way to Cairo. These young men from Sierro Leone and Liberia, Ethiopia and Eritrea, Sudan, Guinea, the Ivory Coast, Rwanda and Burundi had witnessed atrocities and were now having to wait for months and sometimes years for United Nations' interviewers to assess their stories and decide whether they could start a new life in a different country. The conditions in which they waited not only made it difficult to survive from a material point of view, but placed them in limbo. Without family or friends, unable to work officially because of their asylum seeker status, and often suffering from severe psychological distress as a result of the events they fled from, the absence of interactions with, and support from, familiar others sometimes drained from them the will to live. As Moorehead (2006) concludes, the high rates of suicide within these groups are an indicator of desperation and desolation.

Elsewhere, refugees faced problems resulting from lengthy stays in detention camps. Moorehead (2006) recounts the case of a five-year-old boy, Shayan, whose family fled from persecution in Iran only to be placed in detention in Woomera, Australia. The conditions in the camp were crowded and extremely hot. Riots and violence were common, and Shayan became withdrawn. After eleven months, his bed wetting, nightmares, refusal to eat and insomnia were diagnosed as post-traumatic stress disorder. Moved to another detention centre, Shayan witnessed more violence, self-mutilation and an attempted suicide. He stopped eating and drinking and refused to talk, and was taken from his parents to live with another Muslim family in the community. Eventually reunited with his parents (once they had secured Temporary Protection Visas), Shayan remained under psychiatric care, sleeping little, having nightmares and rarely choosing to mix with children his own age because 'they do not know what it is like to have lived inside a prison' (Moorehead, 2006: 115).

If these refugees felt they had to flee their country of origin, they were at least doing something active in an attempt to improve their circumstances. Bales's (2002) research into those children and women kidnapped or sold into prostitution in Thailand (and sometimes sold on to brothels in Japan, Europe and America) details journeys literally forced upon their victims. Bales (2002) details the case of a fifteen-year-old girl called Siri who was sold by her parents to an intermediary and then drugged, raped and beaten as part of her initiation into life in a brothel. Siri's identity had been devastated by the adjustments she had made in order to survive in and 'make sense' of her situation. Her resistance and desire to escape broke down, and she was reduced to taking a 'pride' in her commodity value (as a young good-looking girl her price was relatively high) and by the number of men who chose her for sex (ibid.: 207–9).

It is not only those fleeing from war and persecution or sold into sex slavery who find their identities under persistent assault. Zarembka's (2002) research focused on domestic workers who arrive in the United States under special conditional visas that allow them to work for diplomats, officials of international agencies and certain other foreign nationals, yet which render them liable for deportation should they leave their employment. Many of these workers are paid significantly below the national minimum wage, are forced to work exceptionally long hours for seven days a week and endure intimidation, sexual exploitation and violence. Reported cases include persistent physical and sexual abuse, being made to sleep on the floor, bathe in a bucket in the yard and having to wear a dog collar and sleep with family dogs outside the house (ibid.: 147).

Women migrant workers also face difficulties resulting from being separated from their own families. Hochschild's (2002) study of legal household workers in the United States, for example, includes a number of mothers who left their children behind in order to earn for them a better future. All expressed guilt and remorse, and many found it difficult to 'keep going' in their new lives. As one migrant mother who left her two-month-old baby at home in the care of a relative said:

> The first two years I felt like I was going crazy. You have to believe me when I say that it was like I was having intense psychological problems. I would catch myself gazing at nothing, thinking about my child. (cited in Hochschild, 2002)

Parrenas's (2002) research reinforces this picture of the pain faced by migrant mothers who look after other people's children while being unable to care for their own. In the absence of their children, these women feel as if they are missing an essential part of themselves which has been 'left behind'. As one migrant mother working in Rome noted: 'If I had wings, I would fly home to my children. Just for a moment, to see my children and take care of their needs, help them, then fly back over here to continue my work' (Parrena, 2002: 42). In each of these cases, bodily relationships of love, care and friendship were broken, while physically embedded habits, routines and familiarities became anachronisms which no longer helped individuals navigate the new environment in which they lived.

Dispossessed travellers faced a variety of problems associated with the journeys they undertook and the circumstances that met them at their destinations. There are few 'happy endings' for those trafficked into the sex industry or chained to their work stations as bonded labourers. Nevertheless, there is also plenty of evidence to suggest that those who possessed the autonomy that made it possible to maintain their identity, took every opportunity available to resist treatment of them that was degrading and oppressive. Such action was made more possible for individuals where there existed networks and communities of immigrants in their new country.

Coping, creating and resisting

Recent waves of immigration to the United States and Europe have done much to fill low-paid, unattractive positions in the labour market. The position of these migrants is frequently used to illustrate the inequalities that continue to characterise relations between the affluent West and its former colonies. Nonetheless, it is also important to note that some of these individuals have succeeded in realising certain of their aims. By scraping and saving, many manage to send home money to benefit their families, while the establishment of lives safer than those they left behind is another valued accomplishment (Sassen, 2002). If we are to gain a wider picture of the success or otherwise of the journeys undertaken by dispossessed travellers, however, we need to look at the collectivities and communities of which they are a part.

Historically, the re-creation or re-establishment of community has been an invaluable source of assistance for refugees and migrants, enabling them to maintain parts of their identity they consider essential by receiving some form of validation for their customs, habits and bodily appearance. This is apparent in the case of the free immigrants who arrived in America during the late nineteenth century. While they settled in ghettos that contributed to the cultural and economic barriers that set them apart from the rest of society, their proximity to others from the same background enabled them to maintain some of their traditions at the same time as they were gradually integrating themselves into American life (Briggs, 1978; Bodnar et al., 1982).

The capacity to sustain certain rituals and habitual actions was also crucial to later groups of immigrants arriving in the United States. This is evident among the 140,000 survivors of the Holocaust who arrived in the country after the Second World War. Those who chose to settle in New York found ready-made Jewish communities and benefited greatly from the assistance they received from Jewish agencies as well as from relatives and friends (Helmreich, 1996). The accounts of these survivors suggest that knowing that the habits that served them successfully in their former lives still had some resonance and relevance provided a tremendous boost to their self-esteem and the hope with which they approached the future (ibid.).

More recently, kinship networks have remained immensely important for other immigrants in the United States. Smith's and Tarallo's (1993) study of California, for example, highlights how settled Mexican families provide new immigrants with shelter and food, and information about jobs. The Catholic Church also serves as an element of religious and institutional continuity for these immigrants: it provides them with acceptance, with practical help and advice. Immigrant groups do not simply adapt to their new environment, of course, but have been able to reshape the social and the physical milieu in which they live. Successive waves of Southeast Asian refugees in California, for example, forged social networks which have intervened in and altered the urban landscape in a manner which resembles the cafes and markets that exist in Vietnam (Smith and Tarallo, 1993). Cases such as these illustrate the very real resource that collectivities provide for individuals seeking to survive and prosper in their new lives.

Even if communities of second-generation immigrants validate and enable new migrants to maintain at least some of their habits and customs, however, the meaning of these phenomena change as they are deployed in a new environment. The very fact that immigrants may appreciate *reflexively* the continued resonance of certain habits, for example, shows that these actions are no longer as automatic as they once were. Furthermore, if the nature of these habits changes in the new environment, so too does the nature of the immigrant community (e.g. Park et al. (1967 [1925]: 107)). Sayad's (2004) study of Algerian immigration in France provides us with a good illustration of this process.

Sayad's typology of the 'three ages' of immigration traces how the actions of individual migrants, and the forms of community they are involved with, change over time. Sayad's *first age* describes an early era involving migrants selected from and by the Algerian community because they were trusted peasants who worked hard with the sole aim of minimising their stay abroad and bringing money back home. On their return, celebrations ritually reintegrated them back into the community in order that their future life continued in harmony with their past. The *second age* of immigration was characterised by a much greater degree of discontinuity, however, with migrants travelling in greater numbers and on their own initiative. As Sayad (2004: 39) notes, this was no longer a collective mission 'entrusted by the group to one of its members', but the act of an individual taken on 'his own initiative and on his own behalf'. Emigration 'was no longer a way of helping the group, but a way of escaping its constraints' (ibid.). Visits home to Algeria became shorter and less frequent, and the migrant became shaped increasingly by 'French habits' and the calculating spirit that comes with working in a developed money economy (ibid.: 49–53). Most recently, the *third age* of immigration is based on the firm establishment of an Algerian 'colony' within France, characterised by family as well as individual emigration. This has meant that every 'new wave' of emigrants that came to France found an existing community made up of earlier emigrants 'into which it could incorporate itself' (ibid.: 57). Individual opportunism may have supplemented and eroded a relatively stable *Gemeinschaft* community structure in parts of Algeria, but a new form of Algerian community was gradually established in France. This was informed, at least in part, by previous habits and traditions, facilitated patterns of mutual aid, and complemented the focus on monetary exchange and ambition which had driven immigration in the second age. Nonetheless, these new communities were infused by patterns of rationality, reflexivity and calculation reflective of their external environment which made them *fundamentally different* from their antecedents.

Not all flows of immigration follow the same pattern as that identified by Sayad, but his model says something more general about the mutual accommodations made between individuals, their communities and the countries to which they move or are moved. For example, while the slave trade forced people into long journeys and a lifetime of servitude, it could not eradicate entirely the communities of the people bought and sold under its auspices. In the United States, slaves used song and music to make their work tolerable, and adapted customs and rituals brought with them from their homelands in order to re-create, albeit in heavily modi-fied forms, communal bonds. Indeed, the extent to which slaves managed to interact and assist each other has led Kulikoff (1986) to conclude that slave society was characterised by hundreds of interlocking friendship and kinship networks that stretched across many plantations. Gilroy's (1993) analysis of the black cultures that grew out of slavery updates this picture, while also providing a temporal dimension which complements that of Sayad (2004). For Gilroy (1993), communities of slaves and their allies initially provided a collective basis for resistance, creativity and political activism in the struggles against forced servitude that were conducted in the New World. The black networks and cultures that followed subsequently provided a collective basis for citizenship campaigns in which free black populations living in modernised, indus-trialised countries secured an extension of *individual* as well as group rights. More recently, the focus has returned to collective issues with campaigns for independent political spaces – including a 'return to Africa' movement – in which 'black community and autonomy' could develop at their own pace.

In analysing the extent to which dispossessed travellers have been able to mitigate the assault on their identity experienced by many, I have focused on the relationship between their own creative actions and the collectivities which provide them with some measure of support and validation for their habits, customs and traditions. There is a process of ongoing mutual accommodation here, but it remains to be seen just how much 'fit' or continuity individuals are able to achieve between their previous identities and their new external milieu. This issue takes us to the heart of the pragmatist concern with character; a concern focused on whether individuals can express themselves within their environments and achieve a degree of consistency between their actions and the external environment (Siegfried, 1996: 35–6).

Character, immigration and the internal rupture

One theme that recurs in the literature about dispossessed travellers is that their journeys are never without cost, even for those who find a new home in which they are able to secure a degree of physical and economic safety and a sense of community belonging. This cost is not simply financial, or a cost to the health and energy of the individual, but a cost levied at the very core of their character. Contacts may be maintained with the original community, communities may be created anew, but for many a fissure opens in the self which seems to leave an indelible mark on identity. Sayad (2004) focuses on this issue and locates this problem of character in the fundamental conditions of immigration itself. Sayad (2004: 3) reminds us that immigration means to immigrate with one's history (with immigration itself being central to that), with one's tradition and with one's ways of living, feeling, acting and thinking, with one's language, one's religion and all the other social, political and mental structures of one's society. Immigration does not just involve taking these things with one, but making a fundamental break from the social, economic, political, cultural and moral orders that sustained these integral features of selfhood (ibid.: 88). This is manifest when migrants return home marked by the break that has been made, and imprinted with the priorities and imperatives that dominate living and working in another country. They return, yet no longer 'fit'.

This break may distance immigrants from their home land, but the history and identity they carry with them means that it is not compensated for by integration into their new land. Instead, migrants live at a distance from their new country, requiring a 'hyper-correction' in their appearance, manner and behaviour if they are to be deemed acceptable (Sayad, 2004: 286). Those who seek to make such a 'correction' cannot rely wholly on previous habits to negotiate the external environment, and tend instead towards introversion, introspection and a preoccupation with getting things 'right'. Switching from habitual to reflexive action in this way, however, constitutes a rupture of 'internal time' which can make the individual experience a separation and a loneliness that comes from not being able to be oneself (Sayad, 2004: 142).

In addition, migrants are often subject to considerable pressures to experience their bodies as different and deviant (Sayad, 2004: 203). Living under French colonial rule in Algeria, Fanon (1984 [1952]: 117) analyses how this occurred in the context of a 'white gaze' that equated the colonised with, and reduced them to, their bodies. Fifty years later, Sayad (2004: 206) talks about how Algerian immigrants in France are still stigmatised, experiencing themselves as a 'shameful body, a shy, clumsy body with little self-assurance, a body that is experienced with unease', a 'body that betrays itself'. This prevents them from experiencing a collective 'being with' others from the host community, and helps mark them out as manual labourers unable to rise above physical labour. As one Algerian comments, 'The worst racism is the racism of the dance hall', while at work 'you can't be anything but a labourer; they're not used to that. If they see you trying to get on a bit, they tell you. "You're not like the rest" ' (Sayad, 2004: 49). In this context, the quest for assimilation becomes impossible. While it might be feasible to remove stigmatised clothes, facial hair, mannerisms and even accent, it would take an obliteration of the body itself to finally 'pass' as fully naturalised.

This is the context in which the immigrant is caught in the lived experience of a triple break; a break with their homeland which cannot be bridged, a break with their new society which is also permanent and, the most difficult of all, a break with their own embodied *selves*. In these circumstances, it becomes exceptionally difficult to establish any satisfactory and creative coherence between their internal and external environments.

> Always torn between his permanent present, which he dare not admit to himself, and the 'return' which, whilst it is never resolutely ruled out, is never seriously contemplated, the immigrant is doomed to oscillate constantly between, on the one hand, the preoccupations of the here and now and, on the other, yesterday's retrospective hopes and the eschatological expectation that there will be an end to his immigration. (Sayad, 2004: 215)

The precise content of these breaks and oscillations varies, of course, depending upon the socio-cultural start and end points of their journeys and the conditions that await them in their new environment. Nevertheless, Sayad's account resonates time and again with the reported experiences of other immigrants. These experiences are neither new and nor are they confined to those with radically different religious beliefs from the majority in the host community. W.I. Thomas and Florian Znaniecki's 1918–20 *The Polish Peasant in Europe and America* explained why it was particularly difficult for early Polish immigrants to the United States to settle in their new country. Coming from a background in which the family was a 'corporate person', dominating and imparting identity to its individual members, the letters young immigrant men wrote home reflected a sense of loss, anomie and the active attempts that they were making to re-establish a new community of which they could feel part.

Such experiences are not confined to those at the lower end of the socio-economic spectrum. High technology workers from India employed on contracts in the United States are often well paid and working with the very latest technology in a prestigious sector of the economy, yet confront similar problems moving between two cultures. Aneesh's (2004) research highlights how these professionals orientated themselves to a life in the United States envisaged on the basis of wealth, glamour and technical sophistication, and distanced themselves from the way of life they left in India. Once settled in their new jobs, however, they became disillusioned by the realities of living among a populace struggling with obesity and striving after ambitions out of reach to all but the privileged few. More difficult still for these young adults, who tend to come from respected, middle-class families in India, is the 'devastating realisation' that they are viewed as 'other' and face social and political exclusion in their new lives.

Again, in their interactions with others they are regularly reduced to their bodies or dress. As one computer programmer notes,

> I have this identity as a Sikh. Going around in the malls you can always see their faces, 'What's that, the funny cap you have?' Or 'I like your cap.' (Aneesh, 2004: 58)

American social mores add to their sense of isolation and alienation: friendships are far more difficult to build, take second place to work and are conducted through appointments. These conditions did not make it easy to return to India, though, and Aneesh (2004) found alienation and dissatisfaction continued amongst those who left America. Memories of the 'good life' in the United States 'haunt all who return to India', while those who stay in the United States 'constantly dream of going back to their true place, their nation, their India' (ibid.: 60–1). There is no settled hybrid identity that emerges from this transnational travelling, but a sense of self that was uneasily split in two, 'constantly shaped and shifted by the possibilities of life in other locations where they were not residing' and divided against itself (ibid.: 63).

Even worse are the experiences of those who flee one country in order to avoid persecution, yet end up finding themselves insufficiently distanced from the community they escaped from and unable to find any sense of belonging in their new environment. Politically moderate Muslims who move to the United States, for example, have found themselves caught between 'the world of the fundamentalists' of their faith and 'the world of those not of [their] faith who misunderstand [their] beliefs', and also suffer from the difficulty of establishing any sense of community in a land so permeated by commercialism and the work ethic (Taghmaian, 2005: 335). As one such immigrant put it 'My soul is not in peace here' (ibid.: 339). Taghmaian's (2005) account of one refugee's escape from Afghanistan exemplifies this situation. Zahra, a young Muslim girl whose parents were killed by the Taliban, eventually resettled in the United States in 2001. Despite being thousands of miles away from her persecutors, Zahra remained scared of any signs that she might come into contact with communities of Islamic 'fundamentalists'. Taunted and scorned by Pakistani boys she encountered in her new high school for her 'inadequate hijab', she would cross the road when confronted with bearded men in Islamic dress, and was scared by the mosque situated near her home in Queens. Far from finding support and sustenance from communities of Islamic immigrants, Zahra found that she could not travel far enough from them. Unable to establish a set of social relations that would make her feel as though she belonged in her new life in America, Zahra was caught between two worlds. Neither provided her with a home.

The inability of many adult immigrants to reconcile adequately their identities with the social and economic environment in which they live may not be a universal outcome of the travels, arrivals and destinations focused on in this chapter. It is also worth noting that there is no shortage of contemporary theorists who suggest that the notion of stable character is a myth in these supposedly post-modern times, and that the increasingly complex interchanges occurring between local and global cultures leave all individuals having to constantly patch together a sense of how their identity relates to the world around. There does, however, seem to be something fundamental about the conditions of dispossessed travellers, which frequently introduces an unwanted fissure into the very core of their character.

Morality, globalisation and travel

Turner (1993, 2003) identifies our universal physical frailty as a basis upon which it is possible to construct an overarching morality that can apply to all peoples, irrespective of their religion, ethnicity or culture. In practice, however, access to rights has frequently been confined to the citizens of the nation-state, and moral questions about these rights are often limited to those living legally within the geographical territory of a nation-state. As Leach and Gabaccia (2004: 191) note, one of the features of such practices and debates is that they are predicated on the notion that 'human beings have a natural tie to their place of birth' and prefer and are able 'to be sedentary'. This ignores the central role that travel has played in human history, neglects the major problems faced by those who have had to flee an area, and is a classic example of what Durkheim (1961) refers to as a 'centrifugal' form of nationalism in which national sentiment conflicts with the broader moral rights of humankind as a whole. It also conveniently ignores the fact that the more affluent nations of the West have historically forced, encouraged and invited certain categories of workers to leave their homelands and make their home in America or Europe. Such practices often weaken the communities from which they come, and continue to deprive certain nations of their most skilled and educated young men and women (e.g. the National Health Service in Britain for decades relied upon the recruitment of doctors and nurses from India and the Caribbean).

Many of the policies and practices that follow from such centrifugal forms of nationalism are in direct conflict with any broader concern with the embodied welfare of humans in general. This is illustrated by the conditions that refugees across the world face in being confined to camps and detention centres characterised by violence, suicide attempts, a lack of basic hygiene, inadequate supplies of food and water, and in having to wait months and even years with no idea of what their future is (Fassin, 2005; Moorehead, 2006). Even for those fortunate enough to secure physical safety and material subsistence in their new surroundings, there remain the problems associated with finding that their existing habits, bodily appearances and identities no longer receive the recognition they once did. Outcomes such as these not only make it difficult for immigrants to feel as though they belong to the larger national community in which they now live (a situation which has itself fuelled discontent and exacerbated political and religious extremism) but perpetuate established-outsider boundaries based on gossip, stereotypes and prejudice rather than discussion and debate based on experiences of physical co-presence (Elias, 1994).

Notes

1 The slave trade drove the development of a new sugar industry in the Caribbean, the conversion of South Carolina to rice cultivation and numerous other industries, which contributed to the growing wealth of the West (Walvin, 2006).

2 The contrast this represents with previous forms of travel is stark indeed. *Flaneurie* was originally associated with Paris in the first half of the nineteenth century. Far from seeking speed, the *flaneur* spends time cultivating knowledge about the sensual pleasures of the city, its sights, sounds, smells, tastes and textures. The *flaneur* may consume these experiences at a certain distance in order to be entertained rather than disturbed by them, but has nothing in common with the *blasé*', rationally calculative and sensorily armoured figures that populate Simmel's vision of the metropolis (Tester, 1994).

7

Ailing

Introduction

Visions of healthy and aesthetically perfect bodies may pervade consumer culture, but the ideal they project is a myth. Sooner or later virtually all of us get sick (defined biomedically as involving a diseased organism) and experience illness (defined sociologically as the subjective encounter with the symptoms and suffering associated with sickness). Health and sickness/illness, indeed, are intimately connected: each is viewed and experienced, at least in part, as the absence of the other. Perhaps this relationality is why Sontag's (1991: 3) suggestion that we all hold dual passports to 'the kingdom of the well' and 'the kingdom of the sick' resonates so strongly. While the technologically driven, performative culture that dominates work, sport and consumption in the West may be predicated upon healthy, productive, fit and adaptable embodied subjects, being sick and being ill are not exceptional experiences and states but can strike anyone at anytime. They are fundamental features of the human condition which every society has to deal with, and are intimately involved in shaping people's actions and identities.

If sickness and illness are part of life itself, so too is the experience of physical and mental impairment. Fading eyesight, hearing, memory and the painful consequences of arthritis, for example, are frequent accompaniments of aging, while the very success of medicine in treating acute illness and deferring death into old age has meant that the lives of increasing segments of the population are 'discharged into chronic illness' (Beck, 1992: 205). Chronic conditions associated with aging may not usually bear comparison with the paralysis that can accompany congenital conditions or accidental spinal injury, for example, but their incidence and ordinariness provide further evidence that the notion of the 'perfect body' constitutes little more than a mythical metric against which we can measure our distance from an unrealistic ideal. This is the context in which I have titled this chapter 'ailing', a less than perfect term but one chosen to denote the fact that we *all* are unfit, degenerate and disordered in relation to the promises of limitless performativity associated with those mythically capable bodies that dominate the world of advertising.

The distance that exists between these cultural images and bodily realities does not, however, make the former irrelevant to people's experiences of health and illness, impairment and disability. These experiences are not determined entirely by processes internal to the organic body, but are also shaped by the cultural meanings attached to health and illness and by the varied physical environments in which they occur. The bubonic plague that devastated Europe in the late Middle Ages, for example, was interpreted in overtly religious terms as resulting from God's wrath and 'man's fallen state of sin and suffering' and this impacted on how people experienced the disease (Kleinman, 1988: 18). Similarly, from late antiquity onwards, 'consumption' was interpreted and often reportedly experienced as a sign of individual moral culpability. In both these cases, moreover, concentrations of populations in urban centres played an important role in the transmission of disease and the chances of remaining healthy or ill. Later, in the twentieth century in particular, cancer became *the* disease that visited itself upon 'deficient' personalities, upon those who had not lived healthy physical, emotional or environmentally balanced lives. Starting from the 1980s, AIDS took its turn as the most resonant sign of individual and societal corruption (Sontag, 1991: 11, 59, 83). In contrast, Western technological culture of the twenty-first century has placed unprecedented emphasis on sickness, illness or impairment of *any kind* as a moral deviation from the ideal; from the ideal of the embodied subject able to exert control over his or her own organism and over the wider social and physical environment.

Diseases are not reducible to these cultural elaborations or the physical milieu in which they are experienced, of course, and it would be wrong to conflate the organic and phenomenological impact of sickness with the external environment. Nevertheless, as numerous auto/biographical narratives of illness illustrate, such classifications and settings do have a widespread impact on how people experience disease. It is against this background that the first half of this chapter examines the external environments of health and illness by focusing on the relatively recent development of a culturally sanctioned 'health role' (Frank, 1991a). This role places increased demands on people, demands that ignore the frailty of human embodiment and the varied physical milieu that shape the incidence of illness and impairment, and revolves around highly instrumentalised notions of health. The chapter then shifts focus to include the internal environments of illness and disability by examining how the experience of ill-health and impairment shape people's actions and identities within this wider context. We see here both the impact that norms of performative perfection have on those unable to approximate to the health role, but also plenty of evidence testifying to the creativity of human action and the strength of character that people can develop when faced with an external environment hostile to lived experience and bodily needs. In conclusion, I examine the moral implications drawn by those who have written about the experience of entering the 'kingdom of the sick', implications that question the humanity of the contemporary health role and take us to the very ends of human life itself.

The external environments of action

The social milieu: from the sick role to the health role

As we have seen, metaphors imparting illness with meaning have historically been used to enliven charges that societies and individuals were sinful, corrupt or unjust. What is peculiar about the modern era, however, is the extent to which metaphors of illness and health have been *institutionalised* within specific social roles. Two of these roles stand out as particularly important; the 'sick role' of the twentieth century, and the more recent emergence of the 'health role' which has risen to dominance in the twenty-first century.

It was Talcott Parsons (1991 [1951]) who first identified the sick role as a temporary role into which all people may be admitted, at some time in their lives, with the permission of doctors. This role consists of certain rights and responsibilities, and functions to minimise the effects of illness on the productive capacities of individuals and societies. Those inhabiting the sick role are exempted from responsibility for their health, and excused temporarily from having to meet the demands of other social roles. However, they are granted these rights on the condition that they seek out and cooperate with a doctor who can assist with their *reintegration* back into 'normal' life (Parsons, 1991 [1951]: 451, 477). The sick role would typically cover an episode of a 'specific, acute illness' in which a patient stays away from work for a specific period to rest and take prescribed medication, but Parsons (1978: 32) also defended the applicability of this role for the analysis of chronic illness.

Developed in the context of his analysis of the cultural patterning of mid-twentieth-century American society, Parsons (1978) shows how metaphors regarding moral culpability were institutionalised into this sick role, and identifies the Protestant work ethic as having exerted an enduring influence over the obligations that must be discharged by the ill if they are to avoid being stigmatised by society. Parsons also acknowledged that the sick role was subject to change as a result of the evolution of these (essentially religious) values, however, and in many ways anticipated the increasing emphasis placed on the relationship between illness and *productivity* during the late twentieth century (Shilling, 2002). As the century came to a close, this emphasis led to a relative shift away from the institutional concern with sickness as a temporary deviation from the norm, towards a focus on the imperative of maintaining health in order to conform to the values of an increasingly competitive and performative society. Emerging initially alongside the sick role, and then rising to a position of increasing dominance over it, developed the 'health role' (Frank, 1991a).

The health role differs from the sick role in terms of its emphasis on the *maximisation* of people's productive capacities and the *prevention* of illness. Whereas once sickness and illness circulated between individual organisms and the social system, health is now the medium of exchange between individuals and the social milieu in which they exist. As Parsons (1978: 69) himself noted, health allows us to perform 'an indefinitely wide range of functions' *in relation to* the needs, demands and disturbances of the social system. While the sick role invests the ill with a responsibility for seeking out medical help, and following professional advice in order to return to their social roles, the health role places on people the responsibility for *not getting ill or impaired in the first place.*

The health role has become institutionalised at the level of the nation-state through the medicalised surveillance of populations (Foucault, 1973). Here, the premise is that productive health is threatened constantly by a variety of behavioural and environmental risk factors that require constant monitoring and regular intervention, and that the government creates the context in which individuals are encouraged to maintain their performative capacity (Armstrong, 1983). Risk assessments are regularly conducted in workplaces, for example, and have resulted in such measures as bans on smoking and the drug testing of employees (Jackson, 1995), while the World Health Organisation as well as individual governments have set targets and implemented strategies designed to reduce accidents in the home, workplace and on the roads (Green, 1995). A further manifestation of the institutionalisation of the health role is apparent in the increasing incidence with which health services and health insurance companies reward and penalise their clients (through the scope of coverage they offer and the premiums they charge) for their lifestyle. Those who smoke, drink 'excessive' quantities of alcohol, and are overweight, face higher premiums and the possibility of being prevented from undergoing certain operations and procedures (e.g. Frank, 1991a: 209).

There are partial historical antecedents to the health role (Armstrong, 1983), but the extent of its concern with productive capacity is unprecedented. It is no longer just temporary or chronic illness preventing people from discharging their usual social roles that is deemed problematic, but *anything* that interferes with individuals looking, feeling and being at their best and most productive in a social milieu in which health is prized, expected and, increasingly, demanded. Individuals are now charged with the responsibility of maintaining their bodies at their fittest and most adaptable in order that they can discharge their existing social roles and seek out new opportunities for engaging in productive activities. In order to do this, the main 'right' invested in the health role is the right to a seemingly ever-expanding quantity of health-related products and services. From fitness programmes, to diet products, to food supplements, to cholesterol lowering drugs, the market for health-enhancing products promises to create a virtually infinite set of needs for 'responsible citizens' (Gabe, 1995). These products and services are complemented by burgeoning product information: foods, drinks and other consumables come packaged with risk calculations and warnings on the assumption that 'knowledge about the dangers of certain lifestyle activities will result in their avoidance' (Lupton, 1994; Gabe, 1995: 2). Similarly, the concern with preventative health is manifest in the growing information about, availability, and use of alternative and complementary medicine (Cant and Sharma, 2000: 430). In this context, the scope of medical advice and services becomes all pervasive, expanding into ever-increasing areas of social and personal life and threatening to leave people unable to do without its services (Illich, 2001).

The rise of the health role does not mean that the sick role has been displaced completely. Nevertheless, the rights and responsibilities traditionally invested in the ill person are mediated increasingly through the overriding imperative placed on maximising health. Thus, the sick role has become the 'poor cousin' of the health role: people's admittance to it is more closely monitored and stigmatised than it used to be, and is often restricted to conditions that fall within the scope of conventional medical diagnoses (Nettleton, 2004). Illness now often only contingently removes people from the burden of being 'front runners in the market-place' or 'stalwart supporters in the home' (Kidel, 1988: 5). Against this background, the health role, like its antecedent sick role, has been assessed as implicating contemporary individuals within a new and more demand-ing 'mechanism of social control' (Parsons, 1991 [1951]: 477) which 'ban-ishes' illness and disability 'from everyday life' and associates infirmity 'with a lack of individual strength' (Kleinman, 1992: 205; see also Wilkinson, 2005). In these circumstances, it is easy for the chronically ill or impaired to 'feel that they are culturally illegitimate, unaccepted in the wider society' (ibid.). This is not only because the health role ignores individual or group differences, but because it ignores the significance that the *physical environment* has on people's capacities to approximate to the health role.

The physical milieu: geographies of health and illness

Sontag's reference to the 'two kingdom's of health and illness' is suggestive not only of different embodied conditions and lived experiences, but of the *spatial* dimensions of well-being and sickness. These undoubt-edly implicate the body – as the 'geography closest in' (Nast and Pile, 1998) – but they also point to the external material spaces and places inhabited by embodied subjects. Geographical studies of health and illness have recognised the importance of not reifying place and space, and of recognising the culturally and socially stratified and mediated character of these phenomena. They also highlight the importance of particular physical environments for the incidence and experience of health and illness.

This is most easily illustrated by recognising that geographical space and place may be more or less conducive or inimical to the maintenance of human life itself. Despite the control that humans have exerted over the natural environment, climatic conditions and natural disasters still place real constraints on the types of milieu conducive to healthy populations. Furthermore, the environmental catastrophes and problems caused by human intervention (e.g. nuclear pollution, ozone depletion) reinforce the point that the physical environment cannot simply be treated as epiphenomenal in relation to the social environment. Specifically, in relation to the spread of disease, the importance of the physical environment is evident in the case of infectious outbreaks. The bubonic plague of the late Middle Ages, for example, spread across the European continent with such devastation that it wiped out three-quarters of the region's population. Dense concentrations of housing, with inadequate drainage and clean water supplies, were particularly badly affected. More recently, the poverty data collected in the late nineteenth century by the social reformer Charles Booth dramatically revealed the geographical clustering of bad housing and poor health in the city of London. While the problems associated with most infectious diseases may have been eradicated in the affluent West, epidemiology (concerned with the relative risk of populations becoming sick when exposed to a specific risk factors) and environmental health (concerned with the relationship between people's material surroundings and health and illness) continue to highlight the importance of space and place (Gabe, 1995; Brown, 1995).

The physical environment in which social action occurs exposes people to health risks in a variety of distinctive ways. What is generally regarded as the first epidemiological study discovered a link between water contamination and a cholera epidemic in London when it was undertaken by John Snow in 1854 (Goldstein and Goldstein, 1986; Paneth, 2004). Access to clean water continues to be a major determinant of health and illness. One of the most widely publicised public health incidents in Britain at the end of the twentieth century was the accidental contamination of the local water supply in Camelford, Cornwall. Twenty tons of aluminium sulphate and other dangerous chemicals were tipped into a tank feeding the waterworks, exposing an estimated 20,000 residents to danger (Gatrell, 2002: 222). More generally, water pollution has exposed swimmers and surfers to gastro-enteritis and a host of other health risks (Balarajan et al., 1991), while the importance of clean water is evidenced most starkly by the numbers of people who die due to its absence. UNESCO estimates that between 1.1 and 2.2 million deaths occur each year as a result of diarrhoeal diseases that can be attributed in part to the lack of clean water. Ninety per cent of these deaths occur in children under the age of five. The overwhelming majority occur in Asia and Africa.

Water quality is not the only determinant of environmental health. Air and earth quality is another important geographically related health variable, with studies showing that proximity to certain types of incinerators, factories and high motor vehicle exhaust emissions are all significant risk factors (Gatrell, 2002). Living near to nuclear processing plants has been linked to increased rates of childhood cancer (Gardner, 1989). Dwelling in areas characterised by high levels of radon has been linked to up to 36,000 deaths from lung cancer each year in the United States alone, while the depletion of the ozone layer is associated with rising forms of skin cancer, especially among those who spend much of their time working outdoors (Lubin, 1997; Gatrell, 2002). Community activism highlights further the importance of the relationship between place and health. There are now numerous examples of local pressure groups who have utilised 'popular epidemiology' to challenge governmental decisions concerning the siting of nuclear power stations, factories, waste disposal and toxic waste facilities and mobile phone masts, on the basis that they are related to ill-health (e.g. Phillimore and Moffat, 1994; Williams and Popay, 1994; Brown, 1995).

There are, of course, many other place-related variables that affect levels of morbidity and mortality. It seems that city life can be bad for our health in comparison to rural life, although the specific characteristics of the local neighbourhood may be even more important. The availability of decent housing, safe recreation, non-hazardous and secure employment, nutritious food, transport, street-cleaning and health services, levels of crime and even the reputation of an area have all been identified as important relevant variables (MacIntyre et al., 1993). Now, there is undoubtedly a strong correlation between socio-economic status and living in neighbourhoods more or less conducive to the maintenance of good health. However, even when class is controlled for, place still matters: the health of people belonging to identical class locations varies according to where they live (Blaxter, 1990; Bryant and Mohai, 1992; MacIntyre et al., 1993). Just one example of this is provided by the so-called post-code lottery in Britain. Here local health authorities have some autonomy over which services and drugs they will pay for, meaning that people with multiple sclerosis, cancer or haemophilia, for example, receive very different treatment depending on where they live (Gatrell, 2002). It is not only social class that interacts with place. Residential segregation *within* the city on the basis of 'race', for example, has been shown to have a detrimental impact on African-American infant mortality rates (LaVeist, 1992; Gesler and Kearns, 2002). Migration into cities can also be damaging to health, perhaps especially for women. Gatrell (2002: 167), for example, focuses on the stress and depression that can accompany the lives of women as they seek to come to terms with having to work and look after a family in a new culture that is itself embedded in unfamiliar spatial structures (Kaplan, 1988).

The physical environment is also relevant to the incidence and experience of impairment. Gleeson (2002) refers to the industrial city as a 'disabling' space, a space predicated on the separation of home and work which accelerated the separation of the sick from the healthy. Historically, the dominant attitude among urban planners was that those suffering from mental illness should be socially and spatially separated from the rest of the population by being moved to the healthier environs of the countryside (Busfield 1986). As Gesler and Kearns (2002: 122) note, 'The idea was that since those with mental illness were victims of the new industrial society and could not cope with it, they should be taken to peaceful, natural environments.' The legacy of this separation lives on. Contemporary urban environments appear to have reinforced feelings of loneliness among the mentally ill, presenting them with surroundings in which it is difficult for them to become involved in accessible community activities.

The built environment can also be highly disabling to people whose bodies do not meet the norms assumed by planners and architects. Here we can see how the values of efficiency and productivity central to the health role have for some time been evident in the assumptions of these professionals. Gleeson (2002: 101) expresses this point succinctly when she notes that the built environment is designed for the healthy human being, while persons with any one of numerous physical disabilities find themselves more or less 'isolated by their environments'. Imrie (1999) expands on why it is that many people with disabilities confront the built environment as hostile. As he notes, contemporary buildings in the West remain based on Le Corbusier's view that the project of architecture should be to overturn the socio-environmental degradation of the city through constructions that embodied health, vigour, youth and cleanliness (Imrie, 1999: 35). The problem here was the exclusion of corporeal diversity from the terrain of the architect: buildings were constructed for capable, competent and able bodies (Tschumi, 1996). It is important to note that in recent years there has been a shift in norms relating to the built environment. Building regulations in the United Kingdom, for example, now require disability access to be taken into account for new and, indeed, older structures. Nevertheless, the physical environment remains far from being equally accessible for all.

If the physical environment in which people live can be linked with isolation, sickness and disability, so too can it be invigorating and health promoting. Gesler (1992) talks of 'therapeutic landscapes', signalling the myriad ways in which the 'ever-changing interplay between human activity and the physical environment' can be associated with health, peace and well-being. Historically, we can see examples of such landscapes in the springs and waters of such places as Bath and South Dakota (Geores, 1998; Gesler, 1998). In the case of the former, Roman physicians used the waters to adjust the four humours by heating, cooling, moistening and drying the body in order to restore its equilibrium (Gesler, 1998: 27). Bath continued to attract pilgrims to its waters from across Europe between the eleventh and fifteenth centuries. It is no coincidence that there has in recent decades been a renewed emphasis on the revitalising properties of therapeutic landscapes (from spas to health clubs to 'get away from it all' relaxation breaks) at the same time that the health role has become dominant.

In considering the external environment in which individuals confront issues of health, illness and impairment in the contemporary era, I have been keen to emphasise the distinctive contribution made by our physical surroundings and landscapes. As geographers of health have demonstrated, however, places and spaces both shape and are shaped by the social processes and relationships which inform people's views, actions and experience (Eyles, 1985; Gesler and Kearns, 2002). There is no getting away from this interrelationship, and much of the literature on place and space explores how location is appropriated in part as a *signifier* of class and status. Location is always more than physical place and reflects a spatialisation of social relations. Savage et al. (2005), for example, explore this in discovering how neighbourhood is vital as a measure of people's consumption practices and how its accessibility to fresh air, gyms, health-food shops and so on can impact on health in this context.

The precise manner in which this relationship between the physical and social milieu develops varies, of course, according to historical and cultural factors. In collectivities characterised more by mechanical than organic solidarity, for example, the relationship between the physical and social milieu tends to be far less differentiated than is the case in urban societies. In the Bolivian Andes, the Qolluaya Indians have developed a series of classificatory equivalencies between the human body and the topography and hydrologic cycles of a mountain which dominates their material landscape and shapes their organic and social existence (Gesler, 1992). Physical health is dependent on possessing a circulatory system which displays affinities with the operation of waterways and tunnels, but is equally reliant upon social rituals which bring together and redistribute materials from the communities living in different areas of the mountain (ibid.). What is interesting about this example is that it depicts a relation-ship of relative harmony between the social and the natural environment; an equilibrium that is associated with good health. What is distinctive about the relationship between the health role and the physical environ-ment in the contemporary West, in contrast, is the total disregard that this performative conception of health has not only for individual differences but for the varied places and spaces in which people live.

The phases of embodied action

Identity and crisis

Historical literature on the interaction between the external and internal environments of health and illness illustrates how physical disease, the mental decay that followed untreated syphilis, and the taunts and jibes aimed at the dying, have long been associated with a loss of social status and a crisis of identity. Disease and illness meant that individuals had to cope with an assault on their social position, as well as with the pain, disorientation and declining capacities associated with a loss of relative health (Aries, 1981 [1977]; Elias, 1985). In one sense, little has changed. More respect (or at least isolation) may be afforded to the dying these days (Elias, 1985), but ill-health continues to confront people with a combination of social and organic distress that impacts cumulatively on their identity. The specific context in which people have to negotiate disease in the contemporary West, however, adds a particular colouring to this crisis.

Drew Leder's (1990) work implies that the health role is predicated on people being well enough to allow their bodies to fade from consciousness. It is the potential to become absorbed in a task, unencumbered by the needs, desires or discomforts of one's physical self that allows individuals to max-imise their productivity or performativity. If this capacity for productive action is central to socially validated conceptions of self in the contemporary West, however, illness may introduce into one's life biographical disruption and vulnerability that derives in part from the potential disapproval and devaluation associated with the return of the 'obstinate body' thrust on one through sickness (Corbin and Strauss, 1987; Charmaz, 2000; Williams, 1999; 2003). From being whole and respected, one's social identity can become spoiled, and the basis on which a sense of self sustained thrown into crisis (Goffman, 1963a). The extent, duration and manner in which people are removed from the health role are, of course, crucial variants to this gen-eral picture. Illness affects individuals in myriad ways. Particularly impor-tant, however, is the issue of whether a temporary or longer-term with-drawal from the demands of living a 'productively healthy' life has been sanctioned by legitimate custodians to the sick role. While entrance to the sick role may increasingly be stigmatised in societies dedicated to robust youth, fitness and the maximisation of instrumentally rational perform-ances, those who find themselves ill yet *excluded* from entry even into this role face a worse situation.

Studies of people experiencing ill-health yet excluded from the sick role frequently report how individuals 'found their social position was eroded, their social identity devalued and stigmatised' (Cooper, 1997: 183; Dyck, 1999). They also highlight how these individuals encountered difficulties in obtaining legitimate absence from work or disability benefit and endured interactions with doubting doctors that were conflictual and emotional. Cooper's (1997) research, for example, details how sufferers from Myalgic Encephalomyelitis (ME) had to play the part of a 'good patient' with par-ticular vigilance if they hoped to get their condition validated by a doctor. The danger of being labelled a 'bored housewife' or 'depressed teenager' was very real. The stigma associated with not having an illness validated compounded a sense of confusion, uncertainty and growing panic among sufferers. A similar situation exists among those with other undiagnosed symptoms. If doctors doubt that an individual is suffering from a genuine condition, this can have implications for their sickness benefit, their employment prospects and, of course, their self-esteem (Nettleton et al., 2006). When professional diagnosis was made, in contrast (albeit some-times following months or even years of 'puzzling, sometimes transient, and debilitating symptoms' [Dyck, 1999: 125]), it at least gave shape and meaning to experience even if it also sometimes confirmed the worst fears of the individual.

Short or long-term removal from the health role and even the sick role is not the only reason that the experience of disease and illness is associated with a crisis of identity. This is because the ill or impaired body confronts people with its *own* obstacles and distresses which are consequential for people, to one degree or other, *irrespective* of their social situation. Thus, the onset of both chronic illness and disability have been analysed *in and of themselves* as resulting in an 'ontological assault' on the embodied self (Pellegrino, 1979: 44). Illness and impairment are associated with the rupture of a phenomenologically unified bodily being and the ushering in of an 'object body' in which the organism is experienced as 'a source of constraint' and 'opposition to the self' (Gadow, 1980; Garro, 1992). Instead of facilitating purposeful action, the body becomes an intimate party to the disruption of previous experience (Bury, 1982). The usual parameters of common sense break down, and the routines that have previously ordered time, space, self, body and action no longer function and have to be revisited and reconstructed.

In analysing these experiences of crisis, I draw on Corbin and Strauss's (1987) influential framework for the analysis of chronic illness (a framework which also illuminates the experiences of people who become disabled). This focuses on how illness disrupts people's 'biographical body conceptions'; conceptions constituted by a sense of (1) biographical time, (2) bodily coherence and (3) functionally coherent and morally valid identities. First, then, exiting the health role as a result of chronic illness or physical disability appears to effect a fundamental break with *biographical conceptions of time*. The future-oriented, instrumentalist orientation that governs the lives of those caught up in a culture that makes it increasingly difficult to juggle work, family and leisure responsibilities is disrupted. The long-term plans and temporal routines that governed daily life are no longer viable or possible, and time no longer facilitates actions. Instead, it becomes a problematic variable. In Dyck's (1995) study of multiple sclerosis (MS) sufferers, for example, time was something that could not be relied upon as a constant; the variability of symptoms meant that it was impossible to make definite plans. It is not just concrete plans and routines that are disrupted, furthermore, but people's dreams, wishes and fancies (Radley, 1999: 781). The confidence in the future that underpins our sense of ontological security (our sense that we and the world we inhabit is secure) is removed, and time forces us instead into 'a conscious or semi-conscious awareness of the very uncertainty of our being' (Kidel, 1988: 7; Giddens, 1991). In these circumstances, time can appear to 'freeze', to admit of no future and to foreclose around the ill or disabled body. The experience of chronic pain, for example, seems to shut out any time other than that inhabited by pain (Kleinman, 1988: 64; Leder, 1990; Good, 1992). When illness or disability seem to rob an individual of the possibility of making any existential investment in the future, time can seem empty and pointless (Webb, 1998).

The disruption of time is not an abstract, theoretical process, but is tied intimately to particular experiences of *bodily (in)coherence*. Chronic illness and disability can make people feel that they are inhabiting 'broken' bodies, or even that they have become 'imprisoned' within a physical shell that has failed them, no longer allowing them to make desired contacts with their environment (Corbin and Strauss, 1987: 263, 278; Bauby, 1997). In the period immediately following the onset of illness or disability, the 'broken body', if that is what it has become to the individual, frequently 'occupies the entire field of experience' (McCrum, 1998; Ville, 2005: 332). There is no possibility here of the body 'fading away' from consciousness in a manner that enables people to focus exclusively on purposeful work (Leder, 1990). Instead, body failure can preoccupy those who have constantly to come to terms with 'how to manage what their body cannot normally or properly do' (Corbin and Strauss, 1987: 278). There is also often a strong, gendered component to this disruption in embodiment brought about by disability or chronic illness. As Seymour's (1998: 147) study into spinal cord injuries shows, restricted capacities for movement and sexual performance can weigh especially heavily on men accustomed to playing an active, initiating role in social and personal relationships, while women can be devastated not only by the loss of these capacities but by their inability to carry out responsibilities for caring. More generally, for the chronically ill, the sick body can become like a volcano, constantly threatening to 'menace', 'erupt' and spin 'out of control' (Kleinman, 1988: 44). Here, individuals may constantly worry over such things as whether 'one can negotiate a curb, tolerate flowers without wheezing, make it to the bathroom quickly enough, eat breakfast without vomiting, keep the level of back pain low enough to get through the workday ... or just plain face up to the myriad of difficulties that make life feel burdened, uncomfortable and all too often desperate' (ibid.). Disability and illness can also often lead to a diminution in people's capacity to utilise space. People in wheelchairs or with sensory impairments such as visual or hearing loss may find getting around the modern city especially challenging and difficult, while those with conditions such as MS can be exhausted by the 'simple' task of negotiating their own homes (Dyck, 1995; Gesler and Kearns, 2002).

The third dimension of Corbin and Strauss's (1987) concern with biographical body conceptions focuses on changing senses of *self-identity*. It is here that the effects of disrupted biographical body conceptions can manifest themselves in a full-scale crisis of selfhood. For Charmaz (1983), chronically ill people face a constant struggle to maintain a positive feeling of self worth, and their loss of identity constitutes a fundamental form of suffering. Part of wanting to hang on to past identities reflects a desire to avoid the stigma associated with illness and disability. This is most evident with such diseases as AIDS, a condition which continues to taint people with the status of 'polluter' and can all too often result in social isolation (Crawford et al., 1997). As one sufferer remarked on the treatment he received, 'What the hell is this? I'm not a leper. Do they want to lock me up and shoot me? I've got no family, no friends' (Kleinman, 1988: 163). The general situation for AIDS sufferers may have improved significantly since the 1980s, at least in the affluent West, but social stigma and discrimination remain a problem.

The concern to hang on to past identities is also associated with the problems associated with a loss of physical competence. Bury's (1982) analysis of arthritis sufferers, for example, traces how the pain of the condition is complemented by the difficulties in maintaining a job when one's basic physical skills begin to decline. More generally, people who are chronically ill or disabled frequently struggle with the problems of maintaining a sense that they are an 'able self', as their 'performative acts no longer consistently matched their former interpretation of their place in the world' (Dyck, 1999: 126). This is particularly evident in Seymour's (1998) study in which those struggling to come to terms with severe spinal injuries experienced a bereavement for their former selves. One respondent, Sally, noted how her sense of personhood, womanhood, cognition and intellect all collapsed when she was first confined to a wheelchair.

Narratives of illness and disability highlight the utility of Corbin and Strauss's (1987) concern with how people cope with serious disruptions to their 'biographical body conceptions'. As Frank (1995) argues, however, there are frequently two sides to these narratives. On the one hand, the threat of disintegration looms large for those struggling to come to terms with an altered body which has thrust on them an altered world. On the other hand, many are able to marshal their resources and begin to seek 'a new integration of the body-self' (Frank, 1995: 171).

Creative coping strategies

Corbin and Strauss's (1987) analysis of biographical body conceptions highlights the social and organic distress that follows when people are removed from the health role and have to struggle with the consequences of chronic illness or disability. As Ville (2005: 325) points out, though, numerous studies have shown that people develop creative coping strategies in managing illness and stigma, in negotiating with health-care professionals, and in seeking to rebuild a coherent and re-embodied sense of self (Seymour, 1998). 'Passing' as 'normal' remains a popular strategy for those able to employ it (Dyck, 1999). Snyder's study illustrates how those with conditions that affected memory, such as Alzheimer's, managed this by slowing their responses during social interactions and avoiding spontaneous comments that might embarrass them. Getting the other person to talk until their name could be recalled and increasing the number of 'praise comments' in a conversation proved other ways of deflecting attention from their illness (Snyder, 2000). In the workplace, another strategy involved taking tape-recorders to meetings and utilising pocket spellers as means of compensating for faltering memory (Snyder, 2000: 38).

Individuals suffering from Parkinson's disease, concealed their condition by hiding a shaking hand behind their back, by holding it steady with their other hand or by placing it in a jacket pocket (Nijof, 1995). Such strategies were often seen as essential by those seeking to hold down jobs. Similarly, Dyck's (1999: 128–9) study of MS sufferers details how individuals took notes home to transcribe themselves (rather than let their shaky handwriting be seen by the company secretary), feigned injuries in order to avoid walking through worksites when fatigued and always allowed clients to leave the office first in order to disguise walking difficulties. Finally, both inside and outside of the workplace, individuals drew on reserves of humour and religious faith in order to cope with their illness and 'get through the day'.

Irrespective of the coping strategies used, people whose lives had been changed permanently by their condition eventually confronted the necessity of re-structuring their responsibilities (Snyder, 2000). This would sometimes be supplemented by attempts to use illness, pain or disability as a way of avoiding situations or people. One of Brodwin's (1992) respondents, for example, used her symptoms to mitigate what she saw as the suffocating demands placed on her by family, church and employer. Here, illness and pain became part of 'both a performance and a protest against the demand to perform' felt across the individual's social life (Brodwin, 1992: 80). In order to cope with such demands when they became absolutely necessary, alternative and complementary therapies and remedies were used by many in conjunction with ortho-dox medicine as a distinctive means of gaining help and support (Lupton, 1996; Cant and Sharma, 2000). Viewed from within the health role as a means of maximising one's sense of well-being, these treatments can also be experienced as a resource that could help in simply making life tolerable.

If creative engagements with the social environment could make life more tolerable for those suffering from pain or disability, those with restricted mobility often needed to make material adjustments to and redefinitions of their use of space. Wheelchair users frequently have to seek out accessible accommodation and require modifications to the bath-room, toilet and stairs. The solutions people find to these problems illus-trate both the vigour and ingenuity with which obstacles are overcome, but also the importance of economic and social capital in shaping the chances of meeting successfully these challenges. Internet access, for example, is an important variable to the extent that it allows those with mobility problems to communicate with others easily and effectively. In this respect, Hardey's (2002) research shows how home web pages allow people to make and maintain social contacts with others without having to cope with the fatigue involved in regular telephone conversations or visits. Hardey also discovered an increasing tendency for those who suf-fered from certain conditions to sell products based on their experiences of successful treatment.

Irrespective of the coping strategies that people use in negotiating the details and difficulties of their working, family and personal lives, the ability to make decisive existential investments in life may be crucial to their preparedness to continue this struggle and to begin to come to terms with the disruptions that illness, pain or impairment has made to their biographical body conceptions. Individuals may be as resilient, creative and adaptable as is humanly possible, but the need to invest in re-embodying their sense of identity in line with new realities seems to be a crucial stage in re-acquiring an equilibrium and a peace in life. This is the period in which people attempt to re-establish viable routines and develop a habitual approach to themselves as well as their environment.

Re-establishing routines, re-establishing identities?

Corbin and Strauss's (1987) analysis of biographical body conceptions suggests that many people are able to re-establish coherent embodied identities despite the crises they encounter during chronic illness. This involves 'discovering what aspects of self have been lost ... discovering what aspects of self remain and can be carried forward to provide biographical continuity, and it means discovering what new aspects can be added, not necessarily to replace the old but to give new meaning to biography' (Corbin and Strauss, 1987: 266). Such processes of integration can be undertaken through 'illness narratives', accounts of illness involving 'plot lines, core metaphors, and rhetorical devices ... drawn from cultural and personal models of arranging experiences in meaningful ways and for effectively communicating these meanings' (Kleinman, 1988: 49, 81). These 'narratives' will frequently be unwritten and even unspoken. They may consist of thoughts and even chains of feeling that involve cognitive or emotional reviews that shuttle backwards and forwards in a person's life, drawing on 'day-dreams and various types of imagery for recapturing the past, examining the present, and projecting into the future – all inter- preted, of course, in light of the present' (Corbin and Strauss, 1987: 268). They also often involve anger, denial and bargaining between different parts of the self as it seeks to come to terms with what has changed.

There is no guarantee of 'adjustment' or successful 're-embodiment', of course, and serious chronic illness or disability can result in people withdraw- ing from social life and even suicide. For others, however, the future can be brighter. Corbin and Strauss (1987: 267) cite the case of Joni, for example, who was left quadriplegic by a driving accident but became an accomplished artist by learning to paint with her mouth instead of her hands. Illness narratives also highlight how the work of biographical reintegration is facilitated by devices and/or changed approaches to the body. Paraplegic and quadriplegic respondents provided examples of how they continued dancing in a wheelchair, visited a sex counsellor in order to continue having mutually satisfying sexual relations with their partner, and exercised a mediated agency through the arms and legs of others (ibid.: 274).

Charmaz (1999) makes the point that the work that goes into such processes of re-embodiment and identity reconstruction sometimes enables people to come to terms with and transcend their losses, and emerge with a stronger and more valued self. In certain of these cases it is possible to observe what Albrecht and Devlieger (1999) describe as 'the disability paradox', a term denoting the high quality of life often reported by persons with serious and persistent disabilities (Ville, 2005: 46). Valentine's (1999) study of 'Paul' provides us with an example of just such a case. Having been disabled as a result of an accident, a chance meeting on a trip to buy a new wheelchair resulted in Paul being invited to join a basketball team. Achieving success in wheelchair basketball, and being selected to play for the British squad, enabled Paul to construct an identity as an international athlete. The new, re-embodied, sense of self-identity that Paul managed to create during this period of achievement drew on his previous sense of masculinity, but developed this in a more body-conscious direction. While he used to take his body for granted, Paul became acutely conscious of the diet and exercise regimes that enabled him to maximise his potential on the basketball court. Ironically, 'even though he is bodily impaired, Paul perceives himself to be more "embodied" (i.e. aware of and in touch with his body) and "able-bodied" (i.e. in terms of his physical health, diet and fitness) than before his accident' (Valentine, 1999: 175). Paul has also become more independent and geographically mobile. Instead of relying upon his mother, as was the case prior to his accident, Paul has become much more capable and active in the kitchen. Similarly, instead of being rooted to his home town, Paul's status as an international sports participant has 'gained access to privileges previously denied him, travelling all over the UK, to Europe and to North America' (ibid.: 176).

Paul's case highlights the importance of distinguishing between disability and illness. While many types of bodies are considered to be 'ailing' in relation to the productive demands of the health role, it is important to understand how these bodies vary and how they are experienced in a multitude of different ways. In this respect, there are important distinctions to be drawn between many types of disability, on the one hand, and chronic illness, on the other. Paul's physical condition after physiotherapy remained relatively stable: he was not ill and had a body which allowed him to engage in socially valued performances and re-establish a set of habits that were efficacious in relation to his environment. People suffering from chronic illness in contrast, rarely experience this degree of predictability or stability. For many, the unpredictable nature of their symptoms mean that it is simply not possible to establish reliable habits that allow them to gain control over their environment, or to partake as they would like in the ordinary, health-oriented, flow of social life. Instead, life can become a constant struggle in which the usually 'taken-for-granted' rules of interaction, representing 'independence, competence and decency', become impossible ideals (Nijof, 1995: 192). Moss (1999) highlights this in talking about how her own experiences of ME gave her an affinity with those she came across when conducting research into chronic illness:

> Like other women, I have lost friends because I could not commit to a pre-arranged time, or if I did, in breaking arrangements too often. When a woman talks about people not being able to 'see' her pain unless there are splints, canes, or wheelchairs, I know what she means. No one 'sees' my disease either, so the dread of having to stand up on the bus for 20 mins, the stopping, the going, the swaying, overwhelms me so much that I break out in a cold sweat at the thought of it. When a woman says she has a good day and ends up cleaning out a closet, but 'pays' for it the next three days from being so stiff she can hardly get out of bed, I know what she means. (Moss, 1999: 158–9)

Predicaments such as the one described by Moss constitute important correctives to overly optimistic accounts of the process of accomplishing a reintegrated sense of embodied self based on a newly achieved equilibrium between the external and internal environments of action. Frequently, nothing seems enabling, facilitative or even tolerable about being ill or becoming disabled. In these cases, life itself seems little more than a continual struggle in which even small victories come at too great a cost to one's energies.

Character and the pedagogics of illness

How people respond to being ill and disabled can illuminate human creativity in repairing or recreating identity, as well as illustrating the limits of creativity in the face of a body that refuses to provide individuals with remission from pain, discomfort and immobility. There is also some agreement that these conditions can teach us about loss, mourning and finding meaning in the inexorable march from life to death (Kleinman, 1988). Technological culture in the West may position frailty and pain as a *lack*, to be overcome as quickly as possible, but this has not prevented people from experiencing these conditions as deeply meaningful (Asad, 1993). Such meanings address the issue of what enables people to develop a character (fragmented or otherwise) able to make contact with those things that take them beyond their physical selves and are of immanent or transcendent significance.

Frank (1991a and b, 1995) examines this issue by exploring what he refers to as the 'pedagogics of suffering'. The bodily bases of this pedagogics are embodied subjects who, by living with and through illness, can teach themselves and us all 'how to live a saner, happier life' (Frank, 1991b: 15). For Frank, witnessing and sharing the suffering of others enables us to become more human: being in touch with what is part of the human condition in these ways enables us to 'live in the light of' what this connectivity 'teaches us we can be' (ibid.: 122). This can prompt people to re-evaluate what is truly important to them, and to reorder their decisions and actions on the basis of newly established priorities. Kitto (1988: 112–13) details how being ill can provide people with the time and motive for 'getting in touch' with what is important to them, for example, and a reason and motive for expressing previously hidden emotions which have stood in their way of achieving a sense of well-being. Carricaburu and Pierret's (1995) interviews with gay men suffering from HIV and AIDS provides many illustrations of how illness was viewed as a motive for investing more in family and friendships and in life more generally. As one thirty-nine year old bank manager noted, 'I'm more attentive and sensitive if something happens to my friends. I get more involved in their troubles than I could have before. I live more intensely whatever happens. I try to be closer to my family in the provinces, and I phone more often' (ibid.: 203).

Similar themes are explored in Snyder's (2000) study of Alzheimer's sufferers. Having discussed the losses brought about by their illness, these respondents talked about finding peace and beauty in the world and about the benefit they gained from focusing on the 'small things in life' and on 'childlike things'. As Corbin and Strauss (1987: 271) note, there is in such cases a real joy taken in living, and even in the prospect of death, despite the diminution of performative capacity. Concerns with 'doing' have in part been replaced by a joy of *being* that makes the most out of life while it remains. Radley's (1999) analysis of 'narratives of illness' identifies this cultivation of immanence, of discovering magic in the apparently mundane, as a recurring tendency in those who seek to reach beyond the currently encountered limitations of their bodies. Taking as his starting point the 'shock' or 'terror' frequently experienced by those who discover they are seriously ill, Radley explores the existential efforts they undertake to prevent themselves from being overwhelmed by 'being sick', from the threat posed to the 'ongoingness of life' they previously took for granted, and from the world of medicine that threatens to colonise their bodies. What he finds is that sufferers frequently sacralise sights, people and events that would ordinarily appear part of the profane world of everyday life. Radley suggests that this involves aesthetic work which allows the sufferer to take 'delight' in aspects of life that enable them to continue to invest in living. This is exemplified by Frank's (1991b) account of his treatment and recovery from cancer. Struggling with pain one night, he managed to break through the 'incoherence' of his experience when he was 'stopped on the landing by the sight – the vision really – of a window':

> Outside the window I saw a tree, and the streetlight just beyond was casting the tree's reflection on the frosted glass. Here surely was beauty, found in the middle of a night that seemed to be only darkness and pain. Where we see the face of beauty, we are in our proper place, and all becomes coherent. (Frank, 1991b: 33)

This aesthetic work can have benefits which extend beyond its intrinsic value and lead to other life changes. One of the respondents in Garro's study, for example, found that her struggles with chronic pain led to a greater appreciation of those periods of time when she was not in distress, and of the beauty of life. This resulted in 'Gail' becoming committed to art. As she explains:

> The joy that I have when I'm drawing, sculpting. It's in the face of pain, you know. It's like a shadow that throws the other parts of my life into brighter contrast. You see my brights are brighter because I have this darkness hovering around all the edges ... the world has become a more precious and beautiful place – because I really see it. (quoted in Garro, 1992: 129)

Such profound experiences can deepen and enrich an individual's character by enabling him/her to make contact with a sense of the magic of life; a magic which may be immanent within the apparently mundane world of everyday objects, or transcendent of this world. The pedagogic effects of such experiences, moreover, do not remain confined to the individual, and Frank's suggestion that sharing the experience of illness can result in the establishment of new social links shows how character can result in the formation of moral relationships between people.

Sickness, illness and morality

Arthur Frank (1995) argues that the narratives written and spoken by the ill, and the dialogues they engage in with others, have the potential to 'create empathetic bonds between themselves and their listeners' based around insights into how life might be conducted in an ethical way that takes into account the realities of human frailty. These bonds have the capacity of 'living on' and positively affecting the quality of other interactions (Frank, 1995: xii). While exclusion from the health role may result in a subsequent exclusion from valuable social networks, support groups that grow out of an individual's search for help can provide an alternative source of social capital that can help make life tolerable (Wellman and Frank, 2001). Additionally, the use of the Internet enables social bonds to be forged between people separated by considerable distances. Hardey's (2002) analysis of illness narratives on the web, for example, notes a move from self-narrative to advice giving. One page, called 'Jooly's Joint', provides an example of how such sites work. It explains its rationale as follows:

> When I was diagnosed, I didn't know anything about MS or anyone else who had it. It was a scary and lonely time. I created Jooly's Joint so that people living with our disease can get to know other 'MSers' around the world, to share experiences and give each other support. Four years on, 100s of people come here every week and Jooly's Joint has 10,000 members. (cited in Hardey, 2002)

The initiation of such bonds between people is not, however, a one way process. For Frank, those who listen to and 'share' the suffering of others, by spending time with and tending the sick, are helping to make life more tolerable (see also Deegan, 1994; Twigg, 2006). The work done by volunteer 'buddies', who provide emotional and practical support to people living with AIDS and HIV, provides one example of this (Brown, 1997). Advocacy or campaigning on behalf of the sick is another activity that can occur as an outgrowth of empathetic bonds, or for a variety of other reasons (Dyck, 1995).[1] In the 1980s, for example, email was used to organise campaigns for the medical recognition of conditions that included Gulf War Syndrome, Repetitive Strain Syndrome and HIV (Boberg et al., 1995; Hardey, 2002). Political activism associated with HIV and AIDs was of particular importance during the 1990. Activist groups here not only had to fight to gain recognition of the disease, but had to battle against deeply held prejudice and discrimination on the part of governmental authorities in order to receive treatment and drugs appropriate to their condition. What is interesting about the fast-changing landscape of AIDS politics (as well as the high number of AIDS-related deaths) was the wide range of opportunistic strategies engaged in by activists who used every means available, working in and outside of the state, to advance their cause (Aggleton et al., 1997; Brown, 1997).

It is also important to note here that social bonds surrounding sickness and impairment are not the exclusive province of 'secular' rights and awareness groups. Religions have historically been key to the provision of meaning systems that locate illness, impairment and death in a wider cosmic context, and provide people with ready-made orientations and normative expectations regarding these experiences (Koenig et al., 2000). Christianity and Islam, for example, both place much significance on the care and treatment of the mortal body in this world as a preparation for eternal life in the next, and also place ethical imperatives on believers regarding the care of the sick and infirm.

Conclusion

Illness may have the potential to teach us about life, but it can also reveal something about the limits of human being. Reflecting on the general implications of human frailty and illness for the body politic, Frank (1991b: 121) suggests that we need to recognise sickness as a core experience which unites us as a species and which demands collective provision for care and treatment. Turner (1993) has sought to extend such insights into a theory of human rights based on the ontology of human frailty. Analyses such as these are enormously important in suggesting moral criteria against which to assess the structures of the external environment. It seems to me, though, that care and treatment for the sick, or a recognition of our frailty as grounds for the right to live a certain quality of life, is only one side of this pedagogics of illness.

Parsons (1978) traced the origins of Western medical ethics to the Christian value placed on the 'gift of life', but also acknowledged that issues concerned with the quality of life had become increasingly important by the late twentieth century. In this context, Lawton's study into contemporary hospice care raises important questions concerning the liminal space that exists between life and death. When the bodies of patients reached a stage where they had no control and were, quite literally, falling apart, Lawton found repeated instances of social withdrawal and a 'shutting down' of the self. When tumours expanded, when colons were blocked and resulted in digested food being brought back up as fecal vomit, when control over body functions ceased, when smells became unbearable, there seemed nothing left to sustain personhood. The 'shock' of physical decay proved too much and the final defence available to these individuals involved a process of 'psychic closure' (Lawton, 1998: 100). Like others exposed to unbearable situations, the self could no longer continue. Human life, truly human life, appeared to have ended. In these circumstances, individuals paved the way for their own death. There were no more 'lessons to be learnt' from such decay and there is a strong case for suggesting that the treatment of sickness and, perhaps, the constitution of morality in these instances needs to be predicated on a recognition that life has reached the very end of its journey and that individuals have gone beyond the state where they can act creatively within this world.

Note

1 In terms of the two-way flow of bonds between people, it is also worth noting that advocacy work does not only benefit those groups targeted for help. There is a growing amount of evidence suggesting that getting involved in the community by volunteering to help those who are ill has a positive effect on mental health and general well-being.

8

Surviving

Introduction

One of the accusations levelled at certain perspectives within the field of body studies is that they engage in what Walter Schulz (1986) has referred to as 'inverted Cartesianism'. Having reacted against the dominant philosophical tradition in the West – a tradition that reduced social actors to thinking minds and marginalised the importance of our sensuous bodily being – such perspectives have exposed themselves to the accusation of equating people entirely with their physical capacities. As Keith Tester (2004: 30) argues, 'all the time we understand ourselves or others in terms of bodies alone, we are denying the humanity of both them and ourselves.' Humans are not just flesh and blood objects, in other words, but are characterised by a wide range of social, moral and intellectual capacities. This is an important point and while such criticism may not apply to sociological studies of the body that attend to the lived experience, or to the collective, cultural or spiritual potentialities of embodied subjects, it should serve as a cautionary note for those who conceptualise social actors simply on the basis of their biological needs. A similar concern should also be extended to those structuralist/post-structuralist analysts who conceptualise social actors as passive bodily canvases on which ideologies, sexual matrixes, micro-powers or governmental strategies are inscribed. Approaches such as these engage in forms of conflationism which rob humans of any genuinely creative, socially agentic capacities.

The problem of reducing embodied subjects to their physical being is not just an *academic* question, however, regarding the best way to conceptualise or theorise individuals. Historically, various political powers have sought to remove from people the ability to shape their environment according to their needs and wishes, and to impose on their enemies an animal existence in which survival is a constant struggle. In cases such as these, do we have to take seriously the possibility that people *are* reduced to their physical bodies and robbed of a significant part of what it is that makes them human? If so, do we need to recognise that there may indeed be at least certain situations in which the 'inverted Cartesians' (of whatever variety) have a point?

In this chapter I examine situations in which embodied subjects are condemned to inhabit a social and physical environment in which the basics of biological life become central preoccupations. I do this by focusing on the Holocaust suffered by the Jews, gypsies, homosexuals and others in the territories occupied by Nazi Germany during the Second World War, and on the system of forced labour established by the Gulags in the former Soviet Union. Despite their undoubted differences, both Nazi and Communist projects involved the construction of environments inimical to human life which resulted in the deaths of millions. Rather than suggesting that the 'throwing back' of individuals onto the basics of bodily survival robs them of their human capacity to act creatively and socially, however, survivor accounts and other evidence demonstrates the existence of 'societies of inmates' within the camps and suggests that embodied individuals retained the capacity to make moral choices in line with their sense of right and wrong. As Des Pres (1976) argues, when humans are placed in situations where their basic biological survival is threatened over a long period of time, they are not necessarily 'reduced to' their bodies. Instead, there remain instances of collective bonding, morality and dignity. Survival, for those who lived through the horrors and hardships of camp life, was an embodied experience characterised by a definite *social* (as well as physical) structure: it was 'neither random nor regressive nor amoral' (ibid.: v–vi). This does not, of course, devalue the significance of people's physical being to camp life. People's corporeal capacities enabled them to continue living as social beings, while their collective struggles to meet life's most basic requirements helped them rise above an existence determined solely by these needs. This transcendence developed by *attending to*, not ignoring, the physicality of embodied existence.

The external environments of action

The social milieu: totalitarian politics

Concentration camps have long been used to incarcerate the opponents of imperialist nations. Spain utilised them in Cuba during the 1890s, as did Britain in South Africa during the Boer War. The camps built and run by Nazi Germany and the Soviet Union were intended to imprison enemies of the state and provide a labour force that would contribute in varying degrees to the economic infrastructure and to their respective war efforts. While the Soviets placed more emphasis on the productive role of the camps in industrialising and colonising its inhospitable regions, Nazi Germany utilised the camps for the genocidal destruction of the Jewish peoples.

Nazi propaganda associated Jews with images of 'vermin, of parasites, of infectious disease', and blamed them for Germany's defeat in the First World War. Nazi 'death factories' existed at Belzec, Chelmno, Sobibor, Treblinka, Auschwitz and Majdanek. Stalin referred to his political opponents using very similar images and blamed them for the economic failures of the Soviet Union (Applebaum, 2003: 19–21). Despite presiding over camps in which millions died from extremes of weather, illness and executions, though, the Soviet camp system was not deliberately organised to mass-produce corpses. Nevertheless, the human costs of both these totalising political projects were huge, and they had at their centre visions of the desirable social body which drew strict boundaries between those individual bodies that could be moulded in their image and those requiring exclusion from the body politic.

The first prisoners who entered Germany's camps were not Jews but the political opponents of the Nazis. As Rees (2005: 23) puts it, 'Jews were taunted, humiliated and beaten up in those early days, but it was the left-wing politicians of the former regime who were seen as being the more immediate threat.' While these camps functioned initially as prisons, their role soon expanded. The German programme of ethnically restructuring Poland employed them as a means of imprisoning and terrorising Poles, and the camps increasingly became central instruments in the search for racial purity and the eradication of those regarded as corporeally polluting. The Nazi leadership had, since coming to power in 1933, been committed to the idea that certain 'races' and individuals had more rights to life than others. The practical implications of this view were first evident in the compulsory sterilisations that took place during the 1930s among the mentally ill. Around 300,000 Germans were subjected to such sterilisations (Rees, 2005: 184). Similarly, the first people to be gassed at Auschwitz were victims of the Nazi 'adult euthanasia' programme which involved doctors selecting and killing chronically disabled patients (ibid.: 59). If the German social body had to be cleansed of these physically and mentally defective bodies, however, it recognised a far greater threat in the form of Jews.

The Nazis saw the Second World War as a fight against Judeo-Bolshevik 'subhumans'. The Russian threat was to be annulled through mass starvation, as the Germans took what they needed from that country in order to feed their troops and assist the war effort, but the Jewish threat was more insidious. Jews were seen as undermining Germany through an economic, social and sexual parasitism that sapped the 'racial strength' of their hosts (Theweleit, 1989 [1978]: 8–10). Viewing the 'Jewish problem' as 'a question of space', a policy of ghettoisation was accompanied by plans for concentration camps to supply forced labour and carry out the wholesale extermination of these people (Rees, 2005: 33, 67). Once they were no longer fit enough to labour productively, the Jews and other inmates of the camps were to be murdered. After experimenting with various means of killing, the Nazis decided that gassing was both economically efficient and shielded those soldiers directly involved from undue psychological distress (ibid.: 72).

Life in the camps themselves was governed by a carefully planned and tightly organised structure that subjected inhabitants to a fundamental unpredictability regarding their conditions of existence. This was institutionalised in places such as Dachau in the 1930s, when prisoners were not told the length of their sentence, but took on a qualitatively new dimension once the policy of genocide was operationalised. From July 1942 in Auschwitz, the Schutzstaffel (SS) divided Jewish arrivals into those 'fit' for work and those 'unfit' for work to be gassed immediately (Rees, 2005: 113). Those deemed fit to work, moreover, soon discovered that they were likely after a few months of mistreatment and starvation to find themselves marked as unproductive and condemned to death. Furthermore, those who managed to avoid being selected for the gas chambers in the short-term could still find themselves beaten to death, tortured in punishment blocks, and even turned into human guinea pigs as Nazi doctors made them the object of experiments involving poisonous gas, dissecting, freezing and boiling. Survival was a matter of slim chance, and the scale of killings in the Nazi camps was staggering. At the height of destruction, over 17,200 corpses were fed into the ovens during each twenty-four hour shift at Birkenau, while about 312,000 people were murdered at Treblinka alone between the end of July and the end of August 1942. The total number of deaths in the Holocaust was over six million (Lengyel, 1959; Rees, 2005: 162).

The system of camps developed in the Soviet Union was known as the Gulag or labour camp. The Gulag system had its immediate origins in Lenin's demand to imprison 'unreliable elements' of the population, but assumed a new significance from 1929, the year Stalin decided to use forced labour to speed up industrialisation and excavate the natural resources that existed in the inhospitable far northern territories of the Soviet Union (Applebaum, 2003: 3–4). The Gulag continued to grow throughout the 1940s – with at least four hundred and seventy-six camp complexes existing during the Soviet Union's lifetime – and by the early 1950s played a central role in the Soviet economy. As Applebaum (2003: 4) notes, the camps produced 'a third of the country's gold, much of its coal and timber, and a great deal of almost everything else'.

Approximately eighteen million people passed through the Soviet camps from 1929 until Stalin's death in 1953, and the camps only began to be abolished by Gorbachov in 1987 (ibid.: 4–5). People were sent to them for a variety of real or imagined offences against the state. Political opponents found themselves accused, but people also received sentences for being twice late for work and for buying and selling cigarettes at a profit. These 'criminals' came under enormous pressure (involving interrogation and sometimes torture) to confess their crimes and inform on collaborators (ibid.: 272). Workmates informed on workmates, children on parents and employers on employees. To be seen speaking to the 'wrong' person could result in a lengthy sentence, and no one was safe from the periodic 'purges' Stalin conducted against his 'enemies' and 'opponents'.

The physical milieu: the limits of human endurance

The physical conditions and organisation of camp life made even basic survival difficult, if not always impossible, for those condemned by the

German and Soviet systems. Transportation to the camps was often an endurance test, lasting sometimes for weeks, and resulted in many deaths. Survivors of the Nazi camps recount how the cattle trucks in which they travelled (in the stifling heat or freezing cold, and without even barely adequate food and water) 'became an abattoir' in which the living had to endure the corpses of the dead as the 'SS would neither let us bury nor remove them' (Lengyel, 1959: 21; Levi, 1987: 24). In the Soviet Union, the journey to Kolyma seemed to present a particularly gruelling ordeal for prisoners. Shalamov (1980: 8) recounts how prisoners would arrive emaciated at the Siberian ports of Vladivostok, Vanino or Nakhodka after trips that often lasted between thirty and forty days, and would then be held at other camps prior to being shipped to their final destination. The actions of the Soviet guards on such trips only made things worse. Described as trigger happy, they often failed to provide prisoners with water, food or opportunities for urinating or defecating outside the train wagons (Noble, 1960: 71; Zabolotsky, 1986: xx).

In these conditions of extreme privation, it is not surprising that social 'veneers cracked', 'serious quarrels' occurred, 'instincts predominated' and people experienced themselves as outsiders placed forcibly into a world of irreality (Lengyel, 1959; Levi, 1987: 24; Wiesel, 1981 [1958]: 34). Conditions on the cargo steamers that took prisoners to Kolyma provide one illustration of the ordeals people faced. Political prisoners were frequently attacked and robbed, and the shipboard gang rapes (the 'Kolyma tram') were talked about throughout the camp system. As one surviving prisoner wrote, 'Anyone who has seen Dante's hell would say that it was nothing beside what went on in that ship' (cited in Applebaum, 2003: 169).

For those who reached their destination, the ordeal of survival they confronted had just begun. Bettleheim's (1960: 108) description of early camp life from 1938 to 1939 in Dachau and Buchenwald provides us with what he refers to as the bare 'minimum facts' regarding the physical conditions of life in the Nazi system. Suffering from extreme malnutrition, prisoners had to perform hard physical labour for up to seventeen hours a day, seven days a week, and were exposed to extremes of weather wearing nothing other than inadequate rags. Olga Lengyel's (1959) account of her time in Auschwitz-Birkenau provides more detail. She describes how 1,500 inmates had to make do with twenty bowls to eat from, how roll calls exposed them to the elements for long periods, thereby hastening 'the work of extermination which was the real purpose of the camp', and how the daily ration of a quarter pint of water left those in the camp constantly 'tortured by thirst' and even ready to risk death by drinking infected water from rusty pipes or stagnant puddles (Lengyel, 1959: 49–57; see also Wiesel, 1981 [1958]). The food supplied to the camp prisoners was rarely more, and often less, than a small portion of bread and a helping of a thin, watery soup, and left inmates starving.

If these conditions were not enough to reduce inmates to suffering bodies – aware of little else other than pain and the constant possibility of death – the prevalence of filth added another dimension to this predicament. Lengyel (1959: 126) describes how Auschwitz-Birkenau was situated on a marshy terrain which meant that the 'mud never disappeared', becoming 'a sly and powerful enemy'. It 'penetrated our shoes, our clothing, and even soaked through our soles, which came off and made our swollen feet even heavier' (ibid.). Dysentery was common and prisoners took all sorts of desperate measures to stop fouling themselves – and thereby infringing camp rules which could lead to beatings and death – including using their own eating bowls as toilets. When people in a block caught typhus, diarrhoea 'became uncontrollable. It flooded the bottom of the cages, dripping through the cracks into the faces of the women lying in the cages below, and mixed with blood, pus and urine, formed a slimy, fetid mud on the floor of the barracks' (Perl, 1948: 171; Des Pres, 1976: 53). Buckets of excrement were collected in a passage by the exit to barracks at night, yet by dawn urine and feces covered the floor, sticking to people's feet and emitting a smell which caused some to faint (Birenbaum, 1971: 226).

The struggle against harsh physical conditions also looms large in survivor's accounts of the Soviet camps. Working days of up to sixteen hours, established in an attempt to meet productivity targets set in Moscow, were an ordeal for malnourished prisoners. Staple food, when available, was a watery soup made from 'spoiled cabbage and potatoes, sometimes with a piece of pig fat, sometimes with herring heads' (Applebaum, 2003: 199). However, food supplies were often ruined by the elements in transit, or stolen, or, at times during the Second World War, simply non-existent. While this situation resulted in woefully inadequate or non-existent provision for those required to undertake factory work indoors, those despatched outside to work also had to endure extreme temperatures and violent storms. Little protection was provided by the living quarters, either, which were sometimes no more than earth dugouts. The barracks in which Nadezhda Grankina found herself, for example, 'were infested with countless bedbugs. There were so many of them that sleeping indoors was impossible, even during the day, and we would lie down outside ... on the ground' (Vilensky, 1999).

The social and physical environments of camp life delivered to camp prisoners the most enormous shock to their identities and threatened their pre-existing sense of self. In this context, the threat of death was accompanied by the possibility of total psychological disintegration.

The phases of embodied action

Identity and crisis

Contemporary debates about identity often focus on difference and diversity, but survivor accounts of camp life are 'invariably group portraits' in which 'the trials of the writer' are also those of thousands of other camp inmates (Des Pres, 1976: 3). The initial 'shock' of imprisonment, of mistreatment, of regimes designed to subjugate or kill, was delivered through a process of objectification that assaulted any pre-existing sense of self. Once in the camps, prisoners were no longer treated as embodied *subjects*, with the right to exercise agency, but as enfleshed *objects* that were to be turned in the most efficient manner possible into units of production or, in the case of the Nazi death camps, bones, smoke and ashes.

The brutality of this regime, and its disorienting effects for those who experienced it, was evident even before prisoners arrived at the German camps. This is illustrated by Primo Levi's (1987: 22) reaction to being hit during the process of roll call immediately prior to transportation. It was not the pain of the blows that affected him most, but the 'profound amazement' he felt on witnessing people hitting others 'without anger'. The assault on identity also occurred in the period prior to being admitted into the Soviet camps. Having been arrested on spurious grounds, prisoners were subject to repeated interrogations designed to break their will and their trust in themselves, and to elicit false confessions (Vilensky, 1999; Applebaum, 2003). As Vilensky (1999) reports, this questioning could last for months, continuing all through the night and leaving the accused with hardly any time for sleep and tormented by the screams of agony coming from those whose interrogations included torture.

Once prisoners were admitted to the camps, the crisis of identity and existence they faced continued apace. Those aware enough to realise what was at stake in the Nazi camps had first to cope with the possibility that they would be selected immediately for death in the gas chambers. Those who avoided this fate were confronted with attempts to remove them of their pre-camp identities. Robbed of the smallest of possessions 'which even the poorest beggar' owned in non-camp life, inmates were stripped, shaved, showered and disinfected; left naked and vulnerable without even their hair to remind them of their former selves (Frankl, 1959; Levi, 1987: 33). If prisoners were reduced to their bodies, these were bodies over which they had little control and no rights. Lengyel's account of her initiation into the German camps details the oral, anal and vaginal searches that took place in the presence of drunken guards. Transforming new prisoners into what Primo Levi (1987: 32) refers to as 'the phantoms' they glimpsed on arrival at the camp continued when they were thrown rags to wear. These provided ill-fitting and wholly inadequate protection against the elements (see also Bettleheim, 1960; Wiesel, 1981 [1958]: 48). As a final mark of humiliation, initiation into camp life in Auschwitz was concluded with the tattooing of prisoners (initially on the chest and later on the arms); an inscription which made it easier to identify corpses (Rees, 2005: 80–1).

In the Soviet camps, men and women were shaved over their entire bodies. This was done ostensibly for reasons of hygiene, but being stripped naked 'under the full gaze of male soldiers' also had a ritual significance, especially for women (Applebaum, 2003: 173). Soviet camp-issue 'uniforms' were 'invariably old, ripped, ill-made and ill-fitting' and appeared to be issued in a deliberate attempt to humiliate inmates (Applebaum, 2003: 174). Humiliation continued with work selection, described in the unpublished memoirs of George Bien as a 'slave market'. Inmates had to strip naked in front of women inspectors dressed in white coats who determined the muscular content of the body in front of them by pulling the skin of their buttocks, a process which provided them with 'little choice from this group of living dead' (Applebaum, 2003: 176).

These conditions meant that inmates had to live in an environment that threatened to reduce them to their organic bodies, and had to endure lives in which the smallest changes in physical comfort or discomfort affected the core of their being. In this respect, Shalamov's (1980) *Kolyma Tales* explains why the bathhouse in the Gulag was so unpopular. At the end of each day, prisoners would have to disguard their old underwear for 'new' and there was no opportunity to select on the basis of fit or condition, or to escape the possible misery of a bad exchange which left grown men in tears. It is in the context of such conditions that Des Pres (1976: 77) describes the first stage of camp experience as 'initial collapse', a period in which the identity and sense of reality of prisoners was torn asunder. Conventional opportunities to acquire respect and autonomy, and to organise life according to past desires, were gone, and inmates were left radically removed from their old selves and in a state of disbelief and psychological paralysis. As Philip Muller explains, 'I couldn't understand any of it. It was like a blow on the head, as if I'd been stunned. I didn't even know where I was ... I was in shock, as if I'd been hypnotised, ready to do whatever I was told. I was so mindless, so horrified' (Felman and Lamb, 1992: 231). In the face of this 'otherness of camp life', this 'horror and apparent chaos' that was 'not real by past standards', the identities of inmates were 'unable to root [themselves] in familiar ground' and soon 'fell apart' (Des Pres, 1976: 78). Commenting on the massively over-crowded Soviet prisons of the 1940s, Zabolotsky (1986: 310–11) describes how this initial 'disintegration of personality' happened for some before they even reached the camps and 'before the eyes of everyone' (Applebaum, 2003: 151). This visual element to the assault on identity effected by the camps, and by the journey to the camps, had other elements for those who saw their own reflection after the ravages of their new life had taken their toll. Commenting on looking at herself in a mirror for the first time in three years, Olga Adamova-Sliozberg's account of life in the Gulag notes how she was unable to identify herself:

> Suddenly I recognised my mother's tired, mournful eyes, her greying hair, the familiar melancholy set of her mouth ... It was me. I stood there gaping, unable to believe that I was no longer a young woman whom strangers in the street would call 'miss', but this sad, middle-aged woman who looked at least fifty years old. (Vilensky, 1999: 47)

The will to live was tested to the extreme. Permanently exhausted, often sick and only able to sleep between four and five hours a night at most,

Frankl (1959: 31) describes the most 'ghastly' moment of the normal twenty-four hours of a survivor at Auschwitz as 'the awakening, when, at a still nocturnal hour, the three shrill blows of a whistle tore us pitilessly from our exhausted sleep and from the longings of our dreams'. With previous habits and identities worthless, inmates were plunged into a state of physical and existential crisis in which they were left with nothing that resembled their former selves (Levi, 1987: 33, Wiesel, 1981 [1958]: 48).

Despite the shared elements to this crisis, foremost among them being the constant threat of death, it would be wrong to overlook how it affected inmates in distinctive ways. For Des Pres (1976: 76, 91), the physical act of getting up in the camps constituted a renewal of will in the face of pain and despair, but this renewal took different forms and exerted a terrible toll on those who chose to get out of their bunks and face the apparent impossibility of surviving. Furthermore, it did not prove possible for all to effect this renewal on a daily basis and there were many who never recovered from the initial shock of camp existence. *Muselmänner*, as they were called in the German camps, were unable to overcome the early trauma of their captive circumstances and could not shake their sense of nightmare and awake to their predicament. *Muselmänner* was the name given to the prisoner who was 'giving up and was given up by his [or her] comrades' (Amery, 1999 [1966]: 9), and it is these individuals who appeared to have been reduced to lifeless flesh. Primo Levi (1987) notes how they were condemned to the gas chambers (appearing unfit for work and unable to take any action that might lessen their chances of selection) or to a life that was even shorter than usual in the camps (not conserving energy or looking after themselves in even the most basic of ways).

> Their life is short, but their number is endless; they, the *Muselmänner*, the drowned, form the back-bone of the camp, an anonymous mass, continually renewed and always identical, of non-men who march and labour in silence, the divine spark dead within them, already too empty to really suffer. One hesitates to call them living: one hesitates to call their death death, in the face of which they have no fear, as they are too tired to understand. (Levi, 1987: 96)

These descriptions recur throughout the survivor accounts of life in the German camps. Amery (1999 [1966]) describes those who had been pushed into this state as staggering corpses and as bundles of physical functions in their last convulsions. Des Pres's (1976: 88) summary of survivor's accounts notes how time and again they are described as having entered a state when 'They starved, they fell sick, they stumbled into situations which got them killed.' For these people 'the collapse was too much, too many public and physical blows too fast, until the momentum of decline increased beyond reversal. They died inwardly, and as their spirit withered their outward aspect was terrible to see' (ibid.). A similar process occurred in the Russian camps (though with the vital difference that these inmates were not subjected to the threat of gassing) with many reaching such a state that they stopped looking after themselves. As Applebaum (2003: 310) summarises, 'This deterioration usually progressed in stages, as prisoners stopped washing themselves, stopped controlling their bowels, stopped having normal human reactions – until they became, quite literally, insane with hunger.'

While life was violent, nasty and often short in the camps, Amery provides a useful account of what separated those who had not yet been totally dehumanised from the *Muselmänner*. Such inmates were 'beaten, but not totally destroyed', 'had wounds but not deadly ones', and still just about possessed 'that substratum on which, in principle, the human spirit can stand and exist' albeit on 'weak legs' and often 'badly' (Amery, 1999 [1966]: 9). The speed at which inmates were able to draw back from the initial shock of camp existence was crucial, exerting a huge effect on how they coped with conditions and on their chances of living (Applebaum, 2003: 141–3). Those able to recover at least in part from the initial trauma of camp existence, though, were still marked for life by the crisis they faced. Jean Amery (1999 [1966]: 33–4), for example, talks about how his torture prior to camp life made his reduction to flesh complete and left him 'unable to feel at home in the world'. The effects of these experiences on his identity were exacerbated by a camp existence in which he realised the impotence of the intellect and the intellectual who had no faith in a religion or transcendent cause. Amery committed suicide in 1978. Solzhenitsyn's novel *One Day in the Life of Ivan Denezivitch* also draws on his sense that those who had such belief (e.g. in Christianity or Marxism) were better able to survive their ordeal as a result of their commitment to a higher, morally superior cause. They possessed a framework in which their ordeal could be placed, and believed in a 'kingdom' that 'was not "the Here and Now", but the Tomorrow and the Someplace' (Amery, 1999 [1966]: 13–14). The external environment for them was not reducible to the horrors of camp life but possessed wider bonds.

Political or religious belief did not, of course, prevent millions dying in the gas chambers or from the conditions in the German Camps and Soviet Gulag. Nor did it prevent the identities of believers from being affected profoundly by their experiences. Elie Wiesel (1981 [1958]: 43), for example, describes his response on seeing the bodies of babies being burnt as one of a nightmarish disbelief, a state which turned in time into a loss of faith and a conviction that God no longer existed. While Wiesel (1981 [1958]: 88) found the strength to go on, he reports on others who 'felt the first cracks forming' in their faith, lost their 'reason for struggling' and 'begun to die'. Faith could also be a problem for the identities of those in the Soviet camps who believed in, yet had become prisoners of, the Stalinist project.

> They kept assuring everyone that there had been a counter-revolutionary plot ...
> All of them were convinced that Stalin had no idea of what was going on ...
> They would accuse themselves of a criminal lack of vigilence ... Hardest of

all was the fact that, while they stubbornly defended the justice and good sense of the authorities' actions, they themselves were gradually losing faith. Yet they had devoted their entire lives to the Party. They had been its children and foot soldiers.

Des Pres (1976: 91) notes how reading accounts of camp conditions leads to a sense that life is 'impossible', and that the survivor's will to 'go on' seems 'illogical' and 'irrational'. Against all odds, however, many prisoners did survive the initial collapse of their identities and recovered a sense of self by moving from 'withdrawal to engagement, from passivity to resistance' and managing 'to face what had to be faced' (ibid.: 77). They were able to do this because, despite appearances to the contrary, camp life was far from the 'state of nature' it sometimes appeared. In contrast, survivors were able to maintain social structures in which it became possible for routinised behaviours to develop that assisted their struggle for life and moral sanity (ibid.: 142).

The recovery of habits

As we have seen, a recurring feature of survivor accounts is the sudden and shocking obsolescence of all previously habitual modes of acting and relating to people. In a world turned 'upside down', past propensities and preferences could result in immediate death, while the 'driving necessity' and 'physical disabilities' associated with the camps meant that 'many social habits and instincts' were 'reduced to silence' (Levi, 1987: 93). For those who managed to survive the initial shock of their new life and its associated assault on their self-identity, however, it was possible to develop an approach towards survival that went beyond just *reacting* to circumstances and involved sedimented orientations towards the maintenance of life. New habits and reactions were an essential prerequisite of such actions, however, and it was first necessary to 'armour' oneself, at least in part, against the horrors of camp life. It was also essential to acquire as quickly as possible *mechanical* habits that coalesced around the most immediate of bodily needs, and remained at the very basic level of day-to-day survival. In addition to these pre-conscious responses, the range of routines, rituals and other forms of action evident in camp life showed how individuals could rise above the level of mere existence.

Writing about life in the Nazi camps, Primo Levi (1987: 177) suggests that survival depended on shutting off ordinary emotional experiences and expressions. Belief in reason and hope for the long term had to be suppressed because they rendered the individual unable to cope with the vagaries of camp life and constituted 'a sensitivity which is a source of pain'. Inmates who wished to have any chance of surviving had also to shield and inure themselves from the pain and suffering of others. Showing any reaction to beatings or shootings, or to the screams of those dying in the gas chambers (on those occasions when they could be heard) could quickly result in one's own death. As one inmate who had endured the death of his father in Auschwitz realised, the only way he could survive was to 'block out what was happening around him ... "The longer I wanted to live", he says "the sooner I had to forget." ' (Rees, 2005: 115–16). It was possible, however, to develop this psychological protection. An inmate who had suffered Auschwitz for nearly two years, for example, testified that 'A human being can get used to anything' (cited in Rees, 2005: 97). Another, a dentist given the job of extracting gold teeth from the corpses left by the gas chambers, reports 'I was emotionless at the time. I wanted to survive' (cited in Rees, 2005: 180). Others, members of the Sonderkommando who worked in and around the gas chambers by undertaking such tasks as cutting hair from and burning the corpses, talked of becoming 'numb', of being like a 'robot', but of finding the strength to carry on, to 'live for the next day' (ibid.: 236–7). Certain prisoners even managed to armour themselves to the extent that they blocked out any knowledge of the real function of the death camps. This was not just because such knowledge was 'too horrendous to contemplate' but because of the habitual orientation towards survival that developed in the camps: the daily humiliations of life in the camp – the lice-ridden clothes, the battle to use the latrine, the struggle to find enough to eat, the filth and dirt that pervaded everything – pushed away any thoughts other than the fight to live for the 'immediate moment' (Rees, 2005: 260).

If previous emotional dispositions disappeared, to be replaced by 'deadened' responses that made it possible to 'go on', the habit of physically 'living for the moment' is another constant theme of survivors' accounts (Berkowitz, 1965: 126). Survivors had by necessity to develop a habitual concern with any opportunities that arose to attend to immediate bodily needs. The urgency and necessity of these tasks – tasks characteristically neglected by those unable to recover from the initial shock of camp life – were associated with the experience of not only 'becoming' a physical organism but of phenomenologically inhabiting a particular body *part*. As Elie Wiesel explains:

> I now took little interest in anything except my daily plate of soup and my crust of stale bread. Bread, soup – these were my whole life. I was a body. Perhaps less than that even: a starved stomach. The stomach alone was aware of the passage of time. (Wiesel, 1981 [1958]: 63–4)

Attending to the body in this way, being wrapped up with the body in this way, was not necessarily a process of being *reduced* to the body. Despite the impossibility of keeping properly clean in the camps, participating in the *ritual* of washing (albeit in cold, unclean water) is viewed repeatedly in survivor accounts as 'most important as a symptom of remaining vitality, and necessary as an instrument of moral survival' (Levi, 1987: 46). This was because washing seemed to be indicative of an intentional orientation towards survival and the future (notable, ceasing to wash was an early indicator of an inmate turning into a *Muselmänner*), and because of its sometimes social character. For inmates, washing could be a sign of resistance, a practice which indicated to themselves and others that they refused to give up on life:

> No spectacle was more comforting than that provided by the women when they undertook to cleanse themselves thoroughly in the evening. They passed the single scrubbing brush to one another with a firm determination to resist the dirt and the lice. That was our only way of waging war against the parasites, against our jailers, and against every force that made us its victims. (Lengyel, 1959: 131)

Des Pres (1976: 65) argues that the conditions of camp life collapsed the distinction between concrete existence and symbolic modes of being that have been basic to the structure of Western, and perhaps all, civilisation. Survivor accounts certainly confirm that the circumstances in which inmates found themselves compelled them to pay unprecedented attention to their bodily needs, and to jettison routinised modes of thought that served them well in their previous lives. The fact that habits such as washing developed a strong social and moral significance, however, shows that not all inmates were reduced to a state of non-voluntaristic flesh. This is also reflected in the creative habits developed in relation to work.

Most of the work inmates were forced to do in the Nazi camps had the effect of hastening their deaths. The work regimes were designed to run on a high turnover of labour that was instantly disposable should it slow down or display incompetency. The gruelling nature of many jobs in the Soviet camps also cost thousands of lives. In both contexts it was vital for inmates to conserve energy, to do as little as was possible without this being apparent, to develop habits which economised 'on everything, on breath, movements, even thoughts' (Levi, 1987: 138). Work practices in the Soviet camps, indeed, show how habits from wider society gradually became revived within the Gulag. *Tufta* (or make-work) was widespread in Soviet society ('They pretend to pay us and we pretend to work'), and became a routinised camp practice (Applebaum, 2003: 231). If these orientations towards work were a prerequisite for survival, camp labour regimes also provided opportunities for more inventive ways of making life bearable. Indeed, the creativity that was shown by many prisoners illustrates that humans are able to join together to utilise productively the possibilities that exist with others in even the most desperate of situations.

Making a difference

Adjusting to the initial shock of life in the camps (an experience that often made inmates feel as if they had entered a world of irreality) was itself a major accomplishment. Nevertheless, if inmates were to stand any chance of survival, this adjustment had to be followed quickly by attempts to minimise their exposure to the worst elements of camp life.

One of the most important variables in this struggle revolved around whether an inmate could find a job or 'function' that was seen as useful by the camp authorities. As Eugen Kogan (1953: 85) notes, there were few 'long-term concentration-camp inmates who did not in the course of time rise to more favourable, if not comfortable, working conditions. Those who failed in this endeavor simply perished' (Des Pres, 1976: 115). Indoor jobs were particularly prized, as these provided protection against the weather. Prisoners used any contacts they had, and invented skills, training and experience in relevant areas, in order to secure such positions. One inmate who had been thrown out of the Auschwitz carpentry shop due to lack of skills, for example, recounts how he managed to save his own life by enlisting the help of a benign Kapo in exaggerating his knowledge and obtaining a job preparing food for the Germans (Rees, 2005: 39). In contrast, outdoor jobs, and the exposure to the elements they involved, hastened death. Referring to the Soviet camps, Applebaum (2003) notes how prisoners went to extreme lengths to make themselves ill and get respite from such work by cutting off fingers, infecting cuts and putting their arms in fire. These actions illustrate just what was at stake in hard outdoor work that involved exposure to unbearable levels of cold and heat.

Another important aid in the struggle for survival involved making use of any material objects that could help prolong life. These included bits of wire used 'to tie up our shoes', scraps of 'rags to wrap around our feet' and 'waste paper to (illegally) pad out our jacket against the cold' (Levi, 1987: 39). The most crucial factor in the search to stay alive, however, involved the social networks and webs of interdependency that endured even in the concentration camps. These were not all benign – far from it. Thefts occurred among prisoners and Primo Levi (1987: 39) writes about how inmates had to learn to sleep with their heads on a bundle made up of clothes, containing 'all our belongings, from the bowl to the shoes', yet there were also numerous examples of group action that saved lives.

Most items of daily need could usually be acquired only through collective action involving stealing, bribing, exchange and other means of acquiring goods from the camp guards and camp supplies (Des Pres, 1976: 104–5). Furthermore, survivors' accounts of German camps frequently make reference to occasions when prisoners no longer able to stand in roll call were propped up by their comrades. Had they fallen, they would have been shot by the guards. More prosaically, inmates would tell each other stories in seeking to make camp existence slightly more bearable. Singing, dancing and being able to play a musical instrument could also save an inmate's life. Many of the German and Soviet camps had orchestras, and being assigned to such work could mean the difference between life and death. Inmates also engaged in acts of 'organisation' and 'resistance' that managed to divert supplies to other prisoners and make life slightly more bearable. As Lengyel (1959) notes, reflecting on her time in the German camps:

> Oppression as violent as that under which we lived automatically provoked resistance. Our entire existence in the camp was marked by it ... When labourers at the spining mills dared to slacken their working pace, it was resistance. When at Christmas we organized a little 'festival' under the noses of our masters, it was resistance. When clandestinely we passed letters from one camp to another, it was resistance. When we endeavoured and sometimes with success to reunite two members of the same family – for example, by substituting one internee for another in a gang of stretcher bearers – it was resistance. (Lengyel, 1959: 162)

More general help could be delivered by those inmates assigned jobs in administrative offices. At great risk to their own lives, it was possible in the German camps to save hundreds of inmates by hiding their existence, moving them between camps and disguising figures of new entrants and numbers killed by the gas chambers (Weinstock, 1947). The large numbers of SS officers who were drunk for much of the time also enabled inmates to exploit opportunities for saving lives (Des Pres, 1976: 120). Some of the lengths inmates went to in order to help others may be difficult to comprehend, as are the costs they incurred in taking such actions, but they belie the idea that the environments of the camps removed people's capacity to exercise choice or act creatively. Perl (1948) is just one survivor who wrote about saving life through taking life, in this case by saving the lives of mothers by destroying their unborn children. Such ultimate life/death exchanges were 'forced upon survivors repeatedly' and involved turning repeatedly 'from horror to the daily business of staying alive' (Des Pres, 1976: 87).

Most of the daily 'victories' the inmates managed to accomplish were relatively minor, and could be heavily compromised by the price they had to pay. Occasionally, though, resistance had spectacular results. Perhaps the best known example of this was the sabotage undertaken by the Sonderkommandos. These prisoners played a major role in the functioning of the Nazi gas chambers, but they also managed to smuggle enough explosives into the camps to burn down parts of Treblinka and Sorbibor, and to blow up the crematorium at Auschwitz (Des Pres, 1976: 100).

One should be careful not to romanticise the resistance that occurred or was possible in the camps. While there were work strikes and even full-scale rebellions in the Soviet camps after Stalin's death – rebellions that were in some cases put down with the assistance of tanks (Applebaum, 2003) – death was the outcome awaiting most prisoners in the German camps. Nevertheless, while the camps may have reduced their inmates to 'a single human mass' characterised by 'the same filthy rags, shaved heads, stick-thin festering bodies' and the same 'hurt and need', this was a *human* mass made up of individuals able to involve themselves in 'the margin of giving and receiving' that is 'essential to life in extremity' and that enabled some to survive

(Des Pres, 1976: 37). Selfish and self-interested acts took place all the time, but there was an inescapable network of interdependence among inmates which maintained sociality and saved lives. As Des Pres (1976: 97) notes, 'Even advice to only look after yourself was advice from another', while this interdependence frequently resulted in much more than simple advice. The marathon 'death marches' (which took place as the war neared its end and the Nazis sought to move the inmates further into occupied territory) took the lives of many (to fall down was to be shot) but survivor testimony is full of examples of people 'giving a vital part of themselves, literally their last reserves, to keep each other going' (Des Pres, 1976: 132).

Survival, character, and the moral order of the camps

The structured interdependence evident among inmates shows that the extreme conditions endured by those subjected to camp life did not eradicate social existence. Similarly, the risks that some individuals took in helping others shows that moral choices continued to be made by those who were themselves close to death. It is worth exploring these actions in a little more detail because they provide a powerful illustration of how people could emerge from the most profound of crises and retain a sense of themselves and others as living in accordance with their deepest ideals and feelings of right and wrong. They also show how social interdependence itself is moulded and steered by moral commitments and norms.

Survivor's accounts emphasise repeatedly the moral commitment of witnessing that was embraced by many of the prisoners, and the inner strength this gave them. This was not an isolated, individualised commitment, but one taken on behalf of the dead as well as the living. If this was felt particularly keenly in the German death camps, it was because the Nazis sought not only to destroy Jews, gypsies, gays and others, but to *eradicate all evidence* of this destruction. As a survivor from Dachau reported:

> The SS guards took pleasure in telling us that we had no chance of coming out alive, a point they emphasised with particular relish by insisting that after the war the rest of the world would not believe what happened; there would be rumors, speculations, but no clear evidence, and people would conclude that evil on such a scale was not possible. (cited in Des Pres, 1976: 35)

It is against this background that the commitment to witnessing the existence of, and what went on inside, the camps assumed such moral importance. Lengyel (1959: 88) reports that she had two reasons to live: to work with the resistance and to tell the world 'This is what I saw with my own eyes. It must never be allowed to happen again.' Many others made the same stand – in both German and Soviet camps. Heimler (1959: 191) writes about wanting to bear witness and be 'the voice' for 'the millions who had seen…but could no longer speak'. Weiss (1961) rejoices that she can bear witness, while Kaplan (1966) refers to witnessing as a 'duty', a 'mission' and a 'sacred task'. Through this moral commitment, survivors not only took on an invaluable historical task, but installed in themselves 'an integrity which contradicts the savagery' surrounding them (ibid.). As Vilensky (1999: 335–6) notes in her collection of survivor accounts from the Russian Gulag and prison system, 'They must speak of, and for, the many that did not return. Often deprived of families themselves, they feel a compelling duty to pass on to others the unique and terrible knowledge that their generations possess: that "these things did happen" – and thus could happen again.'

This integrity of individual character comes across in many survivor accounts. Lengyel (1959: 220) recounts how 'many internees [clung] to their human dignity to the very end.' They may have been degraded physically, but the camps 'could not debase them morally' (ibid.). Des Pres (1976: 202) summarises 'the stubborn refusal' of those who refused to be 'completely shaped by their environment' by illustrating how 'dignity was equated with selfhood because it was the only thing left, the one dimension of inmate existence beyond the enemy's reach.' As Perl (1948: 60) noted 'All we had was our human dignity ... and the moral strength to defend it with'. Talking of his own survival, Primo Levi (1987) notes the significance for survival of recognising this dignity in *others*, 'in my companions and in myself, men, not things, and thus to avoid that total humiliation and demoralisation which led so many to spiritual shipwreck'.

These displays of integrity and character suffused the social networks in camps: inmate life was not simply characterised by patterned interactions but by *moral orders*. According to Des Pres (1976: 146), these orders were based around an economy of gift-exchange based on a reciprocity that was 'perpetual' and that could cement people together in a sacred bond. When men and women were abused, starved and moving, day by day, closer to death, the 'smallest favours can shake the frail world of their being with seismic force' (ibid.). Such moral orders imposed just as strong sanctions against those who transgressed their boundaries. Food sharing was a particularly charged mode of exchange, for obvious reasons, and often made the difference between life and death. In this context, stealing part of another's meagre ration could have fatal consequences. As Weinstock (1947: 120–1) writes, such individuals were not reported but were punished when the opportunity arose: if they did not die from the beating, they were 'so incapacitated' that they were 'fit only for the crematorium'. Such actions were approved because they helped 'maintain a certain standard of moral and mutual trust' (ibid.) and seemed widespread through German and Soviet camps (Applebaum, 2003: 205).

These moral orders were not universal among all inmates and were often overlaid by considerations of nationality: 'all survivors recall occasions when they received help from, or offered help to, a stranger who was a fellow countryman' (Des Pres, 1976: 122). Groupings based on nationality were also sometimes supplemented, or complicated, by other allegiances. Commenting on the Soviet camps, Applebaum (2003: 283) notes how the more militant national groups, the Marxists, the religious sects and even the criminal gangs 'provided instant communities, networks of support, and companionship'. The criminal world had its own moral hierarchy: it was not only that different types of criminals had different levels of status, but that rules of behaviour were rigorously enforced. Criminal judicial rituals included 'courts', 'trials' and 'sentences' that could entail beatings, humiliation, the loss of fingers and death (Applebaum, 2003: 269). Sexuality also proved a basis for moral relationships of mutual support, although those known to engage in 'passive' gay sex were often stigmatised (Vilensky, 1999), and people even engaged in marriage ceremonies across walls in the Gulag without ever having met. Solzhenitsyn (Gulag Archipelago, II: 248–9) talks about hearing 'a choir of angels' during such occasions in which there was no reduction to animal need but a 'pure contemplation of heavenly bodies'.

Those individuals who did not fit easily with such groups, in contrast, 'found it more difficult to know how to live life in the camp, more difficult to cope with camp morality and the camp hierarchy' (ibid.). Such groups could lead to factionalism, but their existence also informed some of the most courageous acts reported on in the camps. In particular, Lengyel (1959) describes how during her time in Auschwitz some 400 Greeks refused to be Sonderkommandos and refused to kill a group of Hungarians. This act of defiance, which resulted in their immediate death, again demonstrated how the camps were not able to turn all of their inmates into lifeless physical automatons. As Lengyel (1959: 123) continues, these prisoners proved that 'in spite of the barbed wire and the lash they were not slaves but human beings.'

Conclusion

The Nazi and Soviet camps condemned millions of people to social and physical environments in which mere survival was minimally an enormous challenge and, for millions, impossible. They were not identical, as the Soviet Gulag was not designed or operated to effect genocidal destruction, but both imposed on people conditions which threatened to reduce existence to an unrelenting struggle to secure the basics of human life. Deprived of even minimally adequate supplies of food, water, clothes, sleep, rest or shelter, and subjected in the case of the Nazi camps to conditions designed to destroy any sense of self or psychological security, it is not surprising that many people buckled under the strain and were unable to go on. In these circumstances the *Muselmänner*, as they were called in the German camps, did indeed appear to be reduced to lifeless physical husks of their former selves. This was not an inevitable fate for camp inmates, however, and numerous survivor testimonies and other evidence demonstrates the existence of networks of interdependence, and mutual aid. The people involved in these collectivities and actions were not reduced to a brute, animalistic bodily existence. Instead, and in contrast to the plans of those in charge of the camps, their physical plight provided a basis on which they were able to continue to be embodied beings able to join with others, act morally and retain at least a semblance of self-identity that was irreducible to their surroundings. It was *through* their bodies, by *attending* to the embodied existence of themselves and those around them that they managed to maintain themselves as *more* than their bodies.

9

Believing

Introduction

Debates about belief have become extraordinarily important in recent years. These have been pushed to the foreground by the establishment of new, religiously divergent, immigrant communities in the West, and by the global spread of fundamentalist groups whose use of violence is justified in significant part on the basis of their religious affiliation (Juergensmeyer, 2000; Herbert and Wolffe, 2004). Yet 'belief' in the West is generally understood in a rather restricted manner as an individual phenomenon consisting of mental or psychological commitments to, and expressions of, core values (Asad, 1993). This characterisation not only obfuscates the great variety of forms belief has taken in the West itself, but misrepresents the very different external and internal environments of religious practice in other regions. It can also lead us to overlook important cultural changes occurring presently in Europe and the United States.

In order to identify these changes, and to explore how individuals have been affected by them and contributed to their development, this chapter progresses in two stages. First, I outline the Western technological environment which consolidated the notion of belief as a psychological property of individuals, and then focus on how recent global developments have undermined the hegemony of this instrumental culture. My argument here is that the rational 'enframing' of people and nature associated with technological culture in the West not only erodes meaning from human life, expelling the spiritual and sacred from its borders, but also creates the conditions in which it is possible for other cultural forms of belief to enter and flourish within this void. Second, I explore how individuals have drawn on such alternative beliefs in responding creatively to the potential difficulties associated with living in a technological culture, and examine some of the moral implications of these choices. Before embarking on this analysis, however, it is useful to provide some background to the historically distinctive meanings associated with belief in the West.

Tracing its origins back to Greek and Hebrew notions of trust and confidence, Ruel (1982) indicates how belief used to denote an emotional commitment to engage in particular relationships, activities or contracts deemed stable and honourable, but gradually lost its social and practical connotations (see also Michel, 1975). Asad's (1993) genealogy of Christianity reinforces this understanding by demonstrating how many belief-oriented religious activities in the Middle Ages which have contemporarily been understood in terms of their *symbolic* significance (e.g. monastic copying of manuscripts, the enactment of the liturgy) are more accurately appreciated as practical *bodily techniques* designed to develop Christian virtue, knowledge and community (Asad, 1993: 34, 64). For the eleventh-century theologian Hugh of St Victor, for example, sacramental rites were instituted not because of what they represented, but because of their role in facilitating humility, instruction and exercise (ibid.: 78–9). Again, belief was tied inextricably to bodily practices and experiences, and to immersion within a collectivity.

Given this past, how has belief in the contemporary West become equated so closely with a psychic commitment to, and cognitive expression of, values that we fail to appreciate the historical specificity of this view or the negative impact it can have on our evaluation of other cultures? How is it that we now tend to view belief as a personal statement of significance and identity that is distinctive from wider social relations, bodily dispositions and physical practices (Ruel, 1982: 9–10)? While the processes behind these changes are complex and long term, several factors are particularly worthy of mention.

The evolution of Christianity itself, and especially the Protestant Reformation, helped loosen the customary links that existed previously between social relations, bodily practices and belief (see Mellor and Shilling, 1997). As Ruel (1982) notes, Martin Luther stands out as *the* person for whom belief was realised fully only after an intense *inner* struggle with the self, and maintained as authentic only in the context of a continued *psychological* fight against doubt. Earlier developments within Court Societies, from the fourteenth century, also contributed towards an increased sense of separation between mental processes and bodily feelings which helped compartmentalise belief. As survival and social mobility gradually came to depend less on the ability to defend oneself physically and more on a person's status within Court, social pressures encouraged a greater degree of reflexivity about one's own behaviour and an enhanced monitoring of the actions of others (Elias, 1983). The successful self now needed the capacity to distance private thoughts from public behaviours, and the individual could ill afford belief–practices to structure how they acted in both contexts. A further factor that stimulated the psychologisation of belief was the demand for the 'mobile personality' associated with the urban centres of the Renaissance which was made more urgent by the accelerated development of modernity (Lerner, 1958: 50; Greenblatt, 1980: 227–8; Asad, 1993: 11). To be successful in these contexts required a personality prepared to move, change, invent and grasp opportunities when they arose in a manner unconstrained by overarching social and moral commitments. Finally, the Enlightenment's assault on the authority and epistemological credibility of religion diminished the power of the Church and did much to promote the idea that 'the only legitimate space allowed to Christianity' was 'the right to individual belief' (Asad, 1993: 45).

These factors did not, of course, *remove* the relationship between the body, sociality and belief. Catholics remained schooled in the collective and sensory nature of their faith, while even Puritan belief was not ruptured entirely from practical concerns. Nevertheless, they did contribute towards the ushering in of a *new type of relationship* in which belief was viewed increasingly as a psychological matter of individual preference. This was well suited to the developing contours of industrial society in the nineteenth and, especially, the twentieth century. As the authority of institutional religion waned within the wider social environment, the embodied self was made available for other purposes, while individuals were free to hold a wide range of beliefs as long as these were confined to the private spheres of mind and home. If the above factors did much to contribute to this situation, however, it was radicalised further as a result of the increasing pervasiveness and influence of *technological culture* during the twentieth century.

The external environments of action

The external environment in which belief is compartmentalised in the contemporary West has been constituted anew by a technological culture that expresses a total mastery over the social and the physical milieu. This culture is predicated on the instrumentalisation of embodied subjects through the social environment of *work* (viewing individuals as vehicles for economic performativity) and the similar *enframing of nature* as a 'standing-reserve' for efficiency-based demands (Heidegger, 1993 [1954]: 320, 329, 333). We have explored its performative basis in previous chapters. What is particularly distinctive about this culture, however, is that it seeks to disconnect the environments of human life from any relationship with spiritual or sacred phenomena that exist outside its borders, thus restricting radically the forms of belief that can exist legitimately within its parameters.

The social milieu: technological culture, work and consumption

Given its commitment to domination and mastery, nothing is more central to technological culture than ensuring that everything in its domain is available as a resource for the demands of pure productivity (Heidegger, 1993 [1954]). In terms of the social environment, it is the pervasive emphasis placed on *performative work* in waged-labour *and* in consumer culture that encourages individuals to instrumentalise their thoughts, their feelings and their bodies. This is evident in the workplace when employees are expected to embody corporate ideals of efficiency in their actions and appearance. Reflected in the widespread attempts by professionals to develop (through diet, exercise and various health regimes) a form of 'physical capital' that makes them a productive resource (Ehrenreich, 1990: 236), this becomes all the more urgent for middle-aged staff under pressure to 'keep up' with their younger colleagues (Sennett, 1998). 'Flexibility' has become a key element of this efficiency; constituting a byword not only for manufacturers producing what customers want, when they want, but also signifying the prized qualities of embodied subjects able to respond quickly to external demands (Shilling, 2005a: 73–100; Wolkowitz, 2006). This is exemplified by those high-flying professionals involved in the more privileged echelons of the labour market whose work requires them to travel extensively, to be constantly available via mobile phones, laptops and conference calls, and to structure their domestic lives around employer priorities (Sassen, 2002). The influence of performativity is further reflected in the increasing demands of 'emotion work'. From the 'smiles' and personalities sold by white-collar staff in the 1950s, to the 'deep acting' required to sustain adherence to the 'feeling rules' in the service sector today, the body again faces pressures to embody corporate ideals (Mills, 1953; Hochschild, 1983; Zapf et al., 2001). Finally, at the opposite end of the labour hierarchy, the focus on performativity central to waged-labour in our technological culture is evidenced by the millions of people who work extra shifts and take extra jobs to survive (Toynbee, 2003).

The centrality of performative work to the social environment of technological culture also extends to the sphere of *consumption*. During an epoch in the West when there has been a decline in the numbers of people living their lives in relation to transcendent religious ideals, and a concomitant valuing of youth in a culture which seeks to shield its members from mortality, conceptions of self-identity are often associated with the aim of maintaining a young, 'appealing' appearance (Featherstone and Hepworth, 1991). As a sign of visual distinction, the size, shape and look of the individual body is increasingly regarded as being 'on call' to be remoulded in line with changing ideals of body fashion. This is reflected in the growing number of businesses (from beauty and slimming salons, to tanning and toning studios, to cosmetic surgery clinics) which treat the body (and encourage their customers to treat their bodies) as an object to be managed, groomed and changed according to contemporary aesthetic norms.

The technological emphasis on performance and achievement has thus been extended from work to consumption. In the context of these developments the social milieu has become increasingly self-referential, excluding people from contact with transcendent or immanent forces outside its rational environs. Whereas individuals once subjected their bodies to mortification for religious ideals, they are now more likely to endure effort, expense, privation and pain in the hope of achieving performative goals related to appearance and the accumulation of physical capital. This 'enframing' of human action, furthermore, is not confined to the sphere of the social but is also associated with an increasingly instru-mentalist approach to the physical milieu. This becomes clear when we compare technological culture with its antecedents.

The physical milieu: technologically enframed nature

Technological culture seeks to harness to its logic the external *physical* environment as well as the social environment, and what Foucault referred to as the biopolitical ordering of society that developed in the nineteenth century, and accelerated in the twentieth century, treated nature as a resource to be exploited for worldy purposes and profits (Rutherford, 1993; Suzuki, 2002).[1] From being a phenomenon of awe and wonder, analysed by Marx as a source of religion itself, nature is viewed and treated by technological culture as mathematical, as measurable and as manageable. The ecological effects of this approach have been accompanied by growing concern about global warming, pollution, flooding, the erosion of agricul-tural heartlands and the extinction of species vital to the ecosystem. In the nineteenth and twentieth centuries alone, for example, the United States lost fifty per cent of its wetlands, ninety per cent of its northwestern old-grown forests, and ninety-nine per cent of its tall-grass prairies, while figures on energy consumption are even more remarkable. From 1940 to the end of the twentieth century, Americans used up as large a share of the earth's mineral resources as all previous generations combined (Suzuki, 2002).

In attempting to exert control over the physical environment, techno-logical culture possesses certain similarities with previous cultural formations. After all, if any society is to remain viable its norms, customs, rituals and practices must facilitate a minimum of control over its physical environment as well its social forms. It would be wrong to depict techno-logical culture as just an extension of previous ways of life, however, as this would overlook the qualitatively distinct and in many ways unique manner in which it seeks to structure the relationship between individuals and their physical surroundings. In pre-modern societies, hunting and gathering involved interacting with agentic beings and forces in the natural world (activities which included bargaining with 'non-humans or with the super-natural beings charged with their protection') (Szerszynski, 2005: 41). This immanent view of nature shares certain continuities with Taoist nar-ratives of the origin of humans (Shilling and Mellor, 2007), and also with those held by a number of more recent indigenous societies. The Micmac tribe of hunter-gatherers, for example, see the environment as a society in which animals, plants and inanimate objects are possessed of forces, spirits and super-human beings (Martin, 1978; Szerszynski, 2005: 35).

The development of monotheistic religions (Judaism, Christianity and Islam) during what Karl Jaspers (1953) calls the 'Axial Age', in contrast, located the perception of nature within a dualistic distinction between 'this world' and another, transcendent, world. As Szerszynski (2005: 18) expresses it, 'with divinity and agency progressively eradicated from the world of empirical phenomena' nature is seen as something which humans could and should control through the medium of work. This approach to the physical milieu was accentuated by Protestantism which, as mentioned previously, did much to advance the psychologisation of belief. Even here, however, the human engagement with the natural world received meaning in relation to its *transcendental* significance. Reinterpreting the Calvinist doctrine of predestination into an ethic which equated worldly success with divine favour, this earthly life was still imparted with meaning through the practical and bodily commitments necessitated by Puritan belief. Thus, even though Protestantism took steps to disenchant the physical environment, this process was far from complete. The Puritan settlers of North America, for example, drew on biblical ideas of the desert as a place for testing and spiritual purification in their depiction of the American wilderness (Albanese, 1990: 35–40; Szerszynski, 2005: 54).

Technological culture took a massive further step in redefining the human relation with nature as well as with the social milieu, however, by rupturing these environments from immanent *or* transcendent forces. As Heidegger (1993 [1954]) argues, the cumulative effect of technological culture resulted in a totalising enframing of our physical and social environment which objectifies these milieu as standing reserves ready to be called upon for the purposes of efficient performance. In this context, belief is psychologised and compartmentalised to the private sphere of human existence. People are entitled in their own time to express and act on the basis of religious values (as well as to hold them as private beliefs in the workplace), but technological culture excludes such principles from its own logic, diminishing the social and physical space that can be occupied legitimately by practical expressions of belief.

Technological culture undermined?

The environments of technological culture became increasingly influential during the twentieth century in the West, and pervaded apparently diverse and otherwise opposite social and political developments. While the Cold War was contested between two ideologically opposed power blocs, for example, communist and capitalist regimes were both predicated on attempting to maximise technological advancement and performative achievement. This is why the race to conquer space, and the emphasis on sporting success, assumed such symbolic significance (see Chapter 4). Despite its continued importance, however, there are increasing signs that the hegemony of technological culture is under threat.

First, there has been a resurgence of religious identification that is focused in the non-Western world but which has become increasingly influential in Europe and the United States. The most frequently cited cause of this resurgence in the Middle East and the Global South involves those processes of social, economic and cultural modernisation that became increasingly international in the second half of the twentieth century. Far from resulting in the world wide 'death of religion', as commonly predicted, these processes – which uprooted individuals from rural backgrounds and placed them in rapidly expanding cities – led to a renewed demand for religious community. In the case of Islam, for example, this revival has generally been an urban phenomenon appealing to people who are modern oriented, well-educated, and pursuing professional careers (Huntington, 2002 [1996]: 101). The Islamic world is also growing, and Islam has become 'Europe's second religion', a situation assisted by postcolonial flows of immigration and the establishment (often with aid from Arab governments) of large mosques in major cities (Ruthven, 1997: 15; Hunter and Serfaty, 2002: xiii; Lewis, 2002 [1994]; Rosen, 2002: 145–6). It is not just Islam that has witnessed a growth in recent decades, however, as Charismatic forms of Christianity have, alongside Catholicism, become increasingly visible in Africa, Asia and South America (Cox, 1995).

This religious revival has not just been confined to the non-Western world, but is also evident among those living *within* the technological culture of the West. On the one hand, part of this seems to be a direct response to the prominence of, and challenges apparently posed by, religions in the rest of the world. In a global context marked by increased tensions between nations and religions, it is perhaps no accident that a large majority of people in England and Wales, for example, commonly identify themselves as Christian. More generally, Draulans and Halman's (2005: 181) analysis of recent European Values surveys argues that a majority of people consider themselves to be religious even in countries where a large part of the population are 'unchurched' (see also Lambert, 2004). This may reflect an 'anxiety' about national identity, as Voas and Bruce (2004: 28) argue, but may also constitute a renewed commitment to a cultural identity that *includes* a particular religious heritage. In the United States there has been a longstanding commitment to the work ethic, associated contemporarily with technological culture, alongside a private expression of and affiliation to Christian values, and a general expectation that political leaders express their belief in God (Parsons, 1978). Since 9/11, however, there has been a renewed emphasis on America's 'Christian heritage' and a concern among the religious Right that the polity should be infused with religious values. On the other hand, this resurgence may also be a direct response to the perceived insufficiencies of technological culture. There has been a marked growth of 'new age' spiritualities within the West that explicitly reject the instrumentalisation of the embodied subject, for example, and Heelas et al., (2004) associate this with the growth of 'post-materialist' values. Surveys suggest that increasing numbers of people prize self-expression and subjective well-being over economic success or security (Inglehart, 1997). Furthermore, the New Age 'holistic milieu' has flourished at both local and national levels in recent decades as individuals seek out and participate in all manner of activities intended to reinstate a sense of the sacred in their lives (Heelas et al., 2004). This is reinforced by the proliferation of earth and nature-based forms of spirituality embedded in ecological perspectives which run directly counter to the productivist enframing of the physical milieu central to Western technology. Finally, no summary of possible religious revival in the West would be complete without mentioning what is probably its most important manifestation. Charismatic Christianity has not just grown in Africa and South America, but has become so popular within the West itself that it has prompted claims of a 'new reformation' (Cox, 1995). Hundreds of new Churches are being established every year in the West, and the hugely successful *Alpha Course* has provided a structured programme through which thousands of new adherents have sought to commune with God.[2] With the development of such activities, Charismatic Christianity is providing a new vehicle through which the performativity of technological culture in the West can be mediated by a sensory focus on *other worldliness*, as well as a renewed emphasis on Christian ethics in this world (Watling, 2005).

The second challenge to technological culture has less to do with the simple growth of religious identification outside and within the West, and more to do with the fact that this resurgence actually offers *different cultural models* for technology's deployment within society. With certain exceptions (including Islamic groups such as the Taliban, and sections of the Deep Green movement), the religious cultures mentioned above are rarely opposed to modernisation per se, yet each of them provides an alternative vision of the relationship between belief and technology in society. As Juergensmeyer (2000) explains, India's Jawaharlal Nehru, Egypt's Gamal Abdel Nasser and Iran's Reza Shah Pahlavi were once committed to creating an essentially Western technological culture in their own countries. With the perceived failure of post-colonial states, however, new generations of leaders no longer believed in the Westernised visions of Nehru, Nasser or the Shah. Instead, they were eager to complete the process of decolonisation and build new states that combined economic growth and technological progress with *indigenous* nationalism and religion. Modernisation in India, for example, has been accompanied by the rejection of Western forms and values, and the construction of a new Hindu identity (Pipes, 1983; Jelen, 1991; Kepel, 1994; Huntington, 2002 [1996]: 98–101). In Singapore during the early 1990s, leaders heralded the rise of Asia and contrasted the values of Confucian culture with the moral vacuity responsible for the 'decline of the West' (Huntington, 2002 [1996]: 98, 108). As new flows of migrants move around the world, and as the news media circulate information about these cultural responses at an unprecedented rate, more individuals in the West are exposed to these alternatives. The diverse forms, practices and social bases of different types of belief are starting to become increasingly visible to those living inside, as well as outside, of our technological culture. This visibility has been heightened further as a result of the recent spate of violent attacks launched upon the Pentagon, the World Trade Centre, and other major symbols of American and Western culture (Juergensmeyer, 2000).

It is no longer viable to claim, then, that the external environment in which technological culture operates is monolithic. Nevertheless, its impact in structuring people's lives remains potent, and many critics continue to suggest that it confronts individuals with major problems by making meaningful actions and identities difficult to sustain.

The phases of embodied action

Crisis and identity

Heidegger (1993 [1954]) emphasised the potency and pervasiveness of technological culture in the twentieth century, and suggested that its instrumentalising effects confronted humans with a major crisis. Initially the product of human action, technological culture threatened to rob people of their creative capacities. Similar assessments of the significance of technological culture for the internal environments of human action had reverberated earlier throughout classical sociological writings on such issues as the alienation of humans from their species being, the erosion of value-rational action by the increasing dominance of means–ends efficiency, and the dominance of cynicism over morally informed actions in the money economy. Furthermore, a growing variety of contemporary analyses, emanating from very different perspectives, have reached complementary conclusions in their suggestion that humans face a crisis as a result of being enveloped by a culture that denies them their evolutionarily developed needs for creative work and for contact with the living environment (e.g. Wilson, 1986; Suzuki, 2002: 176–8).

What unites these contrasting analyses is their judgement that it has become increasingly difficult for people to forge lives characterised by the interconnectedness of beliefs, bodily practices and social relations. Technological culture, so its critics argue, promotes the pursuit of material goals over the achievement of a meaningful continuity in our identities and actions (Berman, 1983). As numerous studies suggest, there appear to be a growing number of individuals who feel that the pressures of work, the pace of change and the emphasis placed on material success, has led to an emptying of values from their lives (e.g. Zizek, 2001; Anway, 1995; Bell, 2006; McGinty, 2006). While it may remain theoretically possible as an individual to maintain psychological belief in a set of values, it is difficult to maintain these as deeply meaningful when they can no longer be attached to social relations and practical actions in the workaday world of daily life.

As we have seen, though, the effects of technological culture on the internal environments of human being are neither guaranteed nor unchallenged by other cultural forms. Certain writers continue to espouse a secularisation thesis with regard to sections of Europe (Bruce, 2003). Yet, as Beyer (1994) has suggested, the international flows of people and ideas accompanying the development of technology (including in the late twentieth century an accelerated influx of Muslims into Europe) have resulted in a complex and in many ways a pluralistic situation (Yao, 2001; Rosen, 2002; Lambert, 2004; Parsons, 2004). Islam and Christianity remain significant global religions, while Heidegger himself looked to Christianity and Taoism to find resources to mitigate the negative aspects of technological culture (Petzet, 1993; Chan, 2003; Parkes, 2003; Elliot, 2004). The significance of religious values for people's lives within Western technological culture, moreover, has become clear in an increasing number of case studies.

Creative habits

If individuals can come to feel that their lives have been made instrumental, discontinuous and episodic as a result of living in the rationalised environs of modernity, James (1982 [1902]) explores a common Christian conversion motif in illustrating how religious experience can impart a renewed sense of being *emboldened*. By drawing on case studies, James notes how individuals experiencing the presence of God for the first time felt 'overcome', 'raised up' and a profound sense of fullness and peace associated with having transcended their previous sense of self (James, 1982 [1902]; see also Watling, 2005; Bell, 2006). In common with the above discussion about culturally specific notions of belief, it would be wrong to assume that narratives such as these (narratives which reiterate a historically Christian emphasis on inner experience and individual insight) represent universal experiences of becoming religious (van der Veer, 1996: 14–15). Other religious cultures place greater emphasis on involvement in practices associated with a gradual embodiment of a truth. Anway's (1995) and McGinty's (2006) studies of Western converts to Islam, for example, find some 'turning points' in the narratives of those they spoke to, but also identify a more common, incremental process of conversion involving reading, learning and interacting with other Muslims over considerable periods of time (a process which is perhaps more consistent with the Islamic idea that we were all born Muslims and that converts are simply 'coming home' to the 'one true faith'). However, this observation should not detract from the sense of fullness, completion, peace or renewed stability that frequently accompanies the embodiment of a great variety of religious beliefs, irrespective of how long that process takes. Nor should it lead us to overlook the crucial significance of socially sanctioned *embodied habits* in developing the huge variety of religious identities that exist in the world today. It is the existence of these habits, as well as their personal and social consequences, which provides us with evidence about their potential significance within technological culture.

James (1982 [1902]: 400) and Mauss (1973 [1934]) provide two of the better known examples of these habits in their analyses of the yoking together, through breath, of mind, spirit and body that occurs in Taoist techniques in China and in mystical practice in India. Other practical, culturally sanctioned body pedagogics are evident amongst Muslims living outside and within Europe. As Ruthven (1997) notes, routinised *behavioural conformity* has been far more important than doctrinal conformity for Muslim authorities: dissent on issues of leadership or theology has been more acceptable historically than deviation from what is regarded as acceptable *practice*. This is reflected in what can be considered the key means through which submission (Islam is the Arabic word for submission) to God is conveyed. *Salat* (prayer in the form of ritual prostration in which the precise bodily movements are as important as the accompanying mental activity) takes place five times a day and requires worshippers to have ritually purified themselves before facing Mecca in a common physical bond with all other Muslims (Ruel, 1982: 22). *Salat* is one of the 'five pillars' of Islam and reflects the more general emphasis placed on practice by these obligations. Thus, the *declaration of faith* requires verbal witness and declaration. *Zala* involves the giving of alms. *Fasting* during the holy month of Ramadan is obligatory, and is meant to stimulate a purification of the heart and the remembrance of God's trials. Finally, the *pilgrimage to Mecca* is a once-in-a-lifetime requirement which in the past could take a Muslim years to complete.

These 'five pillars' show the significance of bodily techniques to Muslim religiosity; to be a Muslim is to be actively oriented to this world, and to paradise, in particular ways. Religion here is not a compartmentalised, purely psychological activity, but is integrated within an individual's existence as a whole. Hence the importance for Muslims of interacting with, and gaining support from, other Muslims, an emphasis that extends frequently for converts into the realm of marriage. All of the Western women converts interviewed by McGinty (2006: 103), for example, expressed 'a desire to be "discovered" and recognised as a Muslim woman by a male spouse', a desire which resulted in marriage to a Muslim man.

The physical act of praying is key to Muslims but prayer also has a more general relevance as an habitual expression of faith. As Simmel (1997: 67) notes, the arrangement of the body in Christian prayer traditionally involved kneeling and a bringing together of the body's extremities in a manner which enhanced the physical compactness, the wholeness and the symbolic unity of the physical self. Furthermore, while belief within technological culture may have become psychologised, the resurgence of Charismatic Christianity in the West has lent a much more physical and social dimension to worship that is designed to make faith an embodied habit as much as a reflexive commitment. In their aim of facilitating direct contact with God, for example, Charismatic Christians seek to utilise *all* of the senses in processes of communion which involve repeated, ongoing and very public forms of prayer, touch and song (Watling, 2005). In this context, while the experience of being 'born again' may involve an epiphany and an overwhelming sense of transformation, it also needs to be instilled in individuals at an habitual level which incorporates culturally sanctioned bodily techniques of prayer and other Christian practices.

The significance of habitual action is also evident in the proliferation of New Age and Green spiritualities evident in the West. At first appearance, the 'pick "n" mix' variety of such activities would seem to indicate the prevalence of a reflexive approach towards these faiths by modern consumers 'shopping' around for new and fulfilling experiences (Aupers and Houtman, 2006). Even here, however, the great variety of activities associated with this development, such as tai chi chuan and yoga, encourage physical techniques designed to stimulate a new experience of the embodied self. Deep Green Ecology, for example, is explicit in trying to link one's orientation to the body to a renewed appreciation of nature as a sacred environment (Taylor, 2001a). Even everyday 'green consumerism' involves a bodily ritualisation of belief 'both in the sense of investing everyday actions – shopping, cooking, discarding – with sacred significance, and in terms of involving a certain habituation of bodily action' (Szerszynski, 2005: 138). As Szerszynski continues, recycling and green consumerism are less to do with a constant purposive process of self-questioning than with the development of 'habits of hand and eye – the sorting of rubbish into different bins, the orientation towards iconic brands such as Ecover and Suma and so on' (ibid.; Harrison et al., 1994: 10–11). Once more, group sanctioned embodied habits are not incidental to the development of religious or spiritual values, but are creative forces key to the provision of alternative ways of acting within the environs of technological culture.

Religious character

James (1982 [1902]) makes the point that developing religious belief commonly provides individuals with the sense of being 'in a wider life' than they had previously inhabited; a life marked by meaning and consistency. This observation may be of limited applicability to the compartmentalised form of belief characteristic of technological culture, but certainly seems to capture an important point about practically and socially based religious belief systems. Indeed, Simmel (1997: 47–8) suggests that individuals who give and take from their environment on the basis of coherent spiritual actions, commitments and values, not only gain a sense of belonging to 'a larger whole' but contribute towards the fulfilment of their personalities.

We have already examined how living within technological culture makes this continuity extremely difficult, yet studies show time and again that people do seek to align their lives on the basis of such broader religious commitments. McGinty (2006: 166) provides a number of examples of how the Western Muslim converts she interviewed coped with prejudice and discrimination in their work by asserting their distinctive sense of self in opposition to local norms. Refusing to hide her identity any longer, one woman convert confronted her employer by insisting that she should be able to wear a veil at the office and threatening to pursue a discrimination grievance if this was opposed. Other Muslims have sought to align various aspects of their lives around pragmatic interpretations of what being Islamic in Europe involves (Rosen, 2002). While this can involve compromise, it can also require of individuals much hard work in undertaking what they see to be their religious duties. Female converts are an important force in the formation of what has been referred to as a 'Swedish Islam', for example, initiating and sustaining religious networks which play an important role in civil society (McGinty, 2006: 154). One woman who undertook school visits in order to talk about being a Muslim explains how draining this can be:

> You do your best to show that you don't match the stereotypes ... You show that you are like any other human being, able to laugh and cry. When visiting senior high school the students often ask about sex and such and then you have to give a lot of yourselves. It is good that there are no other Muslims present listening because sometimes it feels like you go too far. You really show them that you are a human being of flesh and blood. (cited in McGinty, 2006)

In contrast, those individuals who develop New Age spiritualities in the West may have more flexibility to align their actions according to a range of alternatives – alternatives which many would suggest are ready made for contemporary consumer culture – but even here there is much evidence of a real commitment that impinges on many aspects of their lives. Aupers and Houtman (2006: 207), for example, note a growing incompatibility between the spiritual commitments of their New Age respondents and the demands of business life; an incompatibility which eventually became intolerable and resulted in changes of job for some of their subjects. In a similar vein, Hollinger (2004: 305) notes how the 'striving for self-perfection in the context of the New Age movement' is associated with social and political *activism* rather than an egoistic absenteeism from the public sphere (see also Heelas et al., 2004). In these cases there are clear attempts to intervene in and change the external environment.

Attempts to organise one's identity and life around a religious character clearly vary on the basis of what is possible within a particular time and place, yet many individuals are uncompromising in undertaking actions they view as consistent with a particular religious identity irrespective of their personal and social consequences. For example, the Reverend Michael Bray was convicted of a series of attacks on abortion clinics in the United States and compared his actions with those who fought against the Nazis (Juergensmeyer, 2000: 20). Having been convicted of participating in the attack on the World Trade Centre, Mahmud Abouhalima talked of realising that he could no longer compromise his Islamic integrity by participating in the 'easy vices' offered by Western society, and of experiencing a 'renewed sense of obligation' to 'struggle against oppression and injustice' wherever it existed (ibid.: 222).

A consideration of actions such as those described above throws into sharp contrast the difference between belief as an individualised, psychologised phenomenon congruent with the performative demands of technological culture, and the possible implications of belief as a thoroughly practical and social form of action. The extent to which religious belief-practice systems provide an alternative to Western technological culture will obviously vary, but radical actions such as those above leave us in no doubt as to their consequentiality for societies based on an instrumental rationalism. They also raise issues regarding the broader moral cultures promoted by particular religious and spiritual forms.

The divergent moralities of religious cultures

Max Weber's writings on religion are best known for their analysis of the 'ethic of world transforming mastery' that lay at the heart of Puritanism and which preceded the dominance of technological instrumentalism (Weber, 1991 [1904–05]). In disenchanting the world and displacing the sacred to the transcendent sphere of the afterlife, Protestantism individualised and isolated individuals as moral beings committed to a *this-worldly* engagement with their environment according to God's Word. Engagement with this world was never an end in itself within Christianity, however, as it was always related to the importance of the *other-worldly* sphere. Through baptism and various forms of communion, Christians have also been called out of this world in order to become reborn as new embodied creations in relation to God's transcendent kingdom (John, 15: 19; Ephesians, 4: 22, 5: 1). This is reflected in the distinction Christianity has made between the 'Spiritual' realm of the Church and the 'Temporal' realm of politics, economics and society, and provides an ethical basis for Christian attempts to intervene in and change *this* world in order to facilitate engagements with the *next* world (Black, 1993: 59). Thus, Parsons (1978) suggests that while contemporary American life is underpinned by an 'institutionalised individualism', this individualism is not without boundaries but is predicated on the Christian 'gift of life' which exhorts followers to do all they can to live this life in a manner which prepares them for eternal life.

In contrast to this Christian ethic (which involves an engagement in this world *in order to* prepare for the next), the Islamic faith can be associated with an ethic of world transforming *reclamation*. Believing that we are all born initially as members of their faith, Muslims have traditionally divided the world into the sphere of peace and Islam (*dar al-Islam*) where this natural state exists, and the sphere of war (*dar al-harb*) where it does not. Within this context, Muslims have an individual and collective obligation to engage in struggle or *Jihad*. Struggle in the path of God (*jihad fi sabil allah*) is, in the Qur'an, a central injunction upon all followers, and has always been one of the major defining features of a distinctively Muslim identity. Distinguished into two broad categories, concerning the struggle for Islamic hegemony (in relation to other religions and the interests of Muslims over non-Muslims in the socio-political sphere), and the struggle within the Islamic community to live, 'body and soul', in a manner pleasing to God, it is understood as a means of separating true belief from infidelity (Heck, 2004: 96–7). Thus, *jihad* cannot be associated only with armed struggle – the struggle is as 'internal' to individuals and the community as 'external' to it – but it does raise important issues about the extent to which the moral culture of Islam allows its followers to integrate socially with members of other faiths. Indeed, Asad (1993: 219) goes so far as to argue that Muslims can only accommodate themselves to public life in the West if they forgo their identities as Muslims. In this respect, it is interesting that Lewis's research (2002 [1994]: 70, 141, 224) details the 'cultural self-sufficiency' and the 'closed system' to which Muslims belong in Bradford, England. This system bolsters their Muslim identities through ongoing links with South Asia, facilitated by satellite television and the Internet, and enables them to 'continue to set themselves morally apart from British society'. Similarly, Rex's (2002: 72) evaluation of private Muslim schools suggests that they 'appear to be preparing their students for living in a Muslim society that does not exist in Britain'.

Christians and Muslims have lived together for centuries, but their moral cultures have not made for easy coexistence. Both Christianity and Islam are monotheistic religions which cannot assimilate easily to their practices additional deities and which view the world in dualistic us-and-them terms. Both are universalistic in their claims to be the one true faith, and both are missionary religions which invest their followers with an obligation to convert non-believers (Huntington, 2002 [1996]: 210–11). Islam expanded by force from its very beginnings, and its proliferation throughout the world 'has been attributed in no small measure to the success of its military leaders in battle' (Bonner, 1992, 1996; Juergensmeyer, 2000: 80). Christianity responded to this via the crusades, which also involved mass killings and forced conversions, and has a history of using violence to enforce doctrinal conformity during such periods as the Inquisition. Contemporarily, of course, the moral forces of Islam and Christianity have been prominent cultural themes in American-dominated military action in Iraq. This is the reason why Huntington (2002 [1996]: 247) referred to the Gulf war as a 'civilisation war'. Westerners generally supported the first Gulf War, while 'Muslims throughout the world came to see that intervention as a war against them and rallied against what they saw as one more instance of Western imperialism' (ibid.). Since that 'rallying' has subsequently involved a series of terrorist attacks on Western soil by extremist Islamic groups, questions about the extent to which Christian and Islamic cultures can coexist peacefully have intensified rather than subsided.

Religious cultures do not always exist in tension with each other, however, or with their social or physical environments. In contrast to Christianity and Islam, Weber (1964) analysed Taoism and Confucianism in China as promoting an 'ethic of world adjustment'. Without any satanic force of evil against which to struggle, and living in a cosmos characterised by a harmonious order in which it was ethically improper to make oneself an 'end' for any external goal, there was no basis on which technological rationalism or an ethic of world mastery or reclamation could follow (Weber, 1964; Kirkland, 2004). Instead, action should occur 'in line with the nature of things' (Capra, 1999: 117), and life should be marked by cultivating a relationship with the world that was *aligned*, rather than in tension, with its inner workings. Being replaces doing, while harmonising one's own energies with the *yin* and *yang* forces that pervade the natural order facilitates an emboldening of the individual in a manner which vitalises the social body as well as the embodied self (Graham, 1989: 197; Kirkland, 2004: 189, 208). Given the pace of economic development in China, it is understandable that such an ethic of adjustment has been accused of doing little more than enabling one 'to fully participate in the frantic pace of the capitalist game while sustaining the perception that you are not really in it' (Zizek, 2001: 15). Traditional aspects of Chinese life have flourished alongside these economic developments, however, and continue to offer for many a spiritual life embedded in the social and natural environment (Kirkland, 2004).

The fourth and final religious culture I want to mention in this section was anticipated by the likes of Durkheim and Simmel and can be viewed as associated with an 'ethic of individual religiosity'. Durkheim distinguished between 'a religion handed down by tradition' and 'a free, private, optional religion, fashioned according to one's own needs and understanding' (cited in Pickering, 1975: 96). This private religion was associated closely with the developing 'cult of the individual' that Durkheim mapped in social and cultural life and which involved 'the glorification not of the self but of the individual in *general*' (Durkheim, 1973 [1898]: 48–9; 1984 [1893]). Writing from a very different philosophical perspective, Simmel (1997) saw religiosity as involving the fulfilment of personality in a manner which developed to its highest extent the specific individuality of the subject. The implications of Durkheim's and Simmel's views of individual religiosity are quite different (Shilling and Mellor, 2001), but can be seen as illuminating distinctive aspects of the growth of New Age spiritualities in the West. Thus, Redden (2005: 231) points out that while the New Age 'movement' possesses no overarching organisation, it is concerned with both personal and collective transformation, the sacralisation of the inner self alongside holistic conceptions of nature and the cosmos, and a recognition that there are many different paths towards spiritual fulfilment. Of course, many individuals who engage in New Age activities are involved in Western translations of Eastern practices which may, as Singleton (2005) suggests, do little more than encourage the individual to relax. For many others, though, there has been a linkage of the personal and the collective through an emphasis on the environment and the development of spiritualities that promote an ethic of individual *and* social responsibility. Here, the world is viewed as an interrelated, living totality on which the future of humanity depends (Taylor, 2001a,b; Szerszynski, 2005).

Conclusion

Sociological analyses of the global influence of Western forms of technology and consumer culture rarely attribute much significance to the importance of belief in mediating and shaping their significance. Instead, belief is often viewed from within the perspective of technological culture as an individualised and psychologised phenomenon that exists increasingly only in the private spheres of people's existence. This not only misrepresents alternative forms of belief that are inextricably bound up with embodied habits and specific communities, but also presents an oversocialised picture of the individual as a subject unable to act differently. Technological culture may encourage people to become individualised and compartmentalised beings, 'standing ready' for the demands of productivity wherever they may occur, but it can also impoverish experience and encourage other cultural responses to living in the modern world. These responses may provide individuals who pursue them with valuable resources through which they are able to reorder their lives. It may also provide them with a basis on which to construct alternative framings of technology.

The importance of these alternative cultural framings has been questioned by those who see them as no more than ideological glosses on the global spread of capitalism. Zizek (2001: 12), for example, dismisses the growth of Eastern religions and spiritualities in the West as a prophylactic against the stresses of a high speed economy. This approach not only treats religious culture as an epiphenomenon, however, but overlooks just how significant Western and non-Western challenges to the *values* of technological culture have been. Thus, the fact that Charismatic Christianity can enthusiastically use media technologies to spread its message across the globe (Coleman, 2000; Noll, 2001; see also MacWilliams, 2002), while simultaneously promoting 'rituals of rupture' that seek to lift individuals out of the enframing of technological culture, means that 'it would be a mistake to reduce it to a mere reflex of the modern' (Robbins, 2004: 137; Droogers, 2001: 54). Islam has embraced the Internet and television to spread its message and maintain a community of believers among its followers dispersed across the world's continents. Similarly, in contrast to fears amongst some scholars that Taoism would suffer in the face of the adoption of Western rational utilitarianism in economic practices (Parkes, 2003), the spread of globalising forms of technology, economics and culture in China has actually led to a *renewal* of traditional religious practices (Yang, 2000).

Despite embracing technology and modernisation it would be wrong to suggest that these, or many other, religious cultures promote instrumentalisation at the expense of transcendent or immanent experiences of the sacred. Hinduism has a long tradition of sacralising nature, for example, while Taoism views the social and physical environments as structured according to the universal forces of *yin* and *yang* (forces that also inhere within the embodied subject) (Coogan, 2005). Instead of dismissing the importance of religious cultures, then, it may make more sense to see their continuation and resurgence in terms of their concern to nurture types of lived experience that invest individuals with a sense of meaning. For all their differences, they are all associated with embracing forms of belief that transcend the individualised, psychologised version accepted as the norm within technological culture. In divesting humans and nature with meaning, indeed, technological culture helped create a void that was ready to be filled by belief systems that could not be confined to the individual and to the mind (Szerszynski, 2005: 18). Weber (1991 [1904–05]) suggested that Protestantism dug its own grave by helping to usher in a capitalist system that no longer needed its ethic. In emptying its own environs of meaning, however, the technological culture that has emerged from advanced capitalism may just have provided the conditions for its own supersession. If the instrumental rationalism of technology in the West is mediated by other cultural influences, however, serious questions remain about the extent to which a resurgence of competing and sometimes antagonist religious practices might contribute to an increase rather than a decrease of global patterns of conflict.

Notes

1 This view of the physical environment as a natural, ecological resource that has been rationalised by technology is frequently depicted as a discursive product of specific social developments and epistemic regimes (Franklin, 2001; Macnaghten and Urry, 2001). However, it would be a mistake to analyse all 'narratives of nature' as social constructions which exist at equal distance from the ontological conditions of what it is to be a human being in particular times and places. Such an approach would overlook just how exceptional technological culture's approach to nature has been, and would also disallow for the possibility that technological culture poses specific, material problems for human being.

2 This development has, however, coexisted with a declining rate of participation in traditional Christian Churches across much of Britain and Europe (Bruce, 2003; Heelas et al., 2004; Thomson, 2006).

10

Conclusion

Sociology's focus on the corporeal dimensions of social action has proven extraordinarily productive. It has facilitated a new perspective on traditional disciplinary problems and dualisms, has encouraged abstract theories to refocus on the material realities of people's lives and has also provided many of the foundations for the interdisciplinary field of 'body studies'. The need for the discipline to go *beyond* bodily behaviour in order to demonstrate the social consequentiality of our physical existence, however, continues to confront analysts with a serious challenge. In seeking to provide a rounded account of the collective phenomenon of *society* without losing touch with the experiencing and active *body-subject*, structuralist and action-oriented approaches have struggled. Despite their best attempts, these theories have ended up portraying either the embodied individual or society as something of an 'absent-presence'. While the material facticity and consequentiality of the body fades from the gaze of the former, it is the relationships, roles, regularities of occurrence and norms and values of social groups that recede into the distant horizons of the latter. Structurationist attempts to solve this problem, furthermore, have yet to prove successful. For all their undoubted inventiveness, the writings of Bourdieu, Grosz, Giddens and others – who engage in what Archer (1995) described as 'central conflationism' – end up reproducing already existing society within the individual body, or positing the embodied subject as the author of all that surrounds them (Shilling, 2005a).

This is where the pragmatist preparedness to recognise the distinctive properties of social relations and their physical surroundings, on the one hand, and of embodied subjects, on the other, is potentially so fruitful. By acknowledging that embodied action is always conducted in an existing external environment, it acknowledges the crucial insight of structuralist theories. By also insisting that the individuals who engage with their surroundings possess emergent capacities and needs, developed over the *longue durée* of human evolution, it also manages to place the crucial insight of individualist theories on a stable footing. Having attributed importance to both the context and the embodied actor, pragmatism then encourages us to analyse embodied action, experience and identity as resulting from the *dynamic interactions* and *transactions* that occur between the external and internal environments. These environments vary in their significance, but these variations are something to be *explored* rather than assumed.

Again, while structuralist or individualist approaches to embodied action tend to assume the causal primacy and efficacy of one or other, pragmatism remains open to processes of flux and change.

It was on the basis of this interpretation that Chapter 2 organised discussion of pragmatism into a flexible framework that could be used to examine the environments of embodied action across diverse areas of human life. Similarly, Chapter 3 interpreted the achievements of the Chicago School of Sociology from this same perspective. In both chapters, discussion moved from the social and physical milieu, to the actions of embodied subjects living in this external environment (informed as these phases of actions are by people's needs and capacities), to the effects of these interactions on character and, finally, to the collective and potentially transformative capacity of groups. My reasons for interpreting and organising the insights of pragmatism in this way were not just theoretical, however, but concerned their potential for being deployed in substantive studies. This is why the bulk of this book is taken up with analyses of issues as diverse as the Holocaust, migration, illness and transgenderism. These areas were chosen as they allow us to explore the relationship between bodily change and social action in circumstances that confront people with radically different opportunities for self-determination. They also provided us with a mix of social activities related directly to modern, technological society, on the one hand, and to aspects of human life more anthropological in their general applicability to human being on the other. Having devoted this space to the application of a broadly pragmatist framework to these areas, though, are there any *general* conclusions that follow from these discussions?

Given its acknowledgement of contingency and sensitivity to the possibilities of change, any attempt to extract overarching theories or grand narratives from these studies would go against the spirit of the pragmatically informed framework utilised in this book. Nevertheless, this framework has yielded several key themes that have been discussed in each chapter. In addition, it has also touched on important issues regarding what it is to be an embodied human being. In this conclusion, I want to approach these by focusing on the issue of *transcendence*; an issue which extends the traditional distinction made in this area between *being* and *having* a body (see Turner, 1984; Frankenberg, 1990; Burkitt, 1999).

The substantive studies in this book repeatedly provide examples of embodied subjects able to *transcend* their purely organic being by *attending to* their own bodies and to the bodies of others. In contrast to the charge that sociological studies of the body engage in an inverted Cartesianism, these chapters demonstrate that the body is not irrelevant to the issue of meaningful social action or to the issue of what it is to be human. Instead, it is the body itself that provides people with the means to go beyond the limits of their purely biological existence. It is by *living in*, *living with*, *attending to* and *caring for* one's own body and the bodies of others, that people become embodied beings with a *wide range* of capacities and potentialities.

Some of the most dramatic examples of this human capacity for transcendence are provided by the Nazi concentration camps and the Soviet labour camps, examined in Chapter 8. Here, people were kept in conditions that made life difficult and even impossible, and were treated by their captors as either sub-human lumps of flesh to be disposed of as quickly as possible or, at best, as labouring bodies made to work up to, and beyond, the point of exhaustion. The moral actions many camp inmates managed to undertake in the most appalling of circumstances, however, demonstrated that not even these environments dehumanised all those subject to them. Yet it was by engaging in physical rituals such as washing and attending to the bodily needs of themselves and others that inmates managed to retain their existence as human beings possessed of more than just a physical organism. These apparently mundane physical techniques actually constituted a means through which inmates were able to garner the strength and moral courage to carry on with life, and to retain a subjectivity that maintained a distance from the objectifying practices of camp life.

The Nazi and Soviet camps constitute extreme examples of political oppression, but processes which apparently work towards reducing individuals to their bodies (albeit it in a very different manner and with very different consequences) are far from alien to contemporary society. Indeed, the performative dimensions of that technological culture dominant in the West evaluate people as bodily *objects* in a number of distinct, yet complementary, ways. In the field of sport examined in Chapter 4, for example, we saw how there is a tendency for elite athletes to be treated as (and to treat themselves as) body-machines whose lives are regulated down to the last detail by training regimes which govern their diet, activity and even sleep patterns. This objectification does not, however, necessarily reduce athletes to an exclusive preoccupation with their organic bodies. Even repetitive and gruelling training schedules could result occasionally in the experience of a transcendent sense of flow akin to a religious experience (James, 1982 [1902]; Jackson and Csikszentmihalyi, 1999). More generally, forms of sport and exercise are not homogenous. In this context, activities such as yoga and tai chi chuan, may involve enormous amounts of effort and a highly disciplined approach to the body, but are focused on seeking to bring together mind, spirit and body in a way that enables practitioners to achieve a communion between, and a union with, forces that exist outside, as well as inside, their bodies.

The productive expectations informing the 'health role', examined in Chapter 7 and possessed of several parallels with the norms of performative sport, are based around the demand of maintaining the body as a fit and flexible resource (Frank, 1991a). As admittance to the traditional 'sick role' becomes more policed and stigmatised, and the contingencies associated with human frailty are disregarded, there is a tendency for people to be perceived increasingly in terms of their capacity for maintaining a fit and active body (Gestaldo, 1997). In this instance, people's worth is tied to their performative health and productive capacity, and the accumulation of economic and social capital is significantly dependent on the maintainance of physical capital. Yet sickness and impairment do not necessarily reduce people's field of experience to their organic bodies, and Chapter 7 reported on how people who were seriously and even terminally ill were able to take an aesthetic and sometimes deeply spiritual delight in the 'small things' of life or, more generally, in the 'wonder of existence' (Frank, 1995). Attending to the new horizons forced on them by their disease did not necessarily result in an experience of helplessness and hopelessness, then, but could sometimes enable individuals to reach beyond the ordinary boundaries of their organic being.

Related examples of people being objectified as bodies, rather than being treated as embodied human beings equipped with a range of capacities and potentialities, were discussed as part of wider analyses in Chapters 5, 6 and 9. Chapter 5, *Presenting*, explored how many transgendered people struggle with a deep sense of being born into the wrong body. Seeking to alter their bodies, to match more closely their sense of self, is only one of the challenges facing these individuals. In addition, transpeople must also cope with the widespread tendency that exists in the sphere of co-present interaction to assign identity on the basis of appearance (Kessler and McKenna, 1978). This visual objectification presents a particular problem to those transgendered individuals who experience a deep discontinuity between their appearance and their subjective sense of self-identity. It is by changing their bodies and working on their habits and appearances, however, that these individuals are able potentially to transcend elements of their previous existence and achieve a greater degree of fit and congruence between their identities and their flesh.

Chapter 6, *Moving*, examined how the refugee and holding camps, border controls, human trafficking and exploitation linked with contemporary global flows of people exert a major cost on those subject to them. Being treated as commodities to be bought and sold into slavery or indentured labour, or problems to be held in camps, or productive resources granted temporary residence because of their value to the economy, can devastate the identities of these people. Even those who migrate legally can find themselves experiencing prejudice and discrimination which objectifies their bodily appearance as 'other' and 'inferior' (Sayad, 2004), or feeling 'empty' and 'lost' as a result of leaving behind their own families and communities (Ehrenreich and Hochschild, 2002). Interestingly, though, it is those who receive some degree of recognition and validation for their habits, customs, appearances and religious practices (often through contact with existing communities of migrants) who are best able to cope with the privations of their new existence and the ruptures from their past (Smith and Tarallo, 1993; Moorehead, 2006). Again, rather than being reduced to their bodies, these individuals are able to maintain or regain a sense of self-respect by receiving favourable recognition of their bodily being from *others*. This illustrates the broader point that transcendence is not something that occurs on the basis of isolated, completely privatised techniques, but has a social and practical foundation.

This mention of religion brings us onto the final substantive chapter, *Believing*. Chapter 9 explored how the centrality of technological culture within affluent nation-states has implications for the character and place of 'belief' in the modern West. Individualised and psychologised, belief has been viewed as a private matter of commitment and expression possessed of a place and significance *outside* of the rationalised environs of the workplace. In this context, people's attempts to achieve a degree of transcendence in relation to the performative principles which pervade work, and so much consumer culture, are expected to accommodate themselves to these structures rather than potentially structuring them. This is one of the reasons that many migrants find life in the West so difficult (Taghmaian, 2005). The notion of belief as individual and psychological is a relatively recent and culturally specific phenomenon, however, and it has not gone unchallenged (Asad, 1993). Indeed, the rational 'enframing' of people and nature associated with technological culture in the West not only erodes meaning from human life, expelling the spiritual and sacred from its borders. It also creates the conditions in which it is possible for other cultural forms of belief to challenge its principles from outside and within its parameters. Islamic nations have often embraced technology, for example, but have developed it on the basis of cultural principles that are very different from those evident in the West. Islam is not unique in its attempts to employ technology within a distinctive cultural basis, moreover, and faiths and spiritualities from Charismatic Christianity to 'new age' movements have sought to mitigate the effects of technological culture in the West (Shilling and Mellor, 2007). None of these can be analysed adequately as purely individual or psychological forms of belief, as they are embedded deeply in practical actions and social relations. In particular, it is by engaging in repetitive physical rites over a long period of time that people *become* the religious subjects they seek to be, possessed of distinctive dispositions to themselves and their external environment.

If these discussions demonstrate how the body provides us with the means to become more than our organic being, they also provide examples of the body's centrality to death. This may seem a banal, unnecessary observation on the grounds that a (living) body is obviously a prerequisite to human life. However, if attending to our fleshy, bodily being provides people with a means of transcending their immediate bodily needs and daily experiences, particular types of bodily neglect are associated closely with a *withdrawal from* and a *giving up on* life. I am not talking here about the highly structured and disciplined asceticism of those religious devotees who undertake lengthy fasts or put themselves through ordeals which can inflict great damage on the body and result in death. Such activities constitute less of a withdrawal from the body than a flight into a religiously structured physicality (Bynum, 1987; Mellor, 1991). In contrast, the neglect of the body evident in the *Muselmänner*, as they were called in the German camps, was associated with an abandonment of life (Amery, 1999 [1966]). A similar process was observed in the Soviet camps as certain prisoners stopped washing themselves, stopped controlling their bowels, stopped having normal human reactions and became close to being lifeless chunks of human flesh.

It is possible to develop parallels between this giving up on life and Durkheim's (1952 [1897]: 276) analysis of fatalistic suicide, a category applied to those 'with futures pitilessly blocked and passions violently choked by oppressive discipline'. Durkheim suggested that this type of suicide was only of historical interest, but in identifying it as relevant to those who take their life as a consequence of suffering from slavery or excessive despotism he allows us to see its continued relevance. It is not simply the positioning of individuals within, or outside, sets of social relations that is relevant to this abandonment of life, however, but people's orientation to their *bodies*.

A very different, but still pertinent, example of those unable to achieve any 'going beyond' of their organic being involves those who could no longer care for their bodies during sickness. Lawton's (1998) research into hospice care found repeated cases of individuals who had lost all control over their bodies, and for whom the shock of physical decay proved too much. Instead of being able to care for their bodies, there was here a process of 'psychic closure' in which the self-identity of the patient 'shut down' and effectively died ahead of the death of the flesh.

Finally, although it does not necessarily result in a 'giving up' on life, the suffering endured by those dispossessed travellers examined in Chapter 6 was based in part on the hostility or even lack of recognition accorded to their habits, appearances and customs. Although the existence of an established migrant community could impart recognition and respect to their bodily being, emboldening them to become economically, socially and even politically active, a lack of respectful recognition was associated with a feeling of being ill-at-ease, homeless and desperate (Moorehead, 2006). Those sold into the sex trade (or into slavery or indentured labour) faced an even bleaker future, sometimes being unable to conceive of their identities in any way other than their status as commodities (e.g. Bales, 2002).

This point about the centrality of the body to human being raises a closely related point about corporeal *experience*. Leder's writings on 'the absent body' have proven influential in their suggestion that it is normal for the direct experience of our bodies to 'fade away' while we are engaged in purposeful tasks (Leder, 1990). Across a range of social, political and spiritual activities, however, it seems that people are able to engage in embodied actions and encounter the variety of human experiences that exist as a result of *engaging with* their bodies. This does not rule out the importance of the body 'fading away' from our consciousness, but Leder's focus is partial as it does not attend to the distinctive body pedagogics that both facilitate and result in quite specific experiences of physical transcendence. Neither does it enable us to illuminate the experiences of transgendered subjects, for example, who feel a chronic dys-ease with their bodies as a result of feeling that they inhabit the wrong type of body.

The notion of an 'absent body' as a way of approaching experience is highly suggestive, however, when it comes to describing how technological culture views the body in the contemporary West. As we have seen, technological culture has approached the body increasingly as a performative resource (Heidegger, 1993 [1954]), and this places many people in a difficult situation. In a marketplace that values health so much, entry into the 'sick role' is regulated and often stigmatised, whereas those who do not possess the sizes, shapes and appearance prized within consumer culture live in a context where cosmetic surgery and other radical body modification techniques are not only available but are increasingly fashionable. The demands of performativity have reached people at younger ages too, and this is evident in the sphere of elite sport. It is not surprising that in a culture where parents enrol their offspring in training programmes at the age of three or four years the term 'battered child athlete' has become commonplace (Wilkinson, 1984; Hargreaves, 1994).

These are manifestations of the many ways in which people are being encouraged to discipline their bodies according to the norms of the external environment of technological culture, and to reduce any *dys-ease* they may feel in doing this. Television is awash with programmes in which people describe as a moral virtue how they put up with the pain of cosmetic surgery, the hunger induced by strict diets, and the discomfort and injuries associated with rigorous training regimes in order to achieve their goals. The body is to be tamed and silenced, not listened to, in order to achieve instrumental goals pertaining to appearance or performance. Thus, the notion of the 'absent body' may not be a valid general account of embodied experience, but it can be seen as an important contribution to understanding the possible effects of technological culture in the West.

The pressures placed on people to absent themselves from their own experiences – in favour of treating their bodies as productive resources in the spheres of work and consumer culture – may help explain the resurgence of activities and forms of belief that enable people to mitigate this situation. Individuals have drawn on belief practices in responding creatively to the potential difficulties associated with living in Western technological culture, for example, while the global force of Islam and the resurgence of Charismatic Christianity provide distinctive visions of technological culture which challenge its instrumentalist parameters.

The relationship between attending to the body and transcending the limits of purely organic existence also has implications for the issue of identity or *character*. It has become very fashionable in analyses of postmodernity to suggest that the notion of identity as something which is more or less fixed is an Enlightenment myth. Far more accurate, so the argument goes, is a recognition of the hybridity and fluidity of contemporary identities

(Haraway, 1994 [1985]). Up to a point, the pragmatist-informed framework utilised in this book is highly sympathetic to the flux and change that is at the centre of this notion of identity. However, pragmatism's concern with habit, and its recognition of the facticity of the body, also displays a sensitivity to the fact that many people have a deeply embedded sense of who they are. This is especially prominent in the chapters on *Presenting* and *Moving*. As numerous studies that have been conducted into migration show, people migrate with their existing histories, habits and bodies, and often experience an enormous sense of dislocation between their existing self-identity and their new external environment (Sayad, 2004). In these circumstances, there is often a search for existing immigrant communities that can provide the recognition and validation of self-identity otherwise missing from their new lives. This is also often associated with a renewed commitment to a religious heritage, and is one of the reasons behind the growth of Islam in the West (Ruthven, 1997: 15; Hunter and Serfaty, 2002: xiii; Lewis, 2002 [1994]; Rosen, 2002: 145–6).

Transsexuals determined to change their bodies to match their sense of self provide another example of how identity can be more stable than allowed for in many theories. While some transpeople enjoy and gain pleasure from playing with the boundaries of male and female, many experience severe difficulties coping with being born into a body from which they feel deeply alienated. For these individuals, their sense of sexed identity is so strong that the only option they feel open to them involves radical hormonal and surgical treatment (see Green, 2004; Rudacille, 2006). This example also illustrates the point that while the properties of the body may not determine individual identity, they are irreducibly important in the ongoing construction of identity.

If the feeling of being born into the wrong body suggests there are limits to how generally relevant notions of identities-in-flux are, so too does the experience of illness. The assault on the self that pain, illness and impairment represent for many can promote a feeling of lost identity even for those who feel they have the most fluid of selves. It is one thing to wonder who you are and to feel ambivalent about your sense of priorities and values when you are relatively well. It seems that far fewer people are in doubt about what they want to regain and maintain about themselves, however, when faced with acute or terminal illness.

The final issue I want to deal with in this conclusion concerns the relevance of attending to and 'going beyond' the body for our concern with those *collective actions* that can have a particularly significant impact in changing the environments in which embodied individuals live. Issues of transcendence may not ordinarily be at the centre of sociological discussions of the moral dimensions of collective action, but pragmatism has long recognised the importance of society's capacity for attending to the needs and desires of its members. A central part of this internal environment has involved aspirational visions of what it is possible to become. These are not necessarily materialistic aspirations, but often focus on questions of meaning and of achieving recognition for people's habits and identities. In a world characterised by major religious conflict, this raises questions about the compatibility of these aspirations and of the extent to which major civilisations can coexist peaceably (Robertson, 2006).

The field of body studies has thus far been characterised by theoretical and philosophically informed studies on the issue of how to approach the analysis of bodies in a social context, and by descriptive empirical studies that have sought to illustrate the importance of people's bodily being via interview and the 'thick description' of ethnography. Rather than adding to either of these, this book has tried to do something different. In the first few chapters I outlined a framework, informed by the insights of pragmatism that provided a theoretically informed context in which substantive studies of embodied action could be conducted. The chapters that followed provided illustrations of how this framework might be utilised and developed. In applying this to studies of survival, competition, illness and impairment, transgenderism, migration and belief, moreover, there have also arisen several key themes which raise questions of fundamental importance to sociology and social theory, and also to the issue of what it is to be human. These demonstrate the continued importance of body studies not only for disciplinary, inter-disciplinary and cross-disciplinary investigations, but also for questions pertinent to the meaning of life itself.

Bibliography

Aggleton, P., Davies, P. and Hart, G. (eds) (1997) *AIDS, Activism and Alliances*, London: Routledge.

Albanese, C. (1990) *Nature Religion in America*, Chicago: University of Chicago Press.

Albrecht, G. and Devlieger, P. (1999) 'The disability paradox: High quality of life against all odds', *Social Science Medicine*, 48(8): 977–88.

Aldridge, J. (1993) 'The effect of injuries on growth', in M. Lee (ed.), *Coaching Children in Sport*, London: E&FN Spon.

Alexander, J.C. (1997) 'The paradoxical relations of self and society in American sociological thought', in J.C. Alexander, R. Boudon and M. Cherkaoui (eds), *The Classical Tradition in Sociology. The American Tradition, Vol. 1*, London: Sage.

Amery, J. (1999 [1966]) *At the Mind's Limits*, London: Granta Books.

Anderson, B. (2002) 'Just another job? The commodification of domestic labour', in B. Ehrenreich and A. Hochschild (eds), *Global Women*, London: Granta.

Anderson, N. (1923–1924) 'The juvenile and the tramp', *Journal of Criminal Law, Criminology and Police Science*, 14: 290–312.

Anderson, N. (1961 [1923]) *The Hobo. The Sociology of the Homeless Man*, Chicago: Phoenix Books/Chicago University Press.

Anderson, N. (1975) *The American Hobo. An Autobiography*, Leiden: E.J. Brill.

Anderson, N. (1998 [1940]) 'Men on the move', extracted in N. Anderson *On Hobos and Homelessness*, R. Rauty (ed.), Chicago: University of Chicago Press.

Aneesh, A. (2004) 'Between fantasy and despair. The transnational condition and high-tech immigration', in D. Gabaccia and C. Leach (eds), *Immigrant Life in the US*, London: Routledge.

Anshel, M. (2003) *Sport Psychology*, San Francisco: Benjamin Cummings.

Anway, C. (1995) *Daughters of Another Path. Experiences of American Women Choosing Islam*, Lee's Summit: Yawna Publications.

Applebaum, A. (2003) *Gulag. A History of the Soviet Camps*, London: Allen Lane.

Archer, A. (1995) *Realist Social Theory*, Cambridge: Cambridge University Press.

Archer, A. (2000) *Being Human. The Problem of Agency*, Cambridge: Cambridge University Press.

Aries, P. (1981 [1977]) *The Hour of Our Death*, New York: Alfred A. Knopf.

Armstrong, D. (1983) *Political Anatomy of the Body*, Cambridge: Cambridge University Press.

Armstrong, K. (2004) *The Battle for God*, London: Harper.

Armstrong, N. and Welsma, J. (1993) 'Children's physiological responses to exercise', in M. Lee (ed.), *Coaching Children in Sport*, London: E&FN Spon.

Asad, T. (1993) *Genealogies of Religion*, Baltimore: John Hopkins University Press.

Atkin, K. and Ahmad, W. (2000) 'Pumping iron; compliance with chelation therapy among young people who have thalassaemia major', reprinted in S. Nettleton and U. Gustafsson (eds) (2002) *The Sociology of Health and Illness Reader*, Oxford: Polity.

Aupers, S. and Houtman, D. (2006) 'Beyond the spiritual supermarket: The social and public significance of new age spirituality', *Journal of Contemporary Religion*, 21(2): 201–22.

Bachelard, G. (1964) *The Poetics of Space*, Boston: Beacon Press.

Baert, P. and Turner, B.S. (eds) (2007) *Pragmatism and European Social Theory*, Oxford: The Bardwell Press.

Bailey, P. (1978) *Leisure & Class in Victorian England*, London: RKP.

Baker, N. and Moreno, D. (2001) *The Ultimate Guide to Windsurfing*, London: CollinsWillow.

Balarajan, R., Soni Raleigh, V., Yuen, P., Wheeler, D., Machin, D. and Cartwright, R. (1991) 'Health risks associated with bathing in sea water', *British Medical Journal*, 303: 1444–5.

Bale, J. (1994) *Landscapes of Modern Sport*, London: Continuum.

Bale, J. and Philo, C. (1998) 'Introduction', in H. Eichberg (ed.), *Body Cultures. Essays on Sport, Space and Identity*, London: Routledge.

Bales, K. (2002) 'Because she looks like a child', in B. Ehrenreich and A. Hochschild (eds), *Global Women*, London: Granta.

Bartky, S. (1988) 'Foucault, feminism and patriarchal power', in I. Diamond and L. Quinby (eds), *Feminism & Foucault*, Boston: Northeastern University Press.

Bartelski, K. and Neillands, R. (1993) *Learn to Ski in a Weekend*, London: Dorling Kindersley.

Bartlett, R. (1999) *Sports Biomechanics*, London: E&FN Spon.

Bauby, J-D. (1997) *The Diving Bell and the Butterfly*, London: HarperPerennial.

Bauman, Z. (1989) *Modernity and the Holocaust*, Cambridge: Polity.

Bauman, Z. (1992) *Mortality, Immortality and Other Life Strategies*, Cambridge: Polity.

Bauman, Z. (1994) 'Desert spectacular', in K. Tester (ed.), *The Flaneur*, London: Routledge.

Baumgartner, M. (1988) *The Moral Order of a Suburb*, New York: Oxford University Press.

Beal, B. (1999) 'Skateboarding. An alternative to mainstream sports', in J. Coakley and P. Donnelly (eds), *Inside Sports*, London; Routledge.

Beck, U. (1992) *Risk Society*, London: Sage.

Becker, H. (1963) *Outsiders*, New York: Free Press.

Becker, H., Geer, G., Hughes, E. and Strauss, A. (1961) *Boys in White*, New York: Transaction Publishers.

Bee, P. (2003) 'Give them a sporting chance', *The Times*, 14 July, p. 8.

Bell, J.S. (2006) *His Forever*, Avon: Adams Media.

Berger, P. (1990 [1967]) *The Sacred Canopy*, New York: Anchor.

Berkowitz, S. (1965) *Where are My Brothers?* New York: Helios.

Berman, M. (1983) *All That is Solid Melts into Air*, London: Verso.

Bettleheim, B. (1960) *The Informed Heart*, Harmondsworth: Penguin.

Beyer, P. (1994) *Religion and Globalisation*, London: Sage.

Billings, D. and Urban, T. (1982) 'The socio-medical construction of transsexualism', *Social Problems*, 29: 266–82.

Birenbaum, H. (1971) *Hope is the Last to Die*, New York: Twayne.

Birley, D. (1993) *Sport and the Making of Britain*, Manchester: Manchester University Press.

Birrell, S. and Theberge, N. (1994) 'Ideological control of women in sport', in D.M. Costa and S.R. Guthrie (eds), *Women and Sport. Interdisciplinary Perspectives*, Champaign: Human Kinetics.

Black, A. (1993) 'Classical Islam and medieval Europe: A comparison of political philosophies and cultures', *Political Studies*, XLI: 58–69.

Blake, A. (1996) *The Body Language: The Meaning of Modern Sport*, London: Lawrence & Wishart.

Blaxter, M. (1990) *Health and Lifestyles*, London: Routledge.

Blumer, H. (1969) *Symbolic Interactionism*, Berkeley: University of California Press.

Boberg, E., McKee, M., Flatley-Brennan, P. and McCarthy, C. (1995) 'Development, acceptance and use patterns of a computer based educational and social support system for people living with AIDS/HIV infection', *Computers in Human Behaviour*, II(2): 289–311.

Bodnar, J., Simon, R. and Weber, M.P. (1982) *Lives of their Own: Blacks, Italians and Poles in Pittsburgh, 1900–1960*, Urbana: University of Illinois Press.

Bogardus, E. (1949) 'The sociology of William I. Thomas', *Sociology and Social Research*, 34: 34–48.

Bollettieri, N. and Schaap, D. (1997) *My Aces, My Faults*, London: Robson Books.

Bologh, R. (1990) *Love or Greatness. Max Weber and Masculine Thinking – A Feminist Inquiry*, London: Unwin Hyman.

Bonner, M. (1992) 'Some observations concerning the early development of Jihad along the Arab-Byzantine frontier', *Studia Islamica*, 75: 5–31.

Bonner, M. (1996) *Aristocratic Violence and Holy War*, New Haven: American Oriental Society.

Booth, D. (1995) 'Ambiguities in pleasure and discipline: The development of competitive surfing', *Journal of Sport History*, 22(3): 189–205.

Borden, I. (2001) *Skateboarding, Space and the City*, Oxford: Berg.

Bornstein, K. (1994) *Gender Outlaw*, New York: Routledge.

Bourdieu, P. (1984) *Distinction*, London: Routledge.

Bourdieu, P. (1986) 'The forms of capital', in J. Richardson (ed.), *Handbook of Theory and Research for the Sociology of Education*, New York: Greenwood Press.

Bourdieu, P. (1988) 'Program for a sociology of sport', *Sociology of Sport Journal*, 5: 153–61.

Bourdieu, P. and Wacquant, L. (1992) *An Invitation to Reflexive Sociology*, Chicago: Chicago University Press.

Brasch, R. (ed.) (1990) *How did Sports Begin?* Thornhill: Tynron Press.

Briggs, J. (1978) *An Italian Passage. Immigrants to Three American Cities, 1890–1930*, New Haven: Yale University Press.

Brodwin, P. (1992) 'Symptoms and social performances: The case of Diane Reden', in M-J. DelVecchio Good, P. Brodwin, B.J. Good and A. Kleinman (eds), *Pain as Human Experience. An Anthropological Perspective*, Berkeley: University of California Press.

Brown, G. (1988) 'Transsexuals in the military', *Archives of Sexual Behavior*, 17(6): 527–37.

Brown, M. (1997) *Replacing Citizenship. AIDS, Activism and Radical Democracy*, New York: The Guildford Press.

Brown, P. (1995) 'Popular epidemiology, toxic waste and social movements', in J. Gabe (ed.), *Medicine, Health and Risk*, Oxford: Blackwell.

Brown, P.G. and Shue, H. (eds) (1983) *The Border That Joins*, New Jersey: Rowan & Littlefield.

Bruce, S. (2002) *God is Dead. Secularisation in the West*, Oxford: Blackwell.

Bruce, S. (2003) 'The demise of Christianity in Britain', in G. Davie, P. Heelas and L.Woodhead (eds), *Predicting Religion*, Aldershot: Ashgate.

Bryant, B. and Mohai, P. (1992) *Race and the Incidence of Environmental Hazards. A Time for Discourse*, New York: Westview Press.

Bulmer, M. (1984) *The Chicago School of Sociology*, Chicago: University of Chicago Press.

Bulmer, M. (1997) 'W.I. Thomas and Robert E. Park: Conceptualising, theorising and investigating social processes', in C. Camic (ed.), *Reclaiming the Sociological Classics*, Oxford: Blackwell.

Burgess, E.W. (1925) 'The growth of the city: An introduction to a research project', in R. Park, E.W. Burgess and R. McKenzie (eds), *The City*, Chicago: University of Chicago Press.

Burgess, E.W. (1927) *The Urban Community*, Chicago: University of Chicago Press.

Burgess, E.W. (1934) 'Sociological aspects of the sex life of the unmarried adult', in I. Wile (ed.), *The Sex Life of the Unmarried Adult*, New York: Vanguard Press.

Burkitt, I. (1991) *Social Selves*, London: Sage.

Burkitt, I. (1999) *Bodies of Thought*, London: Sage.

Bury, M. (1982) 'Chronic illness as biographical disruption', *Sociology of Health & Illness*, 4(2): 167–82.

Busfield, J. (1986) *Managing Madness*, London: Routledge.

Butler, J. (1993) *Bodies Matter*, London: Routledge.

Butler, J. (1994) 'Gender as performance: An interview with Judith Butler', *Radical Philosophy*, Summer, 67.

Bynum, C.W. (1987) *Holy Feast and Holy Fast*, Berkeley: University of California Press.

Califia, P. (2006) 'Manliness', reprinted in S. Stryker and S. Whittle (eds), *The Transgender Studies Reader*, London: Routledge.

Camic, C. (1986) 'The matter of habit', *American Journal of Sociology*, 91(5): 1039–87.

Campbell, M. (2007) 'Migrants risk all in new assault on fortress Europe', *The Sunday Times*, 3 June.

Cant, S. and Sharma, U. (2000) 'Alternative health practices and systems', in G. Albrecht, R. Fitzpatrick and S. Scrimshaw (eds), *Handbook of Social Studies in Health and Medicine*, London: Sage.

Capra, F. (1999) *The Tao of Physics*, Boston: Shambhala.

Carricaburu, D. and Pierret, J. (1995) 'From biographical disruption to biographical reinforcement: The case of HIV-positive men', *Sociology of Health and Illness*, 17: 65–88.

Cashmore, E. (2000) *Making Sense of Sports* (third edition), London: Routledge.

Chambers, P. (2006) 'Secularisation, Wales and Islam', *Journal of Contemporary Religion*, 21(3): 325–40.

Chan, W-C. (2003) 'Phenomenology of Technology: East and West', *Journal of Chinese Philosophy*, 30(1): 1–18.

Charmaz, K. (1983) 'Loss of self: A fundamental form of suffering in the chronically ill', *Sociology of Health and Illness*, 5(2): 168–95.

Charmaz, K. (1999) 'Stories of suffering: Subjective tales and research narratives', *Qualitative Health Research*, 9: 362–82.

Charmaz, K. (2000) 'Experiencing chronic illness', in G. Albrecht, R. Fitzpatrick and S. Scrimshaw (eds), *Handbook of Sociological Studies in Health and Medicine*, London: Sage.

Chase, C. (2006 [1998]) 'Hermaphrodites with attitude', reprinted in S. Stryker and S. Whittle (eds), *The Transgender Studies Reader*, London: Routledge.

Chouinard, V. (1999) 'Body politics: Disabled women's activism in Canada and beyond', in R. Hester and H. Parr (eds), *Mind and Body Spaces*, London: Routledge.

Coakley, J. (1994) *Sport in Society: Issues and Controversies*, St Louis: Mosby.

Coleman, S. (2000) *The Globalisation of Charismatic Christianity*, Cambridge: Cambridge University Press.

Collins, R. (1988) *Theoretical Sociology*, Orlando: Harcourt Brace.

Colomy, P. and Brown, D. (1995) 'Elaboration, revision, polemic and progress in the second Chicago School', in G.A. Fine (ed.), *A Second Chicago School?* Chicago: University of Chicago Press.

Connell, R.W. (1990) 'An iron man: The body and some contradictions of hegemonic masculinity', in M. Messner and D. Sabo (eds), *Sport, Men and the Gender Order*, Champaign: Human Kinetics.

Coogan, M. (ed.) (2005) *Eastern Religions*, London: Duncan Baird.

Cooley, C.H. (1909) *Social Organisation*, New York: Charles Scribner & Sons.

Cooley, C.H. (1922 [1902]) *Human Nature and Social Order*, New Brunswick: Transaction Publishers.

Cooper, L. (1997) 'Myalgic encephalomyelitis and the medical encounter', reprinted in S. Nettleton and U. Gustafsson (eds) (2002), *The Sociology of Health and Illness Reader*, Oxford: Polity.

Corbin, J. and Strauss, A. (1987) 'Accompaniments of chronic illness: Changes in body, self, biography and biographical time', *Research in the Sociology of Health Care*, 6: 249–81.

Cornwell, J. (1984) *Hard Earned Lives*, London: Tavistock.

Coser, L. (1971) *Masters of Sociological Thought*, New York: Harcourt Brace Jovanovich.

Cotterell, P. (2006) 'Conversion and apostasy', in C. Partridge and H. Reid (eds), *Finding and Losing Faith*, Milton Keynes: Paternoster Press.

Cox, H. (1995) *Fire From Heaven*, Reading: Addison-Wesley.

Crawford, J., Lawless, S. and Kippax, S. (1997) 'Positive women and heterosexuality: Problems of disclosure of serostatus to sexual partners', in P. Aggleton, P. Davies and G. Hart (eds), *AIDS Activism and Alliances*, London: Falmer.

Creasey, M., Shepard, N. and Gresham, N. (2000) *An Introduction to Rock Climbing*, London: Southwater.

Cressey, P. (1929) *The Closed Dance Hall in Chicago*, MA thesis, University of Chicago.

Cressey, P. (1932) *The Taxi-Dance Hall*, Chicago: University of Chicago Press.

Cromwell, J. (2006) 'Queering the binaries', in S. Stryker and S. Whittle (eds), *The Transgender Studies Reader*, London: Routledge.

Cross, M. and Keith, M. (eds) (1993) *Racism, the City and the State*, London: Routledge.

Crossley, N. (2001) *The Social Body*, London: Sage.

Csikszentmihalyi, M. (1975) *Beyond Boredom and Anxiety*, San Francisco: Josey Bass.

Csordas, T. (ed.) (1994) *Embodiment and Experience*, Cambridge: Cambridge University Press.

Curry, T. (1991) 'Fraternal bonding in the locker room', *Sociology of Sport Journal*, 8: 119–35.

Dacyshyn, A. (1999) 'When the balance is gone. The sport and retirement experiences of elite female gymnasts', in J. Coakley and P. Donnelly (eds), *Inside Sports*, London: Routledge.

Dant, T. (1999) *Culture in the Social World*, Buckingham: Open University Press.

Davis, F. (1963) *Passage Through Crisis*, Indianapolis: Bobbs-Merrill.

Dawe, A. (1970) 'The two sociologies', *The British Journal of Sociology*, 21(2): 207–18.

de Beauvoir, S. (1993 [1949]) *The Second Sex*, London: Everyman.

Deegan, P.E. (1994) 'Recovery: The lived experience of rehabilitation', in W.A. Anthony and L. Spaniol (eds), *Readings in Psychiatric Rehabilitation*, Boston: Boston University, Center for Psychiatric Rehabilitation.

Des Pres, T. (1976) *The Survivor*, New York: Oxford University Press.

Dewey, J. (1896) 'The reflex arc concept in psychology', *Psychological Review*, 3: 357–70.

Dewey, J. (1927) *The Public and Its Problems*, New York: Holt.

Dewey, J. (1958) *Experience and Nature* (second edition), New York: Dover.

Dewey, J. (1969 [1916]) *Democracy and Education*, New York: Macmillan.

Dewey, J. (1980 [1934]) *Art as Experience*, New York: Perigee.

Dewey, J. (2002 [1922]) *Human Nature and Conduct*, New York: Dover.

Dorow, S. (2004) 'Adopted children's identities at the China/US border', in D. Gabaccia and C. Leach (eds), *Immigrant Life in the US*, London: Routledge.

Douglas, M. (1970) *Natural Symbols*, London; Routledge.

Downer, S. (2004) 'I've been there and done that', *The Times*, 17 November, p. 16.

Draulans, V. and Halman, L. (2005) 'Mapping contemporary Europe's moral and religious pluralist landscape', *Journal of Contemporary Religion*, 20(2): 179–93.

Droogers, A. (2001) 'Globalisation and pentecostal success', in A. Corten and R. Marshall-Fratani (eds), *Between Babel and Pentecost*, Bloomington: Indiana University Press.

Dunning, E. (1999) *Sport Matters*, London: Routledge.

Dunning, E. and Sheard, K. (1979) *Barbarians, Gentlemen and Players*, Oxford: Martin Robertson.

Duquin, M. (1994) 'She flies through the air with the greatest of ease: The contributions of feminist psychology', in D.M. Costa and S.R. Guthrie (eds), *Women and Sport. Interdisciplinary Perspectives*, Champaign: Human Kinetics.

Durkheim, E. (1952 [1897]) *Suicide*, London: Routledge.

Durkheim, E. (1955) *Pragmatisme et Sociologie*, Paris: Vrin.

Durkheim, E. (1961) *Moral Education*, New York: Free Press.

Durkheim, E. (1973 [1898]) 'Individualism and the intellectuals', in R. Bellah (ed.), *Emile Durkheim On Morality and Society*, Chicago: University of Chicago Press.

Durkheim, E. (1984 [1893]) *The Division of Labour in Society*, London: Macmillan.

Durkheim, E. (1995 [1912]) *The Elementary Forms of Religious Life*, New York: Free Press.

Duroche, L. (1990) 'Male perception as a social construct', in J. Hearn and D. Morgan (eds), *Men, Masculinities and Social Theory*, London: Hyman.

Dyck, I. (1995) 'Hidden geographies: The changing lifeworlds of women with MS', *Social Science and Medicine*, 40(3): 307–20.

Dyck, I. (1999) 'Body troubles: Women, the workplace and negotiations of a disabled identity', in R. Hester and H. Parr (eds), *Mind and Body Spaces*, London: Routledge.

Dyer, K. (1982) *Challenging the Men*, New York: University of Queensland.

Ehrenreich, B. (1990) *The Fear of Falling. The Inner Life of the Middle Class*, New York: Harper Perennial.

Ehrenreich, B. and Hochschild, A. (2002) (eds), *Global Women*, London: Granta.

Eichberg, H. (1984) 'Olympic sport: Neocolonialism and alternatives', *International Review for the Sociology of Sport*, 19: 97–105.

Eichberg, H. (1998) *Body Cultures. Essays on Sport, Space and Identity*, London: Routledge.

Eisenberg, C. (1990) 'The middle class and competition. Some considerations of the beginnings of modern sport in England and Germany', *The International Journal of the History of Sport*, 7(2): 265–82.

Elias, N. (1983) *The Court Society*, Oxford: Blackwell.

Elias, N. (1985) *The Loneliness of the Dying*, Oxford: Blackwell.

Elias, N. (1991) *Symbol Theory*, London: Sage.

Elias, N. (1994) 'A theoretical essay on established and outsider relations', in N. Elias and J. Scotson. *The Established and the Outsiders*, London: Sage.

Elias, N. (2000 [1939]) *The Civilizing Process*, Oxford: Blackwell.

Elias, N. (2000 [1939]) *The Civilizing Process* (revised edition), edited by E. Dunning, J. Goudsblom and S. Mennell, Oxford: Blackwell.

Elias, N. and Dunning, E. (1986) *The Quest for Excitement*, Oxford: Blackwell.

Elias, N. and Scotson, J. (1994 [1965]) *The Established and the Outsiders*, London: Frank Cass.

Elliot, B. (2004) 'Existential scepticism and Christian life in early Heidegger', *The Heythrop Journal*, 45(3): 273–89.

Engerman, S., Drescher, S. and Paquette, R. (eds) (2001) *Slavery*, Oxford: Oxford University Press.

Ericsson, K., Krampe, R. and Tesch-Romer, C. (1993) 'The role of deliberate practice in the acquisition of expert performance', *Psychology Review*, 100: 363–406.

Erikson Educational Foundation (1974) *Guidelines for Transsexuals*, Louisiana: Baton Rouge.

Evans, H., Jackman, B. and Ottaway, M. (1978) *We learned to Ski*, London: Collins.

Eyles, J. (1985) *Senses of Place*, Warrington: Silverbrook Press.

Faldo, N. with Saunders, V. (1989) *Golf – The Winning Formula*, London: Stanley Paul.

Fanon (1984 [1952]) *Black Skin, White Masks*, London: Pluto.

Farias, M. and Lalljee, M. (2006) 'Empowerment in the New Age: A motivational study of autobiographical life stories', *Journal of Contemporary Religion*, 21(2): 241–56.

Faris, R. (1967) *Chicago Sociology 1920–32*, Chicago: University of Chicago Press.

Fassin, D. (2005) 'Compassion and regression: The moral economy of immigration policy in France', *Cultural Anthropology*, 20(3): 362–87.

Fausto-Sterling, A. (1993) 'The five sexes: Why male and female are not enough', *The Sciences*, May/April: 20–5.

Featherstone, M. (1982) 'The body in consumer culture', *Theory, Culture and Society*, 1: 18–33.

Featherstone, M. and Hepworth, M. (1991) 'The mask of aging and the postmodern life course', in M. Featherstone, M. Hepworth and B.S. Turner (eds), *The Body. Social Process and Cultural Theory*, London: Sage.

Featherstone, M., Thrift, N. and Urry, J. (2005) *Automobilities*, London: Sage.

Feinberg, L. (2006) 'Transgender liberation. A movement whose time has come', reprinted in S. Stryker and S. Whittle (eds), *The Transgender Studies Reader*, London: Routledge.

Felman, S. and Lamb, D. (1992) *Testimony*, New York: Routledge.

Ferguson, P. (1994) 'The flaneur on and off the streets of Paris', in K. Tester (ed.), *The Flaneur*, London: Routledge.

Fields, K. (1995) 'Introduction', in E. Durkheim (1995 [1912]) *The Elementary Forms of Religious Life*, New York: Free Press.

Fine, G.A. (1995) 'A 2nd Chicago School?', in G.A. Fine (ed.), *A Second Chicago School? The Development of a Postwar American Sociology*, Chicago: University of Chicago Press.

Fisher, B. and Strauss, A. (1997) 'George Herbert Mead and the Chicago tradition of sociology', in J.C. Alexander, R. Boudon and M. Cherkaoui (eds), *The Classical Tradition in Sociology. The American Tradition, Vol.1*, London: Sage.

Foley, M., Frew, M. and McGillivray, D. (2003) 'Rough comfort: Consuming adventure on the "edge" ', in B. Humberstone, H. Brown and K. Richards (eds), *Whose Journeys*, Penrich: The Institute for Outdoor Learning.

Foucault, M. (1970) *The Order of Things*, London: Tavistock.

Foucault, M. (1973) *The Birth of the Clinic*, London: Tavistock.

Foucault, M. (1979a) *Discipline and Punish*, Harmondsworth: Penguin.

Foucault, M. (1979b) 'Governmentality', *Ideology and Consciousness*, 6: 5–22.

Foucault, M. (1981) *The History of Sexuality, Vol. 1*, Harmondsworth: Penguin.

Foucault, M. (1988) 'Technologies of the self', in L. Martin, H. Gutman and P. Hutton (eds), *Technologies of the Self. A Seminar with Michel Foucault*, Amherst: The University of Massachusetts Press.

Frank, A. (1991a) 'From sick role to health role: Deconstructing Parsons', in R. Robertson and B. Turner (eds), *Talcott Parsons*, London: Sage.

Frank, A. (1991b) *At the Will of the Body*, Boston: Houghton Mifflin.

Frank, A. (1995) *The Wounded Storyteller. Body, Illness & Ethics*, Chicago: Chicago University Press.

Frankenberg, R. (1990) 'Review article: Disease, literature and the body in the era of AIDS – a preliminary exploration', *Sociology of Health and Illness*, 12(3): 351–60.

Frankl, V. (1959) *From Death Camp to Existentialism*, Boston: Beacon Press.

Franklin, A. (2001) *Nature and Social Theory*, London: Sage.

Frazier, E.F. (1932) *The Negro Family*, Chicago: University of Chicago Press.

Freidson, E. (1970) *Profession of Medicine: A Study in the Sociology of Applied Knowledge*, New York: Harper and Row.

Fusco, C. (1998) 'Lesbians and locker rooms: The subjective experience of lesbians in sport', in G. Rail (ed.), *Sport and Postmodern Time*, New York: SUNY Press.

Gabaccia, D. and Leach, C. (eds) (2004) *Immigrant Life in the US*, London: Routledge.

Gabe, J. (1995) 'Health, medicine and risk', in J. Gabe (ed.), *Medicine, Health and Risk*, Oxford: Blackwell.

Gadow, S. (1980) 'Body and self: A dialectic', *Journal of Medicine and Philosophy*, 5: 172–85.

Gaffney, C. and Bale, J. (2004) 'Sensing the stadium', in P. Vertinsky and J. Bale (eds), *Sites of Sport, Space, Experience*, London: Routledge.

Gardner, M. (1989) 'Review of reported increases of childhood cancer rates in the vicinity of nuclear installations', *UK Journal of the Royal Statistic Society, Series A*: 307–25.

Garfinkel, H. (1963) 'A conception of and experiments with "trust" as a condition for concerted stable actions', in O.J. Harvey (ed.), *Motivation and Social Interaction*, New York: Ronald Press.

Garfinkel, H. (1967) *Studies in Ethnomethodology*, Englewood Cliffs: Prentice-Hall.

Garfinkel, H. (2006 [1967]) 'Passing and the managed achievement of sex status in an "intersexed" person', reprinted in S. Stryker and S. Whittle (eds), *The Transgender Studies Reader*, London: Routledge.

Garro, L. (1992) 'Chronic illness and the construction of narratives', in M-J. DelVecchio Good, P. Brodwin, B.J. Good and A. Kleinman (eds), *Pain as Human Experience. An Anthropological Perspective*, Berkeley: University of California Press.

Gatrell, P. (2002) *Geographies of Health*, London: Blackwell.

Geores, M. (1998) 'Surviving on metaphor', in R. Kearns and W. Gesler (eds), *Putting Health into Place*, New York: Syracuse University Press.

George, A. (1996) 'The anabolic steroids and peptide hormones', in D. Mottram (ed.), *Drugs in Sport*, London: E & FN Spon.

Gesler, G. (1992) 'Therapeutic landscapes: Medical issues in light of the new cultural geography', *Social Science Medicine*, 34(7): 735–46.

Gesler, G. (1998) 'Bath's reputation as a healing place', in R. Kearns and W. Gesler (eds), *Putting Health into Place*, New York: Syracuse University Press.

Gesler, W. and Kearns, R. (2002) *Culture/Place/Health*, London: Routledge.

Gestaldo, D. (1997) 'Is health education good for you? Re-thinking health education through the concept of bio-power', in A. Peterson and R. Bunton (eds), *Foucault, Health and Medicine*, London: Routledge.

Gibson, W. (1979) *The Ecological Approach to Visual Perception*, Boston: Houghton Mifflin.

Giddens, A. (1984) *The Constitution of Society*, Oxford: Polity.

Giddens, A. (1991) *Modernity and Self-Identity*, Cambridge: Polity.

Gilliat-Ray, S. (2005) ' "Sacralising" sacred space in public institutions: A case study of the prayer space at the Millenium Dome', *Journal of Contemporary Religion*, 20(3): 357–72.

Gilroy, P. (1993) *The Black Atlantic*, London: Verso.

Gilroy, P. (2000) *Between Camps*, London: Penguin.

Girardot, N.J. (1999) 'Finding the way: James Legge and the Victorian invention of Taoism', *Religion*, 29: 107–21.

Glasser, W. (1976) *Positive Addiction*, New York: Harper & Row.

Gleeson, B. (2002) 'Can technology overcome the disabling city?' in R. Hester and H. Parr (eds), *Mind and Body Spaces*, London: Routledge.

Goffman, E. (1956) 'Embarrassment and social organisation', *American Journal of Sociology*, LXII(3): 264–71.

Goffman, E. (1961) *Asylums*, New York: Anchor Books.

Goffman, E. (1963a) *Stigma*, London: Penguin.

Goffman, E. (1963b) *Behaviour in Public Places*, New York: The Free Press.

Goffman, E. (1969 [1959]) *The Presentation of Self in Everyday Life*, London: Penguin.

Goffman, E. (1977) 'The arrangement between the sexes', *Theory and Society*, 4: 301–31.

Goffman, E. (1983) 'The interaction order', *American Sociological Review*, 48: 1–17.

Golden, M. (1998) *Sport and Society in Ancient Greece*, Cambridge: Cambridge University Press.

Goldman, R. and Papson, S. (1998) *Nike Culture*, London: Sage.

Goldstein, I. and Goldstein, M. (1986) 'The Broad Street pump', in J. Goldsmith (ed.), *Environmental Epidemiology*, Boca Raton: CRC Press.

Good, B. (1992) 'Work as a haven from pain', in M-J. DelVecchio Good, P. Brodwin, B.J. Good and A. Kleinman (eds), *Pain as Human Experience. An Anthropological Perspective*, Berkeley: University of California Press.

Goodger, J. and Goodger, B. (1989) 'Excitement and representation: Toward a sociological explanation of the significance of sport in modern society', *Quest*, 41: 257–72.

Gottdiener, M. (2001) *Life in the Air. Surviving the New Culture of Air Travel*, London: Rowen & Littlefield.

Goudie, A. (2000) *The Human Impact on the Natural Environment*, Oxford: Blackwell.

Graham, A. (1989) *Disputers of the Tao*, La Salle: Open Court.

Green, J. (1995) 'Accidents and the risk society', in R. Bunton, S. Nettleton and R. Burrows (eds), *The Sociology of Health Promotion*, London: Routledge.

Green, J. (2004) *Becoming a Visible Man*, Nashville: Vanderbilt University Press.

Green, J. (2006) 'Look! No don't! The visibility dilemma for transsexual men', in S. Stryker and S. Whittle (eds), *The Transgender Studies Reader*, London: Routledge.

Greenblatt, S. (1980) *Renaissance Self-Fashioning*, Chicago: University of Chicago Press.

Gunnell, S. (1994) *Running Tall*, London: Bloomsbury.

Gusfield, J. (1963) *Symbolic Crusade* (second edition), Urbana: University of Illinois Press.

Guthrie, E.R. (1952) *The Psychology of Learning*, New York: Harper & Row.

Guttman, A. (1994) *Games and Empires*, New York: Columbia University Press.

Haake, S. (ed.) (1996) *The Engineering of Sport*, Rotterdam: A.A. Balkema.

Halton, E. (1995) *Bereft of Reason*, Chicago: University of Chicago Press.

Hanson, A. (1999) *A Matter of Opinion*, London: Bantam Books.

Haraway (1994 [1985]) 'A manifesto for cyborgs: Science, technology and socialist-feminism in the 1990s', in S. Seidman (ed.), *The Postmodern Turn*, Cambridge: Cambridge University Press.

Hardey, M. (2002) ' "The story of my illness": Personal accounts of illness on the Internet', *Health*, 6(1): 31–46.

Harding, J. (2000) *The Uninvited*, London: Profile Books.

Hargreaves, J. (1994) *Sporting Females*, London: Routledge.

Harrison, C., Burgess, J. and Filius, P. (1994) *From Environmental Awareness to Environmental Action?* Unpublished Report, Department of Geography, University College London, cited in B. Szerszynski (2005) *Nature, Technology and the Sacred*, Oxford: Blackwell.

Hatton, T. and Williamson, J. (1998) *The Age of Mass Migration*, Oxford: Oxford University Press.

Hausman, B. (1995) *Changing Sex*, Durham: Duke University Press.

Heap, C. (2003) 'The city as a sexual laboratory: The queer heritage of the Chicago School', *Qualitative Sociology*, 26(4): 457–87.

Heck, P.L. (2004) 'Jihad Revisited', *Journal of Religious Ethics*, 32: 95–128.

Heelas, P. (1996) *The New Age Movement*, Oxford: Blackwell.

Heelas, P., Woodhead, L., Seel, B., Szerszynski, B. and Tusting, K. (2004) *The Spiritual Revolution*, Oxford: Blackwell.

Heidegger, M. (1993 [1954]) 'The question concerning technology', in D. Krell (ed.), *Martin Heidegger. Basic Writings*, London: Routledge.

Heimler, E. (1959) *Night of the Mist*, New York: Vanguard.

Helmreich, W. (1996) *Against All Odds*, New York: Simon and Schuster.

Henry, A. (1991) *Autocourse*, London: Hazleton Publishing.

Herbert, D. and Wolffe, J. (2004) 'Religion and contemporary conflict in historical perspective', in J. Wolffe (ed.), *Religion in History. Conflict, Conversion and Coexistence*, Milton Keynes: Open University Press.

Heywood, I. (1994) 'Urgent dreams: Climbing, rationalisation and ambivalence', *Leisure Studies*, 13: 179–94.

Higdon, H. (1992) 'Is running a religious experience?' in S. Hoffman (ed.), *Sport and Religion*, Champaign: Human Kinetics.

Hilton, C. (2003) *Inside the Mind of the Grand Prix Driver*, Sparkford: Haynes.

Hoberman, J. (1992) *Mortal Engines*, New York: The Free Press.

Hochschild, A. (1983) *Managed Heart. Commercialization of Human Feeling*, Berkeley: University of California Press.

Hochschild, A. (2002) 'Love and gold', in B. Ehrenreich and A. Hochschild (eds), *Global Women*, London: Granta.

Hoerder, D. (2002) *Cultures in Contact. World Migrations in the Second Millenium*, Durham: Duke University Press.

Hoffman, S. (1992) 'Nimrod, nephilim and the athletae dei', in S. Hoffman (ed.), *Sport & Religion*, Champaign: Human Kinetics.

Hollinger, F. (2004) 'Does the counter-cultural character of new age persist? Investigating the social and political attitudes of new age followers', *Journal of Contemporary Religion*, 19(3): 289–309.

Holt, R. (1989) *Sport & the British*, Oxford: Oxford University Press.

Honneth, A. and Joas, H. (1988 [1980]) *Social Action and Human Nature*, Cambridge: Cambridge University Press.

Horne, J., Tomlinson, A. and Whannel, G. (1999) *Understanding Sport*, London E&FN Spon.

Huizinga, J. (1970 [1938]) *Homo Ludens*, London: Temple Smith.

Humberstone, B. (1998) 'Re-creation and connections in and with nature', *International Review for the Sociology of Sport*, 33(4): 381–92.

Hunter, S. (ed.) (2002) *Islam, Europe's Second Religion*, Westport: Praeger Publishers.

Hunter, S. and Serfaty, S. (2002) 'Introduction', in S. Hunter (ed.), *Islam, Europe's Second Religion*, Westport: Praeger Publishers.

Huntington, S. (2002 [1996]) *The Clash of Civilizations and the Remaking of World Order*, New York: Free Press.

Illich, I. (2001) *Limits to Medicine* (new edition), New York: Marion Boyars.

Imrie, R. (1999) 'The Body, disability and le Corbusier's conception of the radiant environment', in R. Hester and H. Parr (eds), *Mind and Body Spaces*, London: Routledge.

Inglehart, R. (1997) *Modernisation and Postmodernisation. Cultural, Economic and Political Change in Forty-Three Societies*, Princeton: Princeton University Press.

Ingold, T. (2000) *The Perception of the Environment*, London: Routledge.

Ingold, T. (2004) 'Culture on the ground', *Journal of Material Culture*, 9(3): 315–40.

Ingold, T. and Kurtilla, T. (2000) 'Perceiving the environment in Finnish Lapland', *Body and Society*, 6(3–4): 183–96.

Jackson, P. (1995) 'The case of passive smoking', in R. Bunton, S. Nettleton and R. Burrows (eds), *The Sociology of Health Promotion*, London: Routledge.

Jackson, S. and Csikszentmihalyi, M. (1999) *Flow in Sports*, Champaign: Human Kinetics.

James, W. (1900) *Psychology. Briefer Course*, New York: Henry Holt.

James, W. (1950 [1890]) *The Principles of Psychology, 2 Vols*, New York: Dover.

James, W. (1982 [1902]) *The Varieties of Religious Experience*, Harmondsworth: Penguin.

Jandy, E. (1969) *Charles Horton Cooley: His Life and His Social Theory*, New York: Octagon.

Janowitz, M. (1991) *On Social Organisation and Social Control*, Chicago: University of Chicago Press.

Jaspers, K. (1953) *The Origin and the Goal of History*, London: Routledge.

Jelen, T. (1991) *The Political Mobilization of Religious Belief*, New York: Praeger Publishers.

Joas, H. (1993) *Pragmatism and Social Theory*, Chicago: University of Chicago Press.

Joas, H. (1996) *The Creativity of Action*, Cambridge: Polity.

Joas, H. (1997) *G.H.Mead. A Contemporary Reexamination of his Thought*, Cambridge, MA: The MIT Press.

Johnston, T. (1995) *Rock Climber's Manual*, London: Blandford.

Jorgensen, C. (1967) *Christine Jorgensen. A Personal Autobiography*, New York: Paul S. Erikson.

Juang, R. (2006) 'Transgendering the politics of recognition', in S. Stryker and S. Whittle (eds), *The Transgender Studies Reader*, London: Routledge.

Juergensmeyer, M. (2000) *Terror in the Mind of God. The Global Rise of Religious Violence*, Berkeley: California University Press.

Kane, M.J. (1995) 'Resistance/Transformation of the oppositional binary: Exposing sport as a continuum', *Journal of Sport and Social Issues*, 19(2): 191–218.

Kane-Demaios, J.A. and Bullough, V.L. (2006) 'Introduction', in J.A. Kane-Demaios and V.L. Bullough (eds), *Crossing Sexual Boundaries*, New York: Prometheus Books.

Kaplan, B. (1988) 'Migration and Disease', in C. Mascie-Taylor and G. Lasker (eds), *Biological Aspects of Human Migration*, Cambridge: Cambridge University Press.

Kaplan, C. (1966) *Scroll of Agony*, London: Hamish Hamilton.

Kepel, G. (1994) *Revenge of God: The Resurgence of Islam, Christianity and Judaism in the Modern World*, University Park: Pennsylvania State University Press.

Kessler, S. and McKenna, W. (1978) *Gender. An Ethnomethodological Approach*, Chicago: University of Chicago Press.

Kidd, B. (1990) 'The men's cultural centre', in M. Messner and D. Sabo (ed.), *Sport, Men and the Gender Order*, Champaign: Human Kinetics.

Kidel, M. (1988) 'Illness and meaning', in M. Kidel and S. Rowe-Leete (eds), *The Meaning of Illness*, London: Routledge.

Kilpinen, E. (2000) *The Enormous Fly-Wheel of Society. Pragmatism's Habitual Conception of Action and Social Theory*, Helsinki: University of Helsinki Press.

Kimbrell, K. (1993) *The Human Body Shop*, London: Harper Collins.

Kirkland, R. (2004) *Taoism. The Enduring Tradition*, London: Routledge.

Kitto, P. (1988) 'The patient as healer: How we can take part in our own recovery', in M. Kidel and S. Rowe-Leete (eds), *The Meaning of Illness*, London: Routledge.

Kleinman, A. (1988) *The Illness Narratives*, New York: Basic Books.

Kleinman, A. (1992) 'Pain and resistance: The delegitimation and relegitimation of local worlds', in M-J. DelVecchio Good, P. Brodwin, B.J. Good and A. Kleinman (eds), *Pain as Human Experience*, Berkeley: University of California Press.

Koenig, H., McCullough, M. and Larson, D. (eds), (2000) *Handbook of Religion and Health*, Oxford: Oxford University Press.

Kogan, E. (1953) *The Theory and Practice of Hell*, New York: Farrar, Strauss.

Kreider, R., Fry, A. and O'Toole, L. (eds) (1998) *Overtraining in Sport*, Champaign: Human Kinetics.

Kruger, A. and Murray, W. (2003) *The Nazi Olympics*, Champaign: University of Illinois Press.

Kulikoff, A. (1986) *Tobacco and Slaves. The Development of Southern Cultures in the Chesapeake, 1680–1800*, Chapel Hill: University of North Carolina Press.

Kusz, K. (2003) 'BMX, extreme sports and the white male backlash', in R. Rinehart and S. Sydnor (eds), *To the Extreme*, New York: State University of New York Press.

Kusz, K. (2004) 'Extreme America', in B. Wheaton (ed.), *Understanding Lifestyle Sports*, London: Routledge.

Lambert, Y. (2004) 'A turning point in religious evolution in Europe', *Journal of Contemporary Religion*, 19(1): 29–45.

Lan, P-C. (2002) 'Among women: Migrant domestics and their Taiwanese employers across generations', in B. Ehrenreich and A. Hochschild (eds), *Global Women*, London: Granta.

Laqueur, T. (1987) 'Orgasm, generation and the politics of reproductive biology', in C. Gallagher and T. Laqueur (eds), *The Making of the Modern Body*, Berkeley: University of California Press.

Laqueur, T. (1990) *Making Sex*, Cambridge, MA: Harvard University Press.

Lasch, C. (1991 [1979]) *The Culture of Narcissism*, New York: W.W. Norton.

LaVeist, T. (1992) 'The political empowerment and health status of African Americans: Mapping a new territory', *American Journal of Sociology*, 97(4): 1080–95.

Lawton, J. (1998) 'Contemporary hospice care: The sequestration of the unbounded body and "dirty dying"', reprinted in S. Nettleton and U. Gustafsson (eds) (2002) *The Sociology of Health and Illness Reader*, Oxford: Polity.

Leach, C. and Gabaccia, D. (2004) 'An afterword', in D. Gabaccia and C. Leach (eds), *Immigrant Life in the US*, London: Routledge.

Leder, D. (1990) *The Absent Body*, Chicago: University of Chicago Press.

Lee, R.L.M. (2003) 'The re-enchantment of the self: Western spirituality, Asian materialism', *Journal of Contemporary Religion*, 18(3): 351–67.

Lengyel, O. (1959) *Five Chimneys*, London: Panther Books.

Lerner, D. (1958) *The Passing of Traditional Society. Modernizing the Middle East*, New York: Free Press.

Levi, P. (1987) *If This is Man and The Truce*, New York: Abacus.

Levine, D. (1991) 'Simmel and Parsons reconsidered', in R. Robertson and B.S. Turner (eds), *Talcott Parsons. Theorist of Modernity*, London: Sage.

Levine, D. (1994) 'Social conflict, aggression and the body in Euro-American and Asian social thought', *International Journal of Group Tensions*, 24(3): 205–17.

Levine, D. (1995) *Visions of the Sociological Tradition*, Chicago: University of Chicago Press.

Lewis, J. and Smith, R. (1981) *American Sociology and Pragmatism*, Chicago: University of Chicago Press.

Lewis, J.D. (1997 [1976]) 'The classic American pragmatists as forerunners to symbolic interactionism', in J. Alexander, R. Boudon and M. Cherkaoui (eds), *The Classical Tradition in Sociology. The American Tradition, Vol. 2*, London: Sage.

Lewis, N. (2000) 'The climbing body, nature and the experience of modernity', *Body and Society*, 6(3–4): 58–80.

Lewis, P. (2002 [1994]) *Islamic Britain*, London: I.B. Tauris.

Liao, W. (2000) *Tai Chi Classics*, Boston: Shambhala.

Light, R. and Kinnaird, L. (2002) 'Appeasing the gods. Shinto, sumo and "true" Japanese spirit', in T. Magdalinski and T. Chandler (eds), *With God on their Side*, London: Routledge.

Loy, J. (1995) 'The dark side of agon', in K. Bette and A. Rutten (eds), *International Sociology of Sport. Contemporary Issues*, Festschrift in Honour of Gunther Luschen, Stuttgart: Naglschmid.

Lubin, J. (1997) 'Lung cancer risk from residential radon: Meta-analysis of eight epidemiological studies', *Journal of the National Cancer Institute*, 89: 49–57.

Lukas, G. (1969) *Die Kooperkultur in Fruhen Epochen der Menschehentwicklung*, East Berlin: Sportverlapg.

Lupton, D. (1994) *Medicine as Culture*, London: Sage.

Lupton, D. (1996) 'Consumerism, reflexivity and the medical encounter', reprinted in S. Nettleton and U. Gustafsson (eds) (2002), *The Sociology of Health and Illness Reader*, Oxford: Polity.

Lyle, J. (2002) *Sports Coaching Concepts*, London: Routledge.

Lyng, S. (1990) 'Edgework: A social psychological analysis of voluntary risk taking', *American Journal of Sociology*, 95: 887–921.

McCrum, R. (1998) *My Year Off. Rediscovering life after a Stroke*, London: Picador.

McDonald, L. (1997) 'Classical social theory with the women founders included', in C. Camic (ed.), *Reclaiming the Sociological Classics*, Oxford: Blackwell.

McEnroe, J. (2002) *Serious*, London: Little, Brown.

McGinty, A. (2006) *Becoming Muslim. Western Women's Conversions to Islam*, London: Palgrave.

MacIntyre, S., MacIver, S. and Sooman, A. (1993) 'Areas, class and health: Should we be focusing on places or people?' *Journal of Social Policy*, 22(2): 213–34.

MacLeod, J. (2004) *Ain't No Making It* (second edition), Boulder: Westview Press.

Macnaghten, P. and Urry, J. (2001) *Contested Natures*, London: Sage.

MacWilliams, M. (2002) 'Virtual pilgrimages on the internet', *Religion*, 32: 315–35.

Magdalinski, T. and Chandler, T. (2002) 'Introduction', in T. Magdalinski and T. Chandler (eds), *With God on their Side*, London: Routledge.

Magill, R. (2003) *Motor Learning and Control. Concepts and Applications*, Boston: McGraw Hill.

Maguire, J. (1999) *Global Sport*, Cambridge: Polity Press.

Maguire, J., Jarvie, G., Mansfield, L. and Bradley, J. (2002) *Sport Worlds*, Champaign: Human Kinetics.

Malachowski, A. (2004) 'Preface', in A. Malachowski (ed.), *Pragmatism. Vol. 1. The Historical Development of Pragmatism*, London: Sage.

Mangan, J. (1992) 'Britain's chief spiritual export: imperial sport as moral metaphor, political symbol and cultural bond', in J. Mangan (ed.), *The Cultural Bond. Sport, Empire, Society*, London: Frank Cass.

Mangan, J. and Walvin, J. (eds) (1987) *Manliness and Morality: Middle-Class Masculinity in Britain and America, 1800–1940*, Manchester: Manchester University Press.

Marsh, S. (2004) 'Competitive spirit turns yoga world on its head', *The Times*, 9 October.

Martin, C. (1978) *Keepers of the Game. Indian Animal Relationships and the Fur Trade*, Berkeley: University of California Press.

Martin, D. (2005) 'Secularisation and the future of Christianity', *Journal of Contemporary Religion*, 20(2): 145–60.

Marx, K. (1975) 'Economic and philosophical manuscripts', in L. Colletti (ed.), *Karl Marx Early Writings*, Harmondsworth: Penguin.

Matthews, F. (1977) *Quest for an American Sociology. Robert E. Park and the Chicago School*, Montreal: McGill-Queen's University Press.

Matthews, S. (2000) *The Way it Was*, London: Headline.

Mauss, M. (1954 [1950]) *The Gift*, London: Routledge.

Mauss, M. (1973 [1934]) 'Techniques of the body', *Economy and Society*, 2: 70–88.

Mead, G.H. (1903) 'The definition of the psychical', in *Decennial Publications of the University of Chicago*, First series, Vol. 3, Chicago.

Mead, G.H. (1904) 'The function of imagery in conduct', reprinted in Mead, G.H. (1962 [1934]) *Mind, Self & Society*, Chicago: University of Chicago Press.

Mead, G.H. (1938) *The Philosophy of the Act*, Chicago: University of Chicago Press.

Mead, G.H. (1962 [1934]) *Mind, Self and Society*, Chicago: University of Chicago Press.

Mead, G.H. (1968) *G.H. Mead: Essays on his Social Philosophy*, J. Petras (ed.), New York: Teachers' College Press.

Mellor, P.A. (1991) 'Self and suffering: deconstruction and reflexive definition in Buddhism and Christianity', *Religious Studies*, 27: 49–63.

Mellor, P.A. and Shilling, C. (1997) *Re-Forming the Body. Elementary Forms of Social and Moral Life*, London: Sage/TCS.

Meredith, S., Hicks, C. and Stephens, J. (2001) *Teach Your Child to Swim*, London: Usborne Publishing.

Merleau-Ponty, M. (1962) *Phenomenology of Perception*, London: Routledge.

Merleau-Ponty, M. (1965) *The Structure of Behaviour*, London: Methuen.

Messner, M. and Sabo, D. (1990) *Sport, Men and the Gender Order*, Champaign: Human Kinetics.

Meyerowitz, J. (2002) *How Sex Changed*, Cambridge: Harvard University Press.

Miah, A. (2004) *Genetically Modified Athletes*, London: Routledge.

Michael, M. (2000) ' "These boots are made for walking" ... Mundane technology, the body and human environment relations', *Body and Society*, 3–4: 107–26.

Michel, O. (1975) 'Faith, persuade, belief, unbelief', in C. Brown (ed.), *The New International Dictionary of New Testament Theology*, Exeter: Paternoster Press.

Mills, C.W. (1953) *White-Collar*, New York: Oxford University Press.

Mills, C.W. (1959) *The Sociological Imagination*, New York: Oxford University Press.

Mills, J. and Dimeo, P. (2003) ' "When gold is fired it shines". Sport, the imagination and the body in colonial and postcolonial India', in J. Bale and M. Cronin (eds), *Sport and Postcolonialism*, Oxford: Berg.

Mize, R. (2004) 'Workplace identities and collective memory. Living and remembering the effects of the Bracero total institutions', in D. Gabaccia and C. Leach (eds), *Immigrant Life in the US*, London: Routledge.

Moorehead, C. (2006) *Human Cargo*, London: Vintage Books.

Morgan, W. (2000) 'Sport as the moral discourse of nations', in R. Tannsjo and C. Tamburrini (eds), *Values in Sports*, London: E&FN Spon.

Morris, J. (2002) *Conundrum*, London: Faber & Faber.

Moss, P. (1999) 'Autobiographical notes on chronic illness', in R. Hester and H. Parr (eds), *Mind and Body Spaces: Geographies of Illness, Impairment and Disability*, London: Routledge.

Mottram, D. (ed.) (1996) *Drugs in Sport* (second edition), London: E & FN Spon.

Munson, H. (2003) 'Fundamentalism', *Religion*, 33: 381–5.

Myrdal, G. (1962) *American Dilemma. The Negro Problem and Modern Democracy*, London: Harper & Row.

Namaste, V. (2006) 'Genderbashing', in S. Stryker and S. Whittle (eds), *The Transgender Studies Reader*, London: Routledge.

Nast, N. and Pile, S. (1998) *Places Through the Body*, London: Routledge.

Neria, Y., Roe, D., Beit-Hallahmi, B., Mneimneh, H., Balaban, A. and Marshalla, R. (2005) 'The Al Qaeda 9/11 instructions: a study in the construction of religious martyrdom', *Religion*, 35: 1–11.

Ness, S. (2004) 'Being a body in a cultural way: Understanding the cultural in the embodiment of dance', in H. Thomas and J. Ahmed (eds), *Cultural Bodies. Ethnography and Theory*, Oxford: Blackwell.

Nettleton, S. (2004) ' "I just want permission to be ill". Towards a sociology of medically unexplained symptoms', *Social Science and Medicine*, 62(5): 1167–78.

Nettleton, S., O'Malley, L., Watt, I. and Duffy, P. (2006) 'Enigmatic illness: Narratives of medically unexplained symptoms', *Social Theory and Health*, 2(1): 47–66.

Newell, R. (2000) *Body Image and Disfigurement Care*, London: Routledge.

Newton, E. (1979) *Mother Camp*, Chicago: University of Chicago Press.

Nijof, G. (1995) 'Parkinson's Disease as a Problem of Shame in Public Appearance', in S. Nettleton and U. Gustafsson (eds) (2002), *The Sociology of Health and Illness Reader*, Oxford: Polity.

Nisbet, R. (1993 [1966]) *The Sociological Tradition*, New York: Transaction.

Noble, J. (1960) *I was a Slave in Russia*, New York: The Devin Adair Co.

Noll, M. (2001) *American Evangelical Chistianity*, Oxford: Blackwell.

Oakley, A. (1972) *Sex, Gender and Society*, London: Temple Smith.

Orlick, T. (1990) *In Pursuit of Excellence*, (second edition), Champaign: Leisure Press.

Overman, S. (1997) *The Influence of the Protestant Ethic on Sport and Recreation*, Aldershot: Ashgate.

Paneth, N. (2004) 'Assessing the contributions of John Snow to epidemiology; 150 years after removal of the broad street pump handle', *Epidemiology*, 15(5): 514–16.

Park, R. (1941) 'Methods of teaching: Impressions and a verdict', *Social Forces*, 20: 36–46.

Park, R. (1987) 'Biological thought, athletics and the formation of a "man of character" ', in J. Mangan and J. Walvin (eds), *Manliness and Morality: Middle-Class Masculinity in Britain and America, 1800–1940*, Manchester: Manchester University Press.

Park, R. and Burgess, E.W. (1969 [1921]) *Introduction to the Science of Sociology*, Chicago: University of Chicago Press.

Park, R., Burgess, E.W. and McKenzie, R. (1967 [1925]) *The City*, Chicago: University of Chicago Press.

Parkes, G. (2003) 'Lao-Zhuang and Heidegger on Nature and Technology', *Journal of Chinese Philosophy*, 30(1): 19–38.

Parrenas, R. (2002) 'The care crisis in the Philippines', in B. Ehrenreich and A. Hochschild (eds), *Global Women*, London: Granta.

Parry, V. (2004) 'Born to row', *The Age (Science)*, 9 August, p. 6.

Parsons, G. (2004) 'How the times they were a-changing: Exploring the context of religious transformation in Britain in the 1960s', in J. Wolffe, (ed.), *Religion in History. Conflict, Conversion and Coexistence*, Milton Keynes: Open University Press.

Parsons, T. (1968 [1937]) *The Structure of Social Action*, New York: Free Press.

Parsons, T. (1978) *Action Theory and the Human Condition*, New York: Free Press.

Parsons, T. (1991 [1951]) *The Social System*, London: Routledge.

Partridge, C. and Reid, H. (eds) (2006) *Finding and Losing Faith*, Milton Keynes: Paternoster Press.

Pederson, K. (1998) 'Doing feminist ethnography in the "wilderness" around my hometown', *International Review for the Sociology of Sport*, 33(4): 393–402.

Peirce, C.S. (1878) 'How to make our ideas clear', *Popular Science Monthly*, January, 12: 286–302.

Peirce, C.S. (1997 [1903]) *Pragmatism as a Principle and a Method of Right Thinking – The 1903 Harvard 'Lectures on Pragmatism'*, Patricia Ann Turisi (ed.), Albany: State University of New York Press.

Pellegrino, E. (1979) 'Towards a reconstruction of medical morality', *Journal of Medicine and Philosophy*, 4: 32–56.

Pels, D., Hetherington, K. and Vandenberghe, F. (2002) 'The status of the object: Performances, mediations, and techniques', *Theory, Culture & Society*, 19(5–6): 1–21.

Perkins, H. (1989) 'Teaching the nations how to play: sport and society in the British Empire and Commonwealth', *International Journal of the History of Sport*, 6: 145–55.

Perl, G. (1948) *I was a Doctor in Auschwitz*, New York: International Universities Press.

Petzet, H.W. (1993) *Encounters and Dialogues with Martin Heidegger*, Chicago: University of Chicago Press.

Phillimore, P. and Moffat, S. (1994) 'Discounted knowledge: Local experience, environmental pollution and health', in J. Popay and G. Williams (eds), *Researching the People's Health*, London: Routledge.

Pickering, W.S.F. (1975) *Durkheim on Religion*, London: RKP.

Pipes, D. (1983) *In the Path of God. Islam and Political Power*, New York: Basic Books.

Plessner, H. (1970) *Laughing and Crying. A Study of the Limits of Human Behaviour*, Evanston: Northwestern university Press.

Portis, E. (1972) 'Max Weber's theory of personality', *Sociological Inquiry*, 48(2): 113–20.

Radley, A. (1999) 'The aesthetics of illness: Horror and the sublime', *Sociology of Health & Illness*, 21: 778–96.

Raine, S. (2005) 'Reconceptualising the human body: Heaven's gate and the quest for divine transformation', *Religion*, 35: 98–117.

Rauty, R. (1988) 'Introduction', to N. Anderson *On Hobos and Homelessness*, Chicago: Chicago University Press.

Raymond, J. (1979) *The Transsexual Empire*, Boston: Beacon.

Reckless, W.C. (1925) *The Natural History of Vice Areas in Chicago*, PhD dissertation, University of Chicago.

Reckless, W.C. (1933) *Vice in Chicago*, University of Chicago Press.

Redden, G. (2005) 'The New Age: Towards a market model', *Journal of Contemporary Religion*, 20(2): 231–246.

Rees, L. (2005) *Auschwitz: The Nazis and the 'Final Solution'*, London: BBC Books.

Reisman, D. (1950) *The Lonely Crowd*, New Haven: Yale University Press.

Rescher, N. (1997) *Profitable Speculations. Essays on Current Philosophical Themes*, Lanham: Rowman & Littlefield.

Rex, J. (2002) 'Islam in the UK', in S. Hunter (ed.), *Islam. Europe's Second Religion*, Westport: Praeger Publishers.

Rex, J. and Moore, R. (1973 [1967]) *Race, Community and Conflict*, London: Oxford University Press.

Rinehart, R. (2000) 'Emerging arriving sport', in J. Coakley and E. Dunning (eds), *Handbook of Sports Studies*, London: Sage.

Rinehart, R. and Sydnor, S. (eds) (2003) *To the Extreme*, New York: State University of New York Press.

Rintala, J. (1995) 'Sport and technology: Human questions in a world of machines', *Journal of Sport and Social Issues*, February, 19: 62–75.

Rippon, A. (2006) *Hitler's Olympics. The Story of the 1936 Olympic Games*, London: Pen and Sword Military.

Robbins, J. (2004) 'The Globalisation of Pentecostal and Charismatic Christianity', *Annual Review of Anthropology*, 33: 117–43.

Robertson, R. (2006) 'Civilization', *Theory, Culture & Society*, 23(2–3): 421–36.

Rochberg-Halton, E. (1987) 'Why pragmatism now?' *Sociological Theory*, 5(2): 194–200.

Rojek, C. (2000) *Leisure and Culture*, Houndmills: Palgrave.

Romain, J. (2006) 'Conversion and Judaism', in C. Partridge and H. Reid (eds), *Finding and Losing Faith*, Milton Keynes: Paternoster Press.

Rorty, R. (1979) *Philosophy and the Mirror of Nature*, Princeton: Princeton University Press.

Rorty, R. (1982) *Consequences of Pragmatism*, Minneapolis: University of Minnesota Press.

Rosen, L. (2002) *The Culture of Islam*, Chicago: University of Chicago Press.

Rubin, G. (1975) 'The traffic in women', in R. Reiter (ed.), *Toward an Anthology of Women*, New York: Monthly Review Press.

Rubin, G. (2006) 'Of catamites and kings. Reflections on butch, gender & boundaries', reprinted in S. Stryker and S. Whittle (eds), *The Transgender Studies Reader*, London: Routledge.

Rubin, H. (2003) *Self Made Men*, Vanderbilt University Press.

Rucker, D. (1969) *The Chicago Pragmatists*, Minneapolis: University of Minnesota Press.

Rudacille, D. (2006) *The Riddle of Gender*, New York: Anchor Books.

Ruel, M. (1982) 'Christians as believers', in J. Davis (ed.), *Religions and Religious Experience*, London: Academic Press.

Russell, K. (1986) 'Competition and the growing child stress or distress?' in G. Gleeson (ed.), *The Growing Child in Competitive Sport*, London: Hodder & Stoughton.

Rutherford, P. (1993) 'The entry of life into history', in E. Darier (ed.), *Discourses of the Environment*, Oxford: Blackwell.

Ruthven, M. (1997) *Islam*, Oxford: Oxford University Press.

Sage, G. (1978) 'American values and sport; formation of a bureaucratic personality', *Journal of Physical Education and Recreation*, 49.

Sassen, S. (2002) 'Global cities and survival circuits', in B. Ehrenreich and A. Hochschild (eds), *Global Women*, London: Granta.

Savage, M., Bagnall, G. and Longhurst, B. (2005) *Globalisation and Belonging*, London: Sage.

Sayad, A. (2004) *The Suffering of the Immigrant*, Cambridge: Polity.

Scheffler, I. (1974) *Four Pragmatists*, London: Routledge.

Schmidt, R. (1991) *Motor Learning and Performance*, Champaign: Human Kinetics.

Schmolinsky, G. (2000) *Track and Field. The East German Textbook of Athletics*, Toronto: Sport Books.

Scholinski, D. (1997) *Last Time I wore a Dress*, New York: Penguin Putnam.

Schulz, W. (1986) *Philosohie in der Veranderten Welt*, Neske: Pfullingen.

Schulze, R. (2002) 'The struggle of past and present in individual identities: The case of German refugees and expellees from the East', in D. Rock and S. Wolff (eds), *Coming Home to Germany?* New York: Berghahn.

Schutz, A. (1967 [1932]) *The Phenomenology of the Social World*, Evanston: Northwestern University Press.

Sennett, R. (1994) *Flesh and Stone*, London: Faber & Faber.

Sennett, R. (1998) *The Corrosion of Character*, New York: Norton.

Seymour, W. (1998) *Re-Making the Body*, London: Allen Lane.

Shalamov, V. (1980) *Kolyma Tales*, New York: W.W. Norton & Co.

Shaw, C. (1930) *The Jack Roller: A Delinquent Boy's Own Story*, Chicago: University of Chicago Press.

Sheehan, G. (1992) 'Playing', in S. Hoffman (ed.), *Sport & Religion*, Champaign: Human Kinetics.

Shibutani, T. (1997) 'Herbert Blumer's contribution to C20th Sociology', in J.C. Alexander, R. Boudon and M. Cherkaoui (eds), *The Classical Tradition in Sociology. The American Tradition. Vol. 2*, London: Sage.

Shilling, C. (1993) *The Body and Social Theory*, London: Sage/TCS.

Shilling, C. (2002) 'Culture, the "sick role" and the consumption of health', *British Journal of Sociology*, 53(4): 621–38.

Shilling, C. (2003) *The Body and Social Theory* (second edition), London: Sage/TCS.

Shilling, C. (2004) 'Educating bodies: Schooling and the constitution of society', Foreword to J. Evans, B. Davies and J. Wright (eds), *Body Knowledge and Control*, London: Routledge.

Shilling, C. (2005a) *The Body in Culture, Technology and Society*, London: Sage/TCS.

Shilling, C. (2005b) 'Embodiment, emotions and the foundations of social order: Durkheim's enduring contribution', in J.C. Alexander and P. Smith (eds), *The Cambridge Companion to Durkheim*, Cambridge: Cambridge University Press.

Shilling, C. (ed.) (2007) *Embodying Sociology. Retrospect, Progress and Prospects*, Oxford: Blackwell/The Sociological Review Monograph Series.

Shilling, C. and Mellor, P.A. (2001) *The Sociological Ambition*, London: Sage/TCS.

Shilling, C. and Mellor, P.A. (2007) 'Cultures of embodied experience: Technology, religion and body pedagogics', *The Sociological Review*, 55(3): 531–49.

Shils, E. (1980) *The Calling of Sociology and Other Essays on the Pursuit of Learning*, Chicago: Chicago University Press.

Shusterman, R. (1992) *Pragmatist Aesthetics. Living Beauty*, Oxford: Blackwell.

Siegfried, C. (1996) *Pragmatism and Feminism*, Chicago: University of Chicago Press.

Simmel, G. (1971 [1903]) 'The metropolis', in D. Levine (ed.), *Georg Simmel on Individuality and Social Forms*, Chicago: University of Chicago Press.

Simmel, G. (1971 [1908]) 'The stranger', in D. Levine (ed.), *Georg Simmel on Individuality and Social Forms*, Chicago: University of Chicago Press.

Simmel, G. (1971 [1910]) 'Sociability', in D. Levine (ed.), *Georg Simmel on Individuality and Social Forms*, Chicago: University of Chicago Press.

Simmel, G. (1971 [1911]) 'The adventurer', in D. Levine (ed.), *Georg Simmel on Individuality and Social Forms*, Chicago: University of Chicago Press.

Simmel, G. (1971 [1918]) 'The transcendent character of life', in D. Levine (ed.), *Georg Simmel on Individuality and Social Forms*, Chicago: University of Chicago Press.

Simmel, G. (1990 [1907]) *The Philosophy of Money*, edited and with an introduction by T. Bottomore and D. Frisby, London: Routledge.

Simmel, G. (1997) *Essays on Religion*, New Haven: Yale University Press.

Singleton, M. (2005) 'Salvation through relaxation: Proprioceptive therapy and its relationship to yoga', *Journal of Contemporary Religion*, 20(3): 289–304.

Smith, M.P. and Tarallo, B. (1993) 'The postmodern city and the social construction of ethnicity in California', in M. Cross and M. Keith (eds), *Racism, the City and the State*, London: Routledge.

Smith, S. (1996) 'Western Buddhism: Tradition and modernity', *Religion*, 26: 311–21.

Snyder, E.E. and Spreitzer, E.A. (1983) *Social Aspects of Sport* (second edition), Englewood Cliffs: Prenticehall.

Snyder, L. (2000) *Speaking Our Minds. Personal Reflections from Individuals with Alzheimer's*, New York: W.H. Freeman and Co.

Solzhenitsyn, A.I. (1997) *The Gulag Archipelago 1918–1956: An Experiment in Literary Investigation II*, Basic Books Inc:US.

Solzhenitsyn, A.I. (2000 [1963]) *One Day in the Life of Ivan Denezivitch*, London: Penguin.

Sontag, S. (1991) *Illness as Metaphors/AIDS and its Metaphors*, London: Penguin.

Spade, D. (2006) 'Mutilating gender', in S. Stryker and S. Whittle (eds), *The Transgender Studies Reader*, London: Routledge.

Sparkes, A. and Silvennoinen, M. (eds) (1999) *Talking Bodies*, Jyvaskyla: SoPhi.

Stevens, J. (2006) 'I lead two lives', in J.A. Kane-Demaios and V.L. Bullough (eds), *Crossing Sexual Boundaries*, New York: Prometheus Books.

Stone, G. (1962) 'Appearance and the self', in A. Rose (ed.), *Human Nature and Social Process*, Boston: Houghton Mifflin.

Stone, S. (1991) 'The Empire Strikes Back: A Posttransexual Manifesto', in J. Epstein and K. Straub (ed.), *Body Guards*, New York: Routledge.

Struna, N. (1994) 'The recreational experiences of early American women', in D.M. Costa and S. Guthrie (eds), *Women and Sport*, Champaign: Human Kinetics.

Stryker, S. (2006) '(De)subjugated knowledges. An introduction to transgender studies', in S. Stryker and S. Whittle (eds), *The Transgender Studies Reader*, London: Routledge.

Stuhr, J. (2002) *Pragmatism, Postmodernism and the Future of Philosophy*, London: Routledge.

Sudnow, D. (1978) *Ways of the Hand. The Organization of Improvised Conduct*, London: Routledge

Sullivan, N. (2006) 'Transmorgification: (Un)becoming other(s)', reprinted in S. Stryker and S. Whittle (eds), *The Transgender Studies Reader*, London: Routledge.

Suzuki, D. (2002) *The Sacred Balance*, Vancouver: Toronto.

Swingewood, A. (2000) *A Short History of Sociological Thought* (third edition), Houndmills: Macmillan.

Szerszynski, B. (2005) *Nature, Technology and the Sacred*, Oxford: Blackwell.

Szerszynski, B., Heim, W. and Waterton, C. (eds) (2003) *Nature Performed. Environment, Culture and Performance*, Oxford: Blackwell.

Taghmaian, B. (2005) *Embracing the Infidel*, New York: Delacorte Press.

Taylor, B. (2001a) 'Earth and nature-based spirituality (Part I): From deep ecology to radical environmentalism', *Religion*, 31: 175–93.

Taylor, B. (2001b) 'Earth and nature-based spirituality (Part II): From Earth First! and bioregionalism to scientific paganism and the new age', *Religion*, 31: 225–45

Terry, J. (1999) *An American Obsession. Science, medicine and Homosexuality in Modern Society*, Chicago: University of Chicago Press.

Tester, K. (1994) 'Introduction', in K. Tester (ed.), *The Flaneur*, London: Routledge.

Tester, K. (2004) 'A critique of humanitarianism', in M. Jacobsen (ed.), *Wild Sociology, Dark Times and the Postmodern World – A Sketchy Introduction to the Sociological Spirit of Keith Tester*, Aalborg: Aalborg University Press.

Thai, H. (2002) 'Clashing dreams', in B. Ehrenreich and A. Hochschild (eds), *Global Women*, London: Granta.

Theberge, N. and Birrel, S. (1994) 'Ideological control of women in sport', in D. Margaret Costa and S.R. Guthrie (eds), *Women and Sport. Interdisciplinary Perspectives*, Champaign: Human Kinetics.

Theweleit, K. (1989 [1978]) *Male Fantasies, Vol. 2. Male Bodies: Psychoanalysing the White Terror*, Minneapolis: University of Minnesota Press.

Thomas, W.I. (1907) *Sex and Society*, Chicago: University of Chicago Press.

Thomas, W.I. (ed.) (1909) *Sourcebook for Social Origins*, Chicago: University of Chicago Press.

Thomas, W.I. (1918) 'The professor's views', *Chicago Daily Tribune*, 22 April, pp. 15–16.

Thomas, W.I. (1937) *Primitive Behaviour*, New York: McGraw Hill.

Thomas, W.I. and Znaniecki, F. (1918–1920) *The Polish Peasant in Europe and America. 5 Vols*, Chicago: University of Chicago Press and Boston: Badger.

Thompson, W. (1999) 'Wives incorporated. Marital relationships in professional ice hockey', in J. Coakley and P. Donnelly (eds), *Inside Sports*, London: Routledge.

Thomson, R. (2006) 'Changing your mother? Hindu responses to conversion', in C. Partridge and H. Reid (eds), *Finding and Losing Faith*, Milton Keynes: Paternoster Press.

Tilley, C. (1994) *A Phenomenology of Landscape*, Oxford: Berg.

Toynbee, P. (2003) *Hard Work: Life in Low Pay Britain*, London: Bloomsbury.

Tschumi, B. (1996) *Architecture and Disjunction*, Cambridge, MA: MIT Press.

Tseelon, E. (1995) *The Masque of Femininity*, London: Sage.

Turner, B.S. (1984) *The Body and Society*, Oxford: Blackwell.

Turner, B.S. (1991) 'Recent developments in the theory of the body', in M. Featherstone., M. Hepworth and B.S. Turner (eds), *The Body. Social Process and Cultural Theory*, London: Sage.

Turner, B.S. (1993) 'Outline of a theory of human rights', *Sociology*, 27(3): 489–512.

Turner, B.S. (2003) 'Biology, vulnerability and politics', in S. Williams, L. Birke and G. Bendelow (eds), *Debating Biology*, London: Routledge.

Turner, R.H. (1967) 'Introduction', in R.H. Turner (ed.), *Robert E. Park on Social Control and Collective Behaviour*, Chicago: Chicago University Press.

Turner, V. (1982) *The Anthropology of Performance*, New York: PAJ Publications.

Twigg, J. (2006) *The Body in Health and Social Care*, London: Palgrave Macmillan.

Tzu, C. (1996) *The Book of Cuang Tzu*, translated by M.Palmer with E. Breuilly, Harmondsworth: Penguin.

Unsdorfer, S. (1961) *The Yellow Star*, New York: Thomas Yoseloff.

Urry, J. (2000) *Sociology Beyond Societies*, London: Routledge.

Urry, J. (2002) *The Tourist Gaze*, London: Sage.

Valentine, G. (1999) 'What it means to be a man: The body, masculinities, disability', in R. Hester and H. Parr (eds), *Mind and Body Spaces*, London: Routledge.

van der Veer (1996) *Conversion to Modernities: The Globalization of Christianity*, New York: Routledge.

Verroken, M. (1996) 'Drug use and abuse in sport', in D. Mottram (ed.), *Drugs in Sport* (second edition), London: E &FN Spoon.

Vertinsky, P. and Bale, J. (eds) (2004) *Sites of Sport, Space, Experience*, London: Routledge.

Vice Commission of Chicago (1911) *The Social Evil in Chicago: A Study of Existing Conditions*, Chicago: Gunthrop-Warren Printing.

Vilensky, S. (1999) *Till My Tale is Told. Women's Memoirs of the Gulag*, London: Virago.

Ville, I. (2005) 'Biographical work and returning to employment following a spinal cord injury', *Sociology of Health and Illness*, 27(3): 324–50.

Voas, D. and Bruce, S. (2004) 'Research note on the 2001 Census and Christian identification in Britain', *Journal of Contemporary Religion*, 19(1): 23–8.

Wacquant, L. (2004) *Body and Soul. Notebooks of an Apprentice Boxer*, Oxford: Oxford University Press.

Walter, K. (1991) *Learning Rock Climbing in a Weekend*, London: Dorling Kindersley.

Walvin, J. (2006) *Atlas of Slavery*, London: Longman.

Warraq, I. (2003) *Leaving Islam*, New York: Prometheus.

Watling, T. (2005) ' "Experiencing" Alpha: Finding and embodying the spirit and being transformed: Empowerment and control in a ("Charismatic") Christian worldview', *Journal of Contemporary Religion*, 20(1): 91–108.

Watson, M. with Bunce, S. (2005) *The Biggest Fight. Michael Watson's Story*, London: Time Warner Books.

Webb, D. (1998) 'A "revenge" on modern times: Notes on traumatic brain injury', reprinted in S. Nettleton and U. Gustafsson (eds), *The Sociology of Health Illness Reader*, Oxford: Polity.

Weber, M. (1964) *The Religion of China*, New York: Free Press.

Weber, M. (1968) *Economy and Society, 2 Vols*, Berkeley: University of California Press.

Weber, M. (1991 [1904–1905]) *The Protestant Ethic and the Spirit of Capitalism*, London: Harper Collins.

Weber, M. (1991 [1919a]) 'Science as a vocation', in H.H. Gerth and C. Wright Mills (eds), *From Max Weber*, London: Routledge.

Weber, M. (1991 [1919b]) 'Politics as a vocation', in H.H. Gerth and C. Wright Mills (eds), *From Max Weber*, London: Routledge.

Weinstock, E. (1947) *Beyond the Last Path*, New York: Bonni & Gaer.

Weiss, R. (1961) *Journey Through Hell*, London: Valentine.

Wellman, B. and Frank, K. (2001) 'Network capital in a multi-level world: Getting support from personal communities', in N. Linn, R. Burt and K. Cook (eds), *Social Capital: Theory and Research*, Chicago: Aldine De Gruyter.

Wheaton, B. (2004) ' "New lads?" Competing masculinities in the wind-surfing culture', in B. Wheaton (ed.), *Understanding Lifestyle Sports*, London: Routledge.

White, E. (2001) *The Flaneur*, London: Bloomsbury.

Whitson, D. (1990) 'Sport in the social construction of masculinity', in M. Messner and D. Sabo (eds), *Sport, Men and the Gender Order*, Champaign: Human Kinetics.

Whittle, S. (2006) 'Foreword', in S. Stryker and S. Whittle (eds), *The Transgender Studies Reader*, London: Routledge.

Whyte, W. (1956) *The Organisation Man*, Harmondsworth: Penguin.

Wiesel, E. (1981 [1958]) *Night*, Harmondsworth: Penguin.

Wilkinson, I. (2005) *Suffering. A Sociological Introduction*, Cambridge: Polity.

Wilkinson, J. (2004) *My World*, London: Headline.

Wilkinson, T. (1984) 'Marathon mentality – the risks sportsmen run', *The Listener*, May.

Williams, G. and Popay, J. (1994) 'Lay knowledge and the privilege of experience', in D. Kelleher, J. Gabe and G. Williams (eds), *Challenging Medicine*, London: Routledge.

Williams, S.J. (1999) 'Is there anybody there? Critical realism, chronic illness and the disability debate', *Sociology of Health and Illness*, 21(6): 797–819.

Williams, S.J. (2003) Beyond meaning, discourse and the empirical world: Critical realist reflections on health', *Social Theory and Health*, 1: 42–71.

Willis, S. (1991) *A Primer for Daily Life*, London: Routledge.

Wilson, B. (1985) 'Secularization: The inherited model', in P. Hammond (ed.), *The Sacred in a Secular Age*, Berkeley: University of California Press.

Wilson, E.O. (1986) *Biophilia*, Cambridge, MA: Harvard University Press.

Wilson, W.J. (1978) *The Declining Significance of Race*, Chicago: University of Chicago Press.

Wilson, W.J. (1987) *Truly Disadvantaged. Inner City, the Underclass and Public Policy*, Chicago: University of Chicago Press.

Wilson, W.J. and Taub, R. (2007) *There Goes the Neighbourhood*, New York: Vintage Books.

Wolffe, J. (ed.) (2004) *Religion in History. Conflict, Conversion and Coexistence*, Milton Keynes: Open University Press.

Wolkowitz, C. (2006) *Bodies at Work*, London: Sage.

Woodward, C. (2004) *Winning! The Story of England's Rise to Rugby World Cup Glory*, London: Hodder & Stoughton.

Yang, M.M. (2000) 'Putting global capitalism in its place: Economic hybridity, Bataille and ritual expenditure', *Current Anthropology*, 41(4): 477–509.

Yao, X. (2001) 'Who is a Confucian today? A critical reflection on the issues concerning Confucian identity in modern times', *Journal of Contemporary Religion*, 16(3): 313–28.

Young, K. and White, P. (1999) 'Threats to sports careers. Elite athletes talk about injury and pain', in J. Coakley and P. Donnelly (eds), *Inside Sports*, London: Routledge.

Zabolotsky, N.A. (1986) 'Istoriya moego zaklyucheniya', *Minuvsheye*, Vol. 2.

Zapf, D., Seifert, C., Schmutte, B., Mertini, H. and Holz, M. (2001) 'Emotion work and job stressors and their effects on burnout', *Psychology and Health*, 16: 527–45.

Zarembka, J. (2002) 'America's dirty work: Migrant maids and modern day slavery', in B. Ehrenreich and A. Hochschild (eds), *Global Women*, London: Granta.

Zizek, S. (2001) *Belief*, London: Routledge.

Zorbaugh, H.W. (1929) *The Gold Coast and the Slum*, Chicago: University of Chicago Press.

Name Index

Subject Index

Judaism 148
Juvenile Protection Agency (JPA) 34

kinaesthetic 10, 52, 85
kingdom of the sick, the 6, 104,
    105, 108
kingdom of the well, the 104, 108
Kolyma 129
    Kolyma Tales 132

labour camps 128, 164
lesbians 65, 83
life histories 30
looking-glass self 31, 38, 64

marginal situations 18
Marxism 134, 142
masculinity 17, 21, 46, 49, 58, 60,
    66, 72, 73, 75–7, 119
ME (Myalgic Encephalomyelitis)
    113, 120
Mecca 154
medic/medical 17, 55, 68–78, 81, 84,
    107, 108, 123
medicine 32, 41, 104, 106, 117, 121
    alternative/complementary 108, 117
metropolis 87, 103
migrant 6, 34, 87–9, 93–7, 99, 151,
    165–7
migrant/migratory workers 6, 33, 87,
    88, 93, 95, 100, 102
migration 5–7, 88–90, 110, 163,
    169, 170
mimesis 50, 63
modernity 25, 50, 87, 88, 145, 153
money economy 87, 97, 152
moral order 99, 140–2
morality 1, 21, 37, 56–63, 83, 84,
    102, 103, 122–4, 126, 142,
    157–60
morbidity 110
mortality 110, 147
motility 50, 63, 85
motor racing 52, 53
mountaineering 59
mourning 120
MS (multiple sclerosis) 110, 114, 115,
    117, 122
muscular consciousness 86
Muselmänner 133, 134, 136,
    142, 167
musicians 15, 20, 86
Muslim 94, 101, 153–8
mutual accommodation 53, 85,
    86, 98

National Health Service (NHS) 102
nationalism 58, 102, 151
    centrifugal 102
Nazi Germany/state 6, 90, 126
Nazis 6, 69, 85, 126–9, 131, 135,
    137, 139, 140, 142, 156, 164
Negro Family, The 37
new age spiritualities 7, 150, 155,
    156, 159, 166
norms 2, 22, 47, 48, 70, 77, 78, 84,
    105, 111, 140, 147, 155, 161,
    164, 168
    collective 32
    cultural 6, 11, 43, 85
    economic 46
    gendered 65–9, 73
    of identity 21
    presentational 6, 64, 65
    racial 65
    sexual 37, 65
    social 19, 23, 25, 40, 44, 65, 69,
        71, 74, 82, 148, 162
North America 67, 70, 71, 89,
    119, 149

Olympic Games 57, 58, 63
ozone layer 109, 110

pain 56, 57, 60, 74, 75, 84, 95, 104,
    112, 114–18, 120–2, 129, 131,
    133, 135, 147, 168, 169
panhandling 34
participant observation 30, 34
'passing' 66, 69, 76, 78, 81–3,
    100, 116
patriarchy 22
pedagogics of suffering/illness
    120–3
performance genes 49
performativity 6, 45–9, 56,
    58, 63, 104, 113, 146, 147,
    151, 168
phenomenology 2, 4, 10, 57, 70, 73,
    93, 105, 114, 136
physical
    capital 147, 148, 165
    determinism 71
    mobility 30, 87, 92
    science 27, 40
physiological division of labour 86
Pilates 15
Polish Peasant, The 29, 30, 37, 100
positivism 39
postmodernity 168
post-structuralism 125

sports (*contd.*)
    skill   6, 44–6, 50–3, 56, 59,
        63, 86
    socialised   44–8, 50, 58, 61
SS *see* Schutzstaffel
Stalin   90, 126, 128, 134, 139
stem cell research   42
stigma   38, 58, 65, 68, 70, 113, 115, 116
stigmatisation   11, 25, 65, 68, 82,
    88, 99, 100, 106, 108, 113, 142,
    164, 168
Stonewall   83
structural functionism   40
structuralism   24, 125, 162, 163
style consultants   1
suicide   74, 94, 102, 118, 134, 167
surfers   59, 60, 109
survival   5, 6, 8–10, 18, 33, 35–7,
    44–8, 85, 86, 94, 96, 97,
    125–43, 145, 147, 170
swimming   48, 51, 55, 109
symbolic interactionism   27, 39
sympathetic introspection   30

tai chi chuan   61–3, 155, 164
Tantra   61
Taoism   23, 61, 62, 148, 153, 154,
    158, 160, 161
taste   10, 103
tattoo   1, 73, 131
Taxi Dance Hall, The   29, 30, 37
techniques of the body   9, 13, 14, 20,
    23, 25, 44, 51, 80, 86, 145, 154,
    155, 164, 166, 168
techniques of the self   23, 25
technological culture   7, 45, 63, 104,
    105, 120, 144, 146–55, 157, 159,
    160, 161, 163, 164, 166, 168
technologies of the self   23
technology   1, 5, 15, 17, 42, 49, 51,
    73, 86, 87, 91, 100, 153, 160,
    161, 166
tennis   14, 46, 49, 55, 86

testicular feminisation syndrome   77
third sex/gender   67, 70, 73
touch   10, 51, 59, 154
tramps   33
transcendence   7, 53–7, 59, 62, 83,
    119, 120, 122, 126, 134, 147, 149,
    153, 157, 160, 161, 163–6,
    168, 169
transgenderism   5, 6, 65, 67–70, 75,
    83, 163, 165, 168, 170
transpeople   65, 66, 69, 70, 74, 82,
    165, 169
transplant surgery   42
transsexuality   65, 66–84, 169
transvestite   67, 68
travel   6, 61, 85–93, 97,
    101–3, 119, 129, 147
Treblinka   126, 128, 139
two-sex model   66–73, 80, 82, 83
typhus   130

unassimiliables   69
urban   26–30, 35, 37, 39, 61, 87,
    90–2, 97, 105, 110–12,
    145, 150
urbanisation   26–8
United Kingdom   55, 111
United Nations   94
United States (of America)   26–30,
    34, 36, 39, 46, 47, 49, 55, 56, 58,
    68–71, 73, 83, 88–91, 94–6, 98,
    100–2, 106, 110, 144, 148–50,
    152, 156–8

waged labour   146, 147
windsurfers   51, 59–61
wheelchair users   115–20
World Health Organisation   107
World Trade Centre   152, 156

yoga   23, 61–3, 155, 164

zen   61